Books without Borders

First published by Respondeo Books in 2019
www.respondeobooks.com

Respondeo Books
P.O. Box 5648
Santa Fe, NM 87502
United States

I have tried to recreate events, locales and conversations from my
memories of them. In order to maintain their anonymity in some instances
I have changed the names of individuals and places, I may have changed
some identifying characteristics and details such as physical properties,
occupations and places of residence.

Names:	Franks, Martha C., author.
Title:	Books without borders : Homer, Aeschylus, Galileo, Melville, and Madison go to China / Martha C. Franks.
Description:	Santa Fe, New Mexico : Respondeo Books, [2019]
Identifiers:	ISBN: 978-0-9993059-2-8 (paperback) | 978-0-9993059-3-5 (ebook) | LCCN: 2018968626
Subjects:	LCSH: Education, Humanistic--Study and teaching (Secondary)--China. | China--Description and travel--2001- | Canon (Literature)--Study and teaching (Secondary)--China. | Change-- Study and teaching (Secondary)--China. | China--Relations--Western countries. | Chinese-- Attitudes.
Classification:	LCC: LC1024.C6 F73 2019 | DDC: 370.112/0951--dc23

Book design by Adam Robinson for Good Book Developers

10 9 8 7 6 5 4 3 2 1

Books
without Borders

Homer, Aeschylus, Galileo,
Melville, *and* Madison
go to China

Martha C. Franks

RESPONDEO BOOKS

Santa Fe, New Mexico

Contents

To all who converse with books and with each other,
awakening the past and the future.

"Conversation is a meeting of minds with different memories and habits. When minds meet, they don't just exchange facts: they transform them, reshape them, draw different implications from them, engage in new trains of thought. Conversation doesn't just reshuffle the cards: it creates new cards."

—*Theodore Zeldin*

Foreword

I t is rare for people with profoundly different cultural backgrounds to come into contact and meditate upon each other's
most essential issues not as politicians, not as admirers of what
is foreign, but as educators. In 2012, Martha Franks and her husband, Grant Franks, both teachers at St. John's College in Santa
Fe, New Mexico, were invited to join the faculty of a Chinese high
school and taught Western Classics there for two years. There
they became witnesses of, and participants in, two events occurring in China. The first is the dispersing of Chinese youths from
the native, historical source of education nourishing their Asian
identity—many choose to study abroad in the West. The second is
the rise of liberal education in China, an attempt to re-ground the
spirit of the country, which has become very technological, com-
mercialized, and globalized.

These two events, in tension with one another, indicate that a
radical change is forthcoming in China. And in the midst of these
social issues a great number of individuals are struggling to find
their own identities and balance themselves upon a yet unbal-
anced bridge of the age. This invisible struggle, happening within
their hearts, is not often explored, but here is where Franks begins.
Keenly aware of the value of Western tradition, including Socratic
wisdom, she pursues a personal approach to the Chinese problem:
her immediate concerns are how she interacts with her students,
how she manages to understand the anxiety and the inherited
beliefs in their hearts, and how she refreshes her own beliefs as she

11

teaches and lives in a place so vastly different from the West. The larger forces of the age are strangely overshadowed by the subtle advances and retreats in a classroom, both teacher and students making efforts to guess at each other's intentions and meaning, to test foreign stories, and finally to have a genuine conversation. Periods of alienness and moments of resonance, both intellectual and emotional, go hand in hand. And it is a marvel to see them thus paralleled. The book is written in a style that reflects a combination of harsh realism and deep empathy, though not without a ring of decisive thoughtfulness. The author once remarks in the book: "As a teacher of humanities, my hope was to help my students to discern their own deepest beliefs in order to bring them into the light of day to be examined."

Such a view of teaching is often obscured in the brightness of modern utilitarianism. It is difficult to fulfill this task when what the social context demands from educational systems is people with special skills to fill predetermined positions. What is often emphasized in Franks' book is the silence of the students. I cannot help but admire this truthfulness of the author's depiction. The students must have found their situation strange at first, reading (in high school Western classics like the *Iliad*, the *Oresteia*, *Moby Dick*, and facing questions that do not have a standard answer: "What is a good life?" "What is justice?" "Can virtue be taught?" Not only is there an exchange of narratives between the East and the West, there is also, and maybe more daringly, a challenge to the unconscious principles of unreflective modernity. The obstacles are great, but when they are overcome, when the student's silence is broken, they reward their teacher in an almost graceful way. They write inspiring stories about truths and lies. They become a jury in the trial of Orestes, repeating faithfully, and also fatefully, the circumstance described in Aeschylus' play, splitting their votes between Orestes and the Furies.

Humanities and the natural sciences mean for Franks something beyond a mere accumulation of knowledge that has been discovered by mankind across history. She suggests that the knowledge should be revived and re-lived; history should be experienced not memorized. All her endeavors contribute to the moment of excitement in which students' insights, either ethical or mathematical, are transfixed as eternal. In a country like China, where people are likely to be temporally overburdened, where anachronism can grow to the point of social divide (thus conflicting all values), such a perspective may prove to be helpful. For the problems at hand are not those of a particular culture but of humankind in general.

In chapter eleven, when talking about the scientific revolution, the author says to her students, and most beautifully: "'Yes, stars move. And almost all of them move in wonderfully regular ways—perfect circles in the sky. Imagine what they looked like to people during times in human history when there was no science and life was much more uncertain that it is now. They would have seemed to reflect grandeur and order and constancy, as in mathematics, entirely different from anything anyone encountered in daily life, with its confusion and meanness…If you lived in such times, you might say to yourself that Heaven must be where the Divine lives.'"

We are now living under the great towers of the sciences. But in a technologically progressing and culturally confused society, which is chaotic in its own way, perhaps the same kind of awe and inspiration can still guide our action—although now it is no longer the spatial movements of the stars that trace out the divine order but the temporal sedimentation of what the great thinkers, Eastern and Western, have thought and written.

I am conscious of the difficulty of such an encounter between East and West, for it can either fall into a vulgar multiculturalism that dissolves both traditions, or it can end up in appreciations reflecting only apparent meanings and immediate usefulness. Yet we should not just avoid such encounters because of contempt for what is foreign or enchanted by a kind of awe that ties our tongues.

When I was still a college graduate back in Santa Fe, I once met Franks after a quiet stroll around the campus of St John's College and struck up a conversation with her. Sunlight was overabundant. I do not remember much of what we talked about, but she certainly made a few remarks about liberal arts programs and, giving me a firm glance, concluded: "I believe in this kind of education." At that moment, I wanted to ask her, half playfully and half sincerely, *But why do you believe in it?* For some reason I didn't say it, and the conversation ended up in peaceful compliance. How I wish that I had asked that question, as I am writing this forward on a rainy evening in Beijing, recalling another line that the author writes in an almost serious tone: "If we respect each other's beliefs to the point of being unwilling to discuss them, then they divide us."

Yang Jinglong
2018. 8. 8

序

来自截然不同的文化的人们，能够相接触，且不凭借政治目的，不眷于求奇慕异，而为彼此之文化的断续存亡，以教育者的身份来谨慎考量，这定是罕见的事了。玛莎·弗兰克斯（Martha Franks）和她的丈夫，葛兰特·弗兰克斯 (Grant Franks) 均是美国圣约翰学院的导师。他们于二零一二年赴华，受北京大学附属中学之邀，负责其古典教育课程的规划与教授。两年期间，他们夫妇二人切身地目睹，也参与了中国教育界饱含预兆意味的两大事件：其一，即中国学生的留学之势，愈趋猛烈。个中影响，自然并非是"访学"，"游历"之词汇所能敷衍。这是整一代人的文化认同，审美与道德传统，都在接受西方文化的洗礼，或者说西方现代性的洗礼。既在语言的变革，又在语言所指的物的迁动；既关乎肉体，也触及魂灵。于此，想必已无人视而不见了。第二件事，则是中国本土的欲图以"历史性的厚重缓解空间上的文化稀释"的通识教育的崛起。八十，九十年代归国的一批学人重新在高等学府的课堂上开讲中西方古典，兴办博雅学院，正为了给从五四以后便断代了的，无处安放的中国文化精神，再立根基。

不难看出，这与彼此相悖相通的两件事，隐隐牵动着未来的社会变迁。但在抽象的问题之下，是许多我们身边的孩子，在为自己生活的抉择，或忧虑或喜悦。作为留学生，还未上升到国族之问，也必得为一己的身份，内心的对异与同的需求，经历不少磨难吧。恰恰是这最私人，最内在的问题，被许多忧国（或者仅仅忧政治）的教育者所忽略了。而忧政治毕竟与忧国，忧人不同。弗兰克斯夫人撰写的这本书，便是以中国孩子们的个人迷茫为起点，想要勾勒出这座东方国度的大问题来。书的表层，不外乎是她如何尝试着理解这些将成为留学生的孩子的信仰和焦虑，还有她自己在远离西方的环境中如何审问自己之所信的一段记载。更汹涌的社会之力仿佛消隐了，只留下课堂里的逐个动定，师生之间的问与答，互相猜测，互相讲述，以至完成一段恳切的作为人与人的交谈。因为是异族，隔阂与共鸣的瞬间，毋论情感或理性的，都被忠实地写下了。看到它们如此并列着，确实让人惊叹。文句中结合了仿佛带有锐意的写实主义，以及深切的同情。而两者的背后，则有着坚定不移的思辨。作者写道：

　　"作为人文课程的教师，我希望能帮助学生们觉察到自己埋藏最深的所信，并把它们置于光明中，诘问它们，审视它们。"

　　这样的理念往往被教育界的功利主义取代了。毕竟，社会需要的是一众能够填补它的空缺的零件，而非活生生的思辨的人。以我的阅读来看，弗兰克斯夫人的书中重复最多的，是学生们的沉默。这一份描写的真实性，十分宝贵。学生们也一定悄悄地惊异着吧。在一所高中，就开始读起《伊利亚特》，《俄瑞斯忒亚》，《白鲸》这些西方古典书籍。而老师的发问更有意思，绝非刻板的是否之辞："什么是好的生活？""什么是正义？""美德能被教授吗？"课堂的内容，不仅有东西方文化的交换，更是对无意识的现代性思维的质疑。任务是何等的艰巨啊！而当沉默被打破，学生们热忱地创造，思想着的时候，他们又是如何地回报了老师的付出。一篇篇灵动的关于真理与谎言的故事。参与对俄瑞斯忒斯弑父事件的审判。并一如剧中描述，近乎宿命地重复了判决的结果：一半同情俄瑞斯忒斯，一半支持复仇女神。

　　弗兰克斯夫人对人文科学与自然科学有着与众不同的理解。它们并不等同于历史上不断衍变的知识的总聚。历史性的瞬间，唯有被再度经历，才能被称为历史。教育的目的，就是为了品味知识被第一次发现的那永恒性的时刻。沐浴在这样的永恒性的光里，哲思得以开始。中国的人文传统之深厚，不单是祝福，也像某种重负。我们因诸多的传统———已经腐朽而又迟迟未去的传统，或者从未腐朽却被时间遗忘的传统———而难于喘息。在中国，复古的思潮与革新的思潮总会处于尖锐的对立中。人人向往的都是"另一个时代"，竟至于无人能够看清此时此地的困境了。我想，弗兰克斯夫人对于永恒性的理解，会对这样一个国家有所帮助。因为我们现在的问题已经不再是某个民族的问题，而是整个人类的问题。

第十一章里，弗兰克斯夫人讲到天文学革命的时候，如此说道：

"没错，星辰在移动。而它们的移动几乎都有着让人叹为观止的规律性———在天空上的完美的圆形。试着想象一下。它们对人类来说曾意味着什么？尤其在那些比如今更动荡不安的荒蛮的年代里。那时看起来一定和现在日常中的它们截然不同。大地之上，一切都不完美，充斥着卑鄙与混乱……而他们仰望星空，却能看到威严而博大的秩序，规律，与美。如果你生在那个年代，也许会不禁对自己说：天上，那一定是神明居住的地方吧！"

我们正生活在自然科学的荫蔽之下。但在技术无止而文化无定的社会中，也自有其混乱之处。也许这样的敬畏与启示仍然能指引我们的言行？只不过，昭示神意的不再是星辰的运动。东西方伟大的思想者的作品，将为我们指点迷津。

当然，我们已经领悟了这么做的困难所在。东西方文化的触碰，极可能坠入一种肤浅的"多元主义"，把双方最深刻的事物，都磨掉了，抚平了。我们学会了欣赏，却只能嗅到彼此的表层，唯可利用者是图。这不啻为一件万分悲哀的事了。但无论如何，我们规避不了这样的接触。我们———必须为之发声。

仍然读书的时候，我曾在一次校园散步中邂逅了弗兰克斯夫人。我们都精神饱满。圣塔菲城里阳光满溢。我不大记得那时谈论的话了。唯一有印象的，是她论及大学的古典通识课，然后坚定地望了我一眼，总结道："我是完全相信这种教育的。"那一刹那，我心中涌起了想要发问的冲动，一半真诚，一半打趣："可你为什么相信它呢？"不知出于什么缘故，我终于没有开口。谈话也在符合晴日氛围的赞和里悄悄告终。可我多么渴望这样问她啊！写下这篇序言，是在雨意绵绵的傍晚。我这样思索着，回忆起那个宁静的晴日，回忆起作者在书中以无比凝重地口吻写下的那句话：

　　"如果我们太过尊敬彼此的信仰，以至于不愿探讨的时候，它们就会把我们相疏离。"

　　杨景龍

　　2018.8.8

Honor 荣誉

Chapter 1

The *Iliad* and the Best Life

Chinese high school is a warrior culture. The students in my classes in the Beijing high school where I taught for two years from 2012 to 2014 were engaged in constant battle. This became clear to me when I took them slowly through Homer's *Iliad*, the first text in a humanities seminar on the question "What is Change?" The Greek society that Homer sang about was based on competition for excellence in battle, which was rewarded by glory, honor, and prizes. My Chinese students, who were fighting through the literal and figurative tests of a competitive high school, understood that down to their bones.

Everyone attending 北大附中, or *Běi Dà Fù Zhōng*, abbreviated BDFZ, was a high achiever. These students had fought all their lives to excel, graduating from test to test, pulling themselves up by academic accomplishments. They were very nice people, but in that competitive atmosphere they knew the temptation to rejoice as much in others' failures as in their own success. They knew what it was to enter a battle in which there would be both losses and glory.

So much was at stake, after all. With a few exceptions, each was an only child, in line with China's one child policy. On each, as if on the tip of an upside-down pyramid, pressed the weight of the hopes of two parents, four grandparents, and possibly as many as eight great-grandparents, all anxiously hovering. I saw this heavy pressure at work during the days of the big test, called the 高考 (*Gāo kǎo*), which Chinese high school students are required to take at the end of their senior year to qualify for admission to any Chinese university. Only those who do well on the test get into prestigious schools that offer the possibility of success in the Chinese hierarchy and a life filled with glory, honor and the prizes of the world. To do badly on the test means a second-rate school, disappointment to the family, perhaps a slide into obscurity and a life of shame, humiliation and want.

The *Gāo kǎo* is administered simultaneously at various sites all over China, including at BDFZ. On *Gāo kǎo* weekend, tension knotted up the air and the gates to the school were locked. Security guards marched importantly about in flak jackets and helmets while an ambulance waited nearby for the not-unlikely possibility that some students would collapse under their burden. Yellow tape marked off the test centers as if they were crime scenes. Red banners raised above the entryway festively but ominously marked the occasion with giant characters: "Welcome students to the 2013 Annual *Gāo kǎo* Examinations." On the afternoon of the last day of the test, a crowd gathered slowly outside the campus gates. Parents, grandparents and great-grandparents were there, each family waiting for a child to return from battle. They stood patiently, many holding flowers. When at last the test was over, exhausted students issued out of the gates to their families. The crowd parted for them, scanning their faces and trying to read expressions. How had the battle gone? Would there be glory, honor and prizes, or would there be shame, humiliation and want?

The students in our section of BDFZ, the Dalton Academy, had chosen a different path. The Dalton Academy catered to students who had decided to go to college or university in the United States. These students did not take the *Gāo kǎo*, but they transferred the cloud of anxiety that would otherwise have surrounded the *Gāo kǎo* to the SAT or the TOEFL (Test of English as a Foreign Language), on both of which they had to do well to get into an American school. Whether because of their early years pointed toward the *Gāo kǎo* or because they had no other concept of education they rarely thought of anything other than how to get the right answers on tests. They spent enormous amounts of time and money on test preparation, sometimes skimping on work I asked of them in my humanities class (I admonished them in study hall: "Stop doing practice tests and read novels!"). I disliked their preoccupation with tests so much that in my classes I never gave them any, which mystified them. As far as they knew, doing well on tests was the only point of school. It was like telling a soldier not to drill for battle, or an Olympic athlete not to train for a sporting event. How could they win the prizes if they did not prepare for the test? How could they ace the test if there wasn't going to be one? My argument—that a person might genuinely be interested in learning—seemed to them a quaint, if charming, frivolity. They could not afford to indulge in it.

I pushed the argument anyway. It was part of the job that my husband Grant and I had come to China to do. The Dalton Academy had hired us to widen its students' classroom experience, to prepare them for the possibility that professors in the United States might want something more from them than skill at multiple choice tests. Our assignment was to swim against the stream of the students' many-years focus on tests and awaken within them new ways of thinking.

Grant and I brought to this task many years of experience teaching at St. John's College, which was founded on the idea that students should experience learning as a reaching towards freedom through reading and conversation. At St. John's, there are no classroom lectures. The curriculum consists almost entirely of reading classic texts and talking about them. Conversations about classic texts, St. John's believes, train the mind by working with examples of excellence that have set the highest of human standards for thought and articulate feeling. At the same time, talking about those texts challenges students to develop and defend their own opinions as well as to think about how all of these ideas, classic or personal, apply to the circumstances of the modern world. This practice of creativity, grounded on excellence, leads to freedom.

Such conversations are also a way of being human together, a means by which people can better understand each other. While students learn together about the ideas that have shaped the world, they learn at the same time to hear each other and respond to each other with an attention and patience that often becomes friendship. From my experience teaching at St. John's I knew this process worked, and I believed it would work in China, too.

I was in my second year of teaching in China when I assigned Homer's *Iliad* as lead-off text for a humanities seminar organized around the topic: "What is Change?" One aspect of my purpose at the Dalton Academy was to familiarize the students with Western intellectual tradition, of which the *Iliad* is one of the most familiar landmarks. Furthermore, I loved the *Iliad* and I believed I could help my students love it, too.

Seeking the possibility of connection between Homer and China, I turned to historian Karl Jaspers' concept of "the Axial Age[1] (800—200 BCE)." The Axial Age was a time of astonishing intellectual and spiritual flowering when Greece, China, India, Iran and Palestine had produced writings—among them the *Iliad*—that indicated a simultaneous waking to consciousness. Widely spread over the globe, with little or no evidence of any exchange between them, philosophers, prophets and poets from vastly different cultures all began to discuss and catalyze writings on what it meant to be alive, or on how people should live. The Chinese philosopher Confucius and Homer both lived within the Axial Age and despite their geographical separation, it was possible to imagine them exchanging poetry and ideas. If they had, they would have found each other interested in the same kind of conversation. Both were asking or answering the question: "What is the best life?"

---

1   Karl Jaspers, *The Origin and Goal of History*, 10th Ed. (Greenwood Press 1977), *passim*.

It seemed right for a humanities class on the topic of change to start with this moment, the first flowering of the most wonderful capacity of our humanity, our ability to be self-conscious. Perhaps this was the most radical change in human history, the moment when people stepped outside of thoughtless experience and began to talk deliberately about the best way to live. Also, this change was related to the change I wanted to encourage in my students' attitude toward learning, to step outside an unthinking focus on tests and wake up, as Homer and Confucius woke up in the Axial Age, to consider how life should be lived.

These immense ideas were curiously appropriate for the students of the Dalton Academy. They had been raised in China and had learned English to launch themselves outside their native culture, seeking some yet-to-be-defined understanding of humanity. More than any generation before them they would be modeling a new global, interconnected existence, reflecting East and West in conversation to create a broader view of humanity than has ever been before.

To get them ready for such a conversation, we would start with the Axial Age and walk through history, finding instances of great change reflected in classic texts and discussing how and why the changes occurred. The Western tradition was what I knew, so I had to focus on that. Somewhere inside these students, however, the wider conversation I hoped for would be beginning. Ideally, they would apply what I showed them to aspects of their own culture and find new ways to understand human experience. It was a grandiose notion, but there was no percentage in thinking small—grandiose ideas cost no more than crabbed, boring little ones.

On the first day of class the students were wary. I settled them into a circle of desks, facing each other, an arrangement they didn't like. They would have felt more at ease neatly arranged in rows and columns facing me, waiting for me to tell them what to think. I didn't want the class to be easy for them in that way, though, and ignored their mild discomfort.

I asked a few questions about the *Iliad*, trying to see where they were with their reading and what they had thought of it. Most had read the book. Almost everybody had looked it up on Wikipedia, from which they had absorbed a few peremptory opinions that they aired in a conclusory way. The strongest feelings were around the battle scenes, which some thought exciting and others found gross. All this was to be expected. In all likelihood, they were simply giving me what they had decided I would expect, in a way that was both polite and cynical at the same time. These students thought they knew how to impress teachers: find the right answer, get credit for saying it first, then move on. We spent some time on administrative matters, including my explanation about what would be expected of them in a discussion class, a new experience for most of them. They were accepting, though wary.

On the second day of class, we began our conversation on the first book of the *Iliad*. It was a challenge. I was a new teacher for many of them, and everybody was hesitant to raise their voices in this strange setting (and in English, too!). The hardest task I faced teaching in China was convincing my students that I genuinely wanted to hear what they had to say. For all their years in the classroom, they had only spoken when they knew the answer to something. They had never been encouraged to speculate aloud and had no experience with conversation as a way to explore ideas. By contrast, in America even shy people believe that they *should* talk, and that airing opinions is a good thing. In America there is a saying "the squeaky wheel gets the grease;" in the East, the saying goes "the nail that sticks up gets hammered." Getting my students to talk in class required making them feel safe from hammering. They would need to feel confident enough to speak out if they went to college in the United States. More immediately, I wanted to offer them my own feeling that conversation among friends is worth risking something for, as a big part of the best life.

"Was Agamemnon, the leader of the Greek armies, a good king?" I asked.

Silence.

I stood up and wrote the question on the whiteboard, then sat in the circle again. "What do you think? Was Agamemnon a good king?"

More silence. Some people looked at each other. Others looked down and fiddled with pens. Finally, the silence became so uncomfortable that one student, Janie,[2] could stand it no longer, and broke it. "No," she said with an angry air, as if it made her mad that she had been driven to speak. "He should not have taken away prizes from his best warrior Achilles and humiliated him in public. That is stupid. A good king isn't stupid."[3]

They were off. It still took time and lots of encouragement, but discussion has a momentum that grows with each new comment. Each expressed opinion calls forth an equal and opposite opinion. After Janie gave her view I asked her a few questions about it (Why do you think Agamemnon did such a stupid thing? What might worry him about Achilles?). This caused Sam to react and

---

2　All of my Chinese students had chosen English names long ago when they first began to study English. I have changed these names here, and the discussions are a distillation and combination of many discussions.

3　In this book I have corrected the students' use of English in the classroom. The students knew English very well, but when it came to speaking they often ignored the parts they found strange, unnecessary or confusing, like verb tenses and articles. Why, they reasoned, did English change the spelling of verbs to express time? What was the point of "I went to the store?" Why not just say "I go to the store yesterday," as Chinese does? They also complained about the use of the English definite article. The rules for how the word "the" works in English are appalling. When challenged, I could not defend those rules on rational grounds. After several long kvetching sessions, I announced that I would hear no more complaints—the rules were the rules. I was vividly aware—having had it pointed out to me gleefully by these astute students—that my authoritarianism when it came to proper English compromised my position as a teacher of critical thinking. My response: "Life is full of contradictions. Live with them." After some plodding classes in which, to the boredom and frustration of all, I tried to combine discussion of the books with the teaching of English, we settled into a *détente*. I did not slow down a conversation to correct anyone's English, although I often restated something in correct English to make sure I had understood it and to show how a native speaker would construct that thought. In their writing, however, I held them to good English grammar. They had to get through college first, I told them, and then they could become linguists and spend their lives taking revenge on English by pointing out its flaws. It was an attractive prospect.

voice the opposite opinion to hers: "A good king should control a powerful warrior, or his authority will be attacked. Agamemnon is smart to think that Achilles is a problem." Anne agreed, saying: "Achilles acting like child weakens the other fighters. A good king must keep the army strong."

Janie was inclined to be offended at Sam and Anne's disagreement. She felt it as a challenge to her and turned on them combatively, saying with some scorn that Agamemnon could have found a less stupid and greedy way to control Achilles if he was afraid of him. Sam swelled a little and for a moment it looked as if there might be a quarrel just like the one in the *Iliad* but other voices quickly calmed the waters. More than American students, Chinese students dislike disharmony in the classroom and will seek to heal it.

Soon we were talking about the problem of authority and kingship. How can a good king deal with the dangerous situation of having as a subject someone who is more divinely gifted and a better warrior than the king himself? The students brought up two or three examples from Chinese history and were surprised when I welcomed these references. They found it odd, it seemed, to talk about history in a humanities class. I thought I could see them processing this oddness cautiously in their minds and concluding that there was no telling what a Western teacher might do. Certainly, they enjoyed telling me about Chinese history; they could practice talking in English, and I could learn from them, which they found satisfying.

In the next class, I brought up the Axial Age as the moment when, all over the globe, people began to be self-conscious. Homer, Confucius, and the Buddha, as well as other great thinkers and religious leaders, all flourished within a few hundred years of each other and all were asking the question at the heart of the humanities: "What is the best life?" It's a question that everyone has, as all people must make decisions about what life to live. Each of these students, for example, had already chosen to be at this school, and soon would have to choose what to study in college and what career they wanted.

I asked them, "What do you think is the best life?"

After a long pause, someone, nearly whispering, ventured: "The best life has lots of money." This prompted suppressed giggles.

"Okay, good," I said. "Suppose you have lots of money. What do you do with money?"

"Buy things," someone else said boldly, getting a laugh.

"All right. Obviously, you don't want money itself, you want the things money can buy. What things?" I wanted to know.

Lots of ideas poured out at that: "Clothes, jewels, travel, a big house …"

"Why do you want these things?" I asked. They thought that was a ridiculous question. There was no *why* about wanting things. You just wanted them.

Tom joked, "I want whatever my friends don't have!"

"So," I said to him, "you want your friends to envy you. You want to impress them?" They looked at me with an "of course!" expression that was tinged with a little surprised embarrassment—I gathered that people rarely said that aloud. "Why do you want that?" I pressed.

"I would feel proud," Tom answered, after a moment.

"You want glory and honor, like a Greek warrior?" He agreed, relieved that we were talking about the book again. Yes, he was like a Greek warrior that way.

I summarized: "All of us want money but not necessarily money itself. We want to be able to buy things. But it's not only things we want. We also want other people to envy us and be impressed by us. That is, we are Greek warriors. We want the prizes that money can buy, and we want people to give us glory and honor." They thought about this.

Allen jumped into the silence and announced: "I want to be rock star."

"You know I'm going to ask," I responded, "why do you want that?" He grinned, sure he had figured out the answer and said, "glory, honor and prizes!"

"Really?" I teased him back. "You don't actually like music? It's just a way to get glory, honor and prizes?" Allen's music was a byword around the campus. He had a band and played in it every extra moment he had. Seeing no way to deny it, he admitted that he loved music for its own sake.

I asked, "If you had to choose between money and music, which would you choose?"

This question seemed to hit a sore place. Nobody liked it. Faces turned downwards. Perhaps it named something that many of them hid within, including Allen. They might like music, or art, or anything, but they had obligations to their families, some of whom had sacrificed a lot to get them into a school like this, with a shot at a future in an American college. They felt a duty to get rich.

"I won't choose," said Allen, bravely. "I want both." The circle lightened, and I thought they would applaud.

"Let's go back to the *Iliad*," I offered. "It turns out that we understand Achilles very well. He's the world's best warrior, which was at the time the way to get glory, honor and prizes—he's the rock star of ancient Greece. It looks like he is living the best life as a celebrated hero in battle before the city of Troy, which the Greeks are trying to conquer. Then a quarrel arises, and, in front of the whole Greek army, Agamemnon the king takes away his prizes and humiliates him. He's still the best warrior, but his glory, honor and prizes have been stolen from him. How does he feel?"

They knew that one. It was the first word of the poem. "Angry!" said several students at once. "Ra-a-ge," said Janie in a deep voice, enjoying the word.

"Yes, angry, full of rage. So, thinking about what we have just said about what you believe is the best life, tell me exactly why he is angry."

They worked out an answer. Achilles wasn't just angry at Agamemnon for humiliating him. There was a deeper matter at stake. Achilles, as we learn later in the poem, had two possible lives. He could choose between a short, glorious life or a long one in obscurity. He had been thoughtlessly living the glorious life when Agamemnon had taken away his glory. Yet Agamemnon still expected him to go into battle and die young, all to support Agamemnon's cause. Achilles had been cheated. No wonder he was angry and walked away from battle, even if that behavior looked shameful to everyone around him. Suddenly Achilles had been forced to consider, as we all must, whether the life he was living was really the best life.

Allen, apparently, was still thinking about his music and suddenly said: "If that happened to me, part of me would be happy."

"Why?" asked many, in astonishment. He didn't want to answer. The question hung in the air, perhaps because people began to guess at what he might mean. When Achilles had his honor stolen he did not have to fight anymore. He could sit safe in his tent, away from battle, and talk of going home. He could take up the lyre and sing songs. Maybe Allen was playing out in his mind what would happen if he were cheated of his success at school. He would be angry but he also wouldn't have to study so hard. He wouldn't have to feel so responsible all the time. He could play his guitar and sing. There would be shame, humiliation, and the risk of want, but there would be some relief, too.

Elaine remarked, "Maybe now Achilles thinks he will make the other choice and live a long life." As class ended we left Achilles in his tent, trying to decide what was the best life. Students stood up chattering excitedly in Chinese, which I took as a good sign that their interest was caught. Across nearly three thousand years these Chinese students were finding a common question with an ancient Greek warrior.

I had asked students to write a paragraph of reaction to the *Iliad,* mostly to get a look at their English writing. Like their speech, it often reflected Chinese grammatical structures, suggesting that they were thinking in Chinese and then translating into English. Perhaps some of them were even doing the translating with Google. Either way, there was a lot of work for me. I was willing to let minor grammatical lapses slide in conversation, but to get through college in America their writing in English needed to be correct. There would be no tests in my class, but there would be papers.

One thing that the assignment made clear was that we would have to talk about religion. Homer's gods mystified many of the students, who regarded them scornfully as superstitions, a reaction not too different from classes I had taught in America. The gods in Homer are childish, whiny, fussy, deceitful, subject to flattery and bribery, and lacking in the smallest self-consciousness or maturity. East or West, readers inevitably wonder whether Homer was primitive, stupid or both to attribute divinity to such trivial characters. My Chinese students had all of these doubts and more besides. Most of them had been raised without any experience of religion at all and they were thus more likely than students I had in the West to assume that Homer was giving an accurate picture of all gods and all religion.

In response, I spent a class suggesting that they think about Homer's gods as if they were embodied powers. "Take music, for example," I said, smiling at Allen. "It's powerful. It affects people. Music, language, beauty, ambition, the capacity to make things—all these relate to human abilities and feelings, but they also seem bigger than humans. People get caught up in their power. But power, just by itself, doesn't necessarily make somebody dignified or mature. It may even do the opposite. When we are in the grip of the powers represented by Apollo, Aphrodite, Zeus or Hephaestus we often do very foolish, undignified, immature, and even awful things. We march to war and get killed under the influence of music and rhetoric. We make idiots of ourselves and cause disastrous consequences for love. We commit crimes in pursuit of ambition. We destroy our world with technology. Homer's poetry treats these powers as if they were divine persons that are themselves undignified and immature, expressing that these abilities are powerful and immortal but also dangerous and arbitrary—they do not always lead to good. There's truth in that, don't you think?"

They mulled this over, still mostly inclined to believe that this Western Homer guy was not actually a great artist, but merely silly and primitive. They suspected I was trying to make Homer look better than he was.

One of the privileges of reading classic texts with students who had never heard of them before was the freshness of their reactions. It was great to pierce the reverence that famous books sometimes command, to the detriment of the freedom of response that they must have met when they were first read. For example, in our first year in China, Grant and I had taught a class on *Hamlet*, which we read slowly, accompanied by plenty of video performances. It was marvelous to listen to the opinions of students who did not yet know how it ended. "I think Hamlet and Ophelia are going to get back together," one student argued, "they are obviously all bound up with each other." These students helped me feel the tragedy more deeply than I ever had when, in the last four minutes of the play, so many people that have loomed so important lie suddenly dead on the stage.

It wasn't clear to me, however, how such a fresh look at classic texts would work with regard to the topic of religion, which has played so big a role in the West. Differences in attitudes toward religion make for knotty issues in any context and can be a threat to conversation. I knew I would have to take care with the subject.

In the classes that followed, we made our way through the *Iliad*, seizing every chance to discuss the ways in which the quarrels, contests, and affections of the characters from Greece and Troy were familiar from our own lives. For the battle books, I assigned everybody a warrior whose story they were to follow and repeat for the class. I tried not to give sensitive people gory deaths to report on, but Homer makes it hard to avoid those horrors. Even some of the students I thought tough and uncaring were a little upset when a spear pierced their warrior's kidney and a character they had come to know clenched the dust in his teeth, his soul chittering away to Hades. Sometimes the poet-narrator pauses the fight and gives the whole life story of a warrior as he faces a charging hero, so that readers come to care about him and feel for his family just before watching him die. Harsh stuff.

As the book and the semester progressed, there were a variety of reactions to how we were reading and talking. A few students, at least at the beginning, wrote the whole class off as an easy credit, because there were no tests and no one was forced to join the conversation. That's always a danger of teaching through reading and conversation, which relies on students' genuine interest. For a few, the idea of school as a source of genuine interest was so foreign that they did not know how to approach it. They had spent so much of their lives looking at school as a source of glory, honor and prizes separate from their real interests that they did not know how to treat it otherwise. Such students spoke in class only to ask about how they would be graded. Some kept their heads down entirely, thinking they were cleverly getting away with something when they skipped the reading or stayed silent during discussion. Slowly, over the year, many of this group warmed to what we were doing, although a small number never did. School as a source of genuine interest was too strange. Perhaps it will open for them some day and they will remember us.

Lots of students, though, loved what went on in our class, even though they still thought it a charming luxury that they could not afford to indulge in very much. If an SAT loomed, or a test in another subject, work for my class was likely to be the first thing shorted. Yet the figure of Achilles became vivid in their minds. Living in their own warrior educational culture, they sympathized with him. They understood how angry he was when the glory, honor and prizes he had worked for were taken from him. They understood, too, why his reaction to that was to wonder whether it had ever been worth spending his life on such things. Once a person gets to that place, it is a small step to the general question of the Axial Age, which applies in every age, to every person, and especially to high school students on the verge of momentous choices: "What is the best life?"

Homer's answer to that question is not obvious. When Achilles hears of the death of his friend Patroclus, he returns to battle, although he knows that the choice to do so will shorten his life. This time he is not looking for glory, honor and prizes, but is in the grip of a new wave of rage. He kills Patroclus' killer, Hector, the son of King Priam of Troy. He doesn't stop there, though. He and humiliates Hector's corpse in every way he can think of, dragging it around the walls of Troy, displaying to the Trojans his contempt for their loved hero, as well as their coming destruction.

Even after all this, Achilles' rage against the dead Hector does not quiet. It is unquenchable, it seems. Then Homer gives us one of the greatest moments in Western literature, a moving image of unexpected human connection. In the final book of the *Iliad*, King Priam comes silently into the Greek camp, by night and alone, to beg Achilles to give him Hector's corpse for honorable burial. Achilles and Priam, enemies, are both victims of war, having lost people they loved and knowing they will themselves die soon. Their hearts touch. As one of my students put it in a lovely English sentence: "Achilles and Priam weep together, in the dark, in the quiet of Achilles' tent, with the army sleeping around them."

So began our educational experiment on the study of change, with Homer's picture of human beings encountering each other through grief and mortal loss. One consequence of the peculiar human ability to become self-conscious to which humanity awoke in the Axial Age, is that we are aware that our time is limited—we should be sure that we spend it on living the best life. The best life might involve turning away from the prizes the world offers in order to think through what we genuinely want. This thinking-through is education. It was what I wanted to give to my Chinese students.

Quietly, too, I harbored hopes of a different kind. Achilles' glory, as Homer sings it, is far greater than it would have been had he merely been famous for winning battles. His lasting glory is that the changes brought about in him lead him to feel for human loss and sorrow, even in his greatest enemy. In a globalizing context in which nationalism, racism, sexism, and other prejudices can cause us to see enemies everywhere, it seemed both truthful and hopeful not only to start with the question common to people the world over at the beginning—what is the best life?—but also to suggest that the answer to the question was bound up with empathy for a common humanity. Possibly the Chinese philosopher Confucius meant something like this when he spoke of "仁 (rén)," or "humaneness." If so—and it will be the job of people like my students, with a foot in both traditions, to decide—then the insight is neither Eastern nor Western but belongs to us all.

In any case, there was no turning back. By coming to the Dalton Academy, my students had already walked away from the battle of the Gāo kǎo. No matter how they had chosen it, they were warriors on Achilles' path instead, defying ordinary expectations and trying out a different approach to the question of what kind of life they wanted. There was nothing to do now but keep moving.

Meaning　含义

Chapter 2

Moby Dick and Seeking Out Mystery

A year and a half before I began my seminar on Change, when Grant and I were first offered the chance to teach in China, the idea was so exciting that, for a long time as we made our preparations, it did not seem important that the invitation did not include any detail about what, exactly, we would be teaching. We did not know if our St. John's College approach was what was wanted or what the curriculum would be. When on a Skype call we raised this subject with H, headmaster of the Dalton Academy, he gave a dismissive, pixilated wave. "We'll talk about that when you get here," he said.

All we knew was that the Dalton Academy section of BDFZ, in addition to its mission to prepare students for an American education, was part of a general experiment in Chinese education to get away from a deadening focus on tests like the *Gāo kǎo* and instead encourage student creativity. In the 1990s, the Chinese bureaucracy, listening to complaints about the *Gāo kǎo*, had become worried that obsessive preparation for a two-day make-or-break examination did not foster creative thought. The Central Committee issued a decree that high schools and universities, in addition to their well-established test-based science and mathematics classes, must require that their students take courses in "general education."

The educators who received this mandate were puzzled. No one was sure what the phrase "general education" meant, as the Central Committee did not say. In their puzzlement, different schools undertook a range of experiments. Some thought that "general education" meant returning to traditional Confucian studies. Others created courses on appreciating Chinese cultural history. Yet others associated the phrase with Western-style liberal arts education, seeing in it an individualistic focus that promised a path to creative confidence. Grant and I, with our years of teaching and learning at St. John's College, had experience with at least one form of that kind of education, so it made sense that H might want us to teach from classic Western texts—or possibly classic Eastern texts, which are also taught at St. John's—in a conversational, seminar style. But if seminar, conversational teaching of texts was what H wanted, which texts should we teach? It seemed odd not to know.

There was too much to do to worry about it much, though. We busied ourselves with the thousand bureaucratic and practical steps that had to be taken before we could take a single step on the actual journey. From time to time in all this activity I was overtaken by a sense of the blankness of the future. During my childhood in the 1960s, China itself had been a blankness, a large, pink empty spot on the globe. Grant and I were American white suburban children of the anti-communist cold war era. We had been raised to shiver at communism. I could not imagine what communist China would look or feel like, even in the most everyday ways. What would our living space be like? What would the school and the neighborhood be like? Every effort to look into the future was like putting my foot on a step that wasn't there.

When we finally touched down in China, the process of filling in the blankness began. My first sight of China was not pink but grey and red, mostly grey. Grey swirled about in the air. Through the pervading greyness there were touches of red on signs and walls that conveyed a few accents of cheerfulness or strength. To be fair, I felt pretty grey and red-eyed myself, after a fifteen-hour plane flight.

H met us at the airport with a school van and driver, a kindness the magnitude of which we did not understand until later. The

Beijing airport is quite far from the city proper, and the route back to Beijing went through some countryside. Trees stood out against the grey and red, although they were oddly regimented, serried in rows rather than looking like unplanned woodland growth. Each carefully spaced tree trunk was painted to the level of about five feet with a grey-white substance, some sort of insecticide, perhaps. I wondered how many centuries it had been since this patch of the world had been wilderness.

Trees gave way to buildings, increasing in density and size. They were grey, sometimes because they were concrete but sometimes because they were painted grey. As the city gathered about us, I was taken aback by the look of the street signs in Chinese. Chinese characters, unlike English words, do not have different widths. Every character can be formed within the same-sized square. That meant that street signs had to my tired eyes an odd, regular, justified look, as if meaning had been serried and regimented like the trees. I tried to flip this around and imagine the look of English words to a Chinese reader. English might look to her the way Arabic looks to me—squiggly and stretched out.

My mother claimed that she could remember the moment she learned to read. She was five years old, riding in her parents' car and looking out the window at a billboard. She saw marks and then, suddenly, the billboard was talking to her, as if a radio had been turned on. For me, here in China, the billboards and signs had gone silent. Entering a city where I could not read the signs felt like deafness. Meaning was in the air around me, but I had no access to it. Suddenly, I wondered whether my new Chinese students would experience my teaching like that. How long it would take before we could hear each other's meaning? I glanced at H. Perhaps the curriculum, which I still knew nothing about, would take our foreignness into account and hurry the process along? I shook my head and went back to rubbernecking.

After several long waits in traffic the van came to a part of Beijing that looked prosperous. The buildings were new and slick, though perhaps a little slapdash. Huge shopping complexes covered with advertisements were everywhere, many of them with English words in addition to Chinese. But the English now also looked strange in its new, subordinate setting, muted and abashed. Already China had changed how I saw.

Until this point the streets had all been wide and crowded with cars, but we turned at last down a narrow lane. Like a splash of red cheer amid grey strangeness, a familiar Seven Eleven sign greeted us just before we entered the iron and stone gateway into the enclosure of the campus of the Affiliated High School of Peking University. The Chinese for the school's name was set in regimented, serried bronze characters above the gate: 北 大 附中. I recognized them! Amazing! Soon all these signs will be talking to me, I thought, hopefully. A uniformed guard stepped from his guardhouse, peered at us and waved us through the gate as it rolled open.

The school van stopped at the first structure, where we got out with our bags. H led us through some doors to an elevator, endearingly old and creaky. The building looked like a 1960s apartment complex in America, once cutting-edge modern and now aging, though still serviceable. When this place was being built, I was in elementary school coloring a pink China on cartoonish world maps. I shook my tired head again and made an effort to stay in the present. The elevator puffed and pulled us up to the fourth floor, where many of the foreign teachers were housed. The numeral four in Chinese rhymes with the word for death, so it's a very unlucky number and Chinese speakers do not want to live on the fourth floor of anything. Fortunately—I suppose people reasoned—foreigners had already had such supreme bad luck in not being born Chinese that no worse could happen to them. There we were.

Our apartment proved to be two former dorm rooms knocked together, about 500 square feet, within which was a bathroom and a tiny kitchen. A shiny new washing machine took up most of the free space in this kitchen, which had no dishwasher and no oven, as Chinese cooking does not rely on ovens. The living room contained a small refrigerator, desks, and sturdy chairs made of thick dark wood, together with a cubelike coffee table (tea table, I guess) and an enormous wardrobe that had a twin in the bedroom. Two windows looked at a brick wall, but a third gave a view of the central courtyard of the school. The bed was hard—all the beds we encountered in China were hard—which proved to be a great thing for Grant's back. Was this an expression of the physical wisdom of the East that it was good for the body to sleep on a hard surface? Or did we happen to visit only places that bought cheap mattresses? During our two years in China, we learned to live with such ambivalence of meaning.

There had been some kind provision for our coming and necessities had been laid in, for which we were grateful. H saw us begin to unpack and then wished us good night, closing the door behind him. As the door shut Grant and I turned to each other. It had been an impossibly long day, after months of planning for we-did-not-know-what. Now we were here. This was the reality about which we had been wondering all that time. The blankness of our future in China had been filled in a little, at least with broad brush marks of our immediate surroundings. We smiled at each other. It all seemed possible. There was nothing too strange.

A knock on the door sounded. H had forgotten to tell us something. "Don't drink the tap water," he said. "It will make you sick." He closed the door again.

Even so. We could do this.

The next day, before our planned meeting with H in his office to talk about the curriculum, we explored the surroundings of our new home, filling in more blankness. We walked first through the campus of BDFZ, dominated by a central, fenced basketball court on which students were shooting hoops in a leisurely way. The dormitories and classroom buildings surrounding the court were all similar to our apartment building, no doubt of the same vintage. On one side of the courtyard, a decorative pool with lily-pads reflected the sky and, as we later learned, bred mosquitoes. A row of notice boards lined our path filled with what appeared to be cheerful public service announcements from the Communist Party. We couldn't read them, but one of them was pretty clearly an anti-smoking message. Nearby, high school students talked and laughed in the September sun. In the center of the space between the buildings, a flagpole proudly flew the Chinese flag, red against a grey sky.

We left the campus by a gate that gave access to a large street with six or eight lanes of traffic loudly roaring, over which was a massive pedestrian bridge that allowed us to cross above the flowing, honking cars. Such bridges are common in Beijing. The city is organized broadly by a series of ring roads concentric to Tiananmen Square, each with a wider perimeter than the one before. Our school was just inside the fourth ring road. The seventh ring road, which was still being planned when we were there, would connect far-flung towns and cities to the capital. We had seen this on maps at home, but now, feeling jet-lagged and vulnerable as I watched the cars whisk under me, I imagined the number of ring roads rising indefinitely, ever greater circles taking over more and more space, engulfing the world. No, I told myself sternly, no fear. It never helps.

On the bridge some vendors were selling cheap goods. Nearby was a beggar who lay flat on his face, unmoving, with a tin can in front of him in mute appeal. More vendors lined the farther sidewalk, and a singer with a portable CD player and a microphone ·belted out a Western song to an audience of twenty or thirty people, many holding shopping bags. Crowds, though cheerful, were unrelenting, pouring on and on like currents and eddies of water. At the street corners that did not have a pedestrian bridge, there were no Walk/Don't Walk safety signs. Traffic seemed to function in an interestingly lawless atmosphere, guided perhaps by the *Dào* (道). People would crowd to the edge of the curb, and then inch into the road until their mass was enough to make the cars slow down and let them cross. When the pressure of pedestrians eased, cars took over until it built up again. Stop signs were mere accents of red, more ornamental than practical.

Apart from people and Chinese characters, very little of what we saw on this first walk in China seemed especially Chinese. One or two buildings were designed to look like structures of the imperial era as commercial attractions, but, for the most part, our surroundings of skyscrapers and tall apartment buildings looked like a high-end shopping district in America or perhaps anywhere in the world. Our Chinese students, when they went to America for college, would feel at home. We heard later that an underground mall that we reached by escalator had originally been built as a bunker to protect government dignitaries if there was nuclear war. The shops there now sold a variety of clothes, expensive toiletries, and plastic tchotchkes—big-eyed cats with clocks in their stomachs waved paws at us. Down one corridor, stored under a staircase, was an enormous dusty dragon's head, waiting for the celebration of the Lunar New Year in February.

Feeling color and line begin to fill up the emptiness of our pre-China imaginings, we headed back to BDFZ for our meeting with H. The moment had finally come, we thought, when H would fill in another blank by revealing what the subject of our classes would be. As soon as we settled into H's office, I asked him pointblank what he wanted me to teach. He responded with a question: "What is your favorite book?" "Well," I replied, taken by surprise, "I suppose my favorite book is *Moby Dick*." "Teach that," he said.

"Wait!" I thought, but did not speak, mulling this idea over. Grant asked H what he meant, and H explained that he wanted teachers to care about the books they taught. He believed that, if a teacher cared about a book, s/he could make the students care, too. His goal was not only to help his Chinese students feel comfortable in the kind of discussion class that they would encounter in humanities classes when they went to college or university in America but also to help them see why people take genuine pleasure or interest in reading—what reading could mean in a life. This is a perspective that these students had rarely met. Their educational lives had focused on reading books solely for the purpose of amassing information in order to do well on tests. H saw this as short-sighted, even on its own terms. Tests at the university level would require a depth of understanding that is best gained, he thought, by being sincerely interested in learning. A life-time of reading pleasure was an added benefit to this strategy. The curriculum at the Dalton Academy, in his view, could offer these double benefits of reading by teaching books that mattered to teachers personally.

While part of me listened to this explanation with strong approval, another part of me was remembering how *Moby Dick* became my favorite book. It happened because my mother was ill and undergoing chemotherapy. Her treatment sessions took place in a large room in which, around a nurse's station, stood a circle of recliners, each with an intravenous drip apparatus beside it. The atmosphere of the room was sad, frightened, and also boring. I volunteered to fight this ambiance by reading something aloud to her during her treatment, a reversal of roles from the many years she had read to me when I was a child. As we were rushing out the door of her apartment to go for a treatment, I grabbed a book from the top of a pile. It was *Moby Dick*. My mother had read it decades before, in high school. She had not thought she liked it much then, but it had haunted her and she had decided to read it again, to see how it would seem to her after seventy years of added experience.

At the hospital, when she had settled into place in her recliner I pulled up a chair and began to read. At first I was sonorous and self-important, conscious of *Moby Dick*'s status as the Great American Novel. That didn't last, though. As my mother and I discovered, the book is—among its other riches—*funny*. Improbably in that somber setting we first giggled in a subdued way and then laughed out loud. That memory is precious to me, the two of us laughing together as poison dripped into my mother's arm.

"Okay, I will," I announced, breaking into what Grant and H were saying. "I'll teach *Moby Dick*." Their conversation was winding down anyway. Grant had just decided to teach the dialogues of Plato in order to confront the students with questions that could not be reduced to clear answers (one dialogue poses the question "Tell me, oh Socrates, can virtue be taught?"—not a question that lends itself to a multiple choice format). We had our direction, although there was still a good deal of blankness staring us in the face. How, we wondered, would Plato and *Moby Dick* work in a Chinese high school classroom? This too was a question that did not have a clear answer. "Oh, well," I thought, as cheerfully as I could. "It will be a good thing to seek out what I did not yet know."

Thus we set sail on two voyages at once. One was the strange new world of China, and the other was the project of trying to pass on to Chinese students our own love of some of the books that have shaped Western culture. Both day-to-day living and our classroom work were to be exercises in learning to read. Trying to read the meanings around us in everyday things would puzzle us as much as we would puzzle our students by teaching them to read meanings in literary and philosophical works outside their culture, and by means of discussion classes that were outside their experience. Sometimes people would get angry, frustrated with questions and mysteries that seemed to have a meaning that was never made clear. More than a few students in Grant's Plato classes fumed at Socrates for refusing to provide answers to the questions he raised, claiming to be glad when he was executed.

The two voyages of exploration naturally mixed. The grey and red, our explorations of the vast, absorbing city of Beijing, together with the later excursions we made into other parts of China, intertwined with what we were trying to offer our students. The intertwining went the other way, too. Especially in that first year of teaching, I learned that books I had loved and taught for years spoke differently because they spoke in China. China spoke back.

Until I saw *Moby Dick* through the eyes of Chinese high school students, for example, I had not realized how many Western stories a reader needed to know to make sense of the book, nor how much my own understanding of the world came from stories I had heard as a child. My students confronted me with the destabilizing realization that these stories had been shaping my way of seeing and reading all my life and had been doing it behind my back. It was an education all by itself to be forced to imagine looking at the world through an entirely different set of stories. I would have to listen to China.

The first three words of *Moby Dick* showed me and my Chinese students something of the task that faced the class with regard to foundational stories. At the beginning of the semester, after introductions and preliminaries, I read aloud the first line of the book: "Call me Ishmael."

The St. John's style of teaching starts every class with an opening question, designed to kick off a conversation. "Why," I asked them, "does the narrator tell us to *call* him Ishmael? Why not just say 'my name is Ishmael?'"

They looked a little surprised and were cautiously silent.

I adjusted a little, asking: "Do you think Ishmael is really his name?"

Still silence, as they looked at each other then down at their books.

I tried a more personal approach: "Have any of you ever thought about what you would call yourself if you could choose your own name?" A few people nodded, and I turned to one of them and asked: "What would it be?" She told me in a soft voice. The others in the group looked at her, obviously trying out this different name in their heads.

"If you started calling yourself this new name, do you think you would feel any different?" I then asked. I watched the class imagining what such a change might be like. The student nodded.

"So what people call you makes a difference?" Another nod, a little less confident.

I read the first line of the book again, "Call me Ishmael," and asked if they thought it was the narrator's real name.

"Maybe a different name for the story?" someone guessed, looking at me to see if that was the right answer.

"Good thought," I affirmed. "It could be that he chooses the name Ishmael because that name means something for the story."

So far, so good. Now came the hard part. I had to give them some idea of what the narrator might be saying by choosing this particular name.

The students settled back into their chairs while I shifted into the lecture mode that they were used to from previous classes. My plan was to tell them the Biblical story of Ishmael and then ask what the name might mean for the book. I explained that Ishmael was the oldest son of the patriarch Abraham by his wife's Egyptian servant Hagar. Seeing puzzlement, I took a step back to try to say what a patriarch was. After quite a few words, I did not feel that I had made it clear. Moving on, I said that Ishmael was not the favored child who answered the promises of God but was cast out of Abraham's family and came near to dying in the desert. Then, in a rush, I reassured them that God saved Ishmael and his mother, and that Ishmael himself became a patriarch of the Arab peoples.

When I was done, the air was filled with polite bewilderment. Obviously, groundwork needed to be laid before any of this would make sense. I stepped further back.

"Ishmael and his story come from the Bible. Have you heard of the Bible?"

They had. In fact the question was a little too elementary. I had stepped back too far, and there was a hint that they felt insulted. Of course they had heard of the Bible and they knew that it was very important to Western religions.

I realized that I could not begin to imagine their attitudes toward religion. Did they despise it? Were they interested in it? If they were like me at their age, it was both. But they also had access to a wholly different perspective than my past self, having been born into a secular society where it was possible to be indifferent to religion. There is no "In God We Trust" on Chinese money, only 毛泽东 (*Máo Zédōng*). Holidays in China celebrate the nation or the family, or poetry, but not God. Until that moment, I had not fully appreciated how thoroughly religion pervaded the America in which I had grown up. It had been unavoidable. Americans could be attracted to religion or contemptuous of it, angrily dismissive or admiring, but nearly oblivious indifference was hard to achieve. In America, God confronted you at every turn.

Would this difference in our experiences pose a problem in reading *Moby Dick*? In order to give them an understanding of this book I might have to find a way to show them what it would feel like to care passionately about religion. There was a nest of thorns! They might think I was trying to proselytize. Already we were plunged into deep waters with who knows what hidden meaning lurking monstrously. There was no help for it, though. I was going to have to tell them Bible stories and try to give them a look at how those stories could shape lives.

I revised all my lesson plans. I would be doing that a lot over the coming two years.

Mindful of my goal to make ideas live, I looked for a common ground that would allow them to read these stories in *Moby Dick* not as signs of Western weirdness, but as offering something that all humans can share. In the next class we had a general conversation about stories. I asked them what stories they had learned as children and still thought about sometimes. I thought I would hear Marxist stories, or heroic stories about *Máo* or possibly Chinese emperors. Instead, I learned about the world of 成语 (*chéngyǔ*).

Chéngyǔ are stories embedded in the Chinese language. Certain ideas are expressed indirectly in Chinese through four-character phrases dropped whole into speech or text. This can be mystifying for a beginning translator. There you are, slowly working your way through a sentence, and suddenly you encounter: "Watch stump, wait rabbit." Really? you think, and look up all the characters again, only to get the same thing. The phrase by itself seems senseless, but it makes sense if you know a certain old story. A Chinese political philosopher named Han Fei told a story about a farmer who happened to see a rabbit knock itself out running into a stump. In the hope of more rabbits doing that, he gave up farming and waited by the stump as his crops died.

Star Trek fans might recognize this linguistic strategy in the episode "*Darmok*" from *The Next Generation* series. Ideas are expressed by reference to stories. Only if you know the stories can you understand what is being said. Fortunately, modern computer dictionaries can play the role of Counselor Troi in developing strategies to help. If you enter the first two characters of a *chéngyǔ* into certain computer dictionaries, the computer will suggest the next two, and explain the idiomatic meaning of the story. In the case of the stump and the rabbit, the four-character phrase "Watch stump, wait rabbit" means to stop working in the hope of a windfall. When a Chinese person wants to express the idea that someone has allowed optimism to trump responsibility, the feckless farmer is remembered.

In the children's section of the local bookstore, I found volumes of illustrated *chéngyǔ*. This kind of book seemed like a great way to learn Chinese, but I never got very far in deciphering the stories. I was so impatient to know Chinese that I undertook things that were too hard for me and then slacked off in despair, getting nowhere. It was a textbook case of "Pull seedling, help grow," an expression that comes from another *chéngyǔ* in which a farmer wanted to make his rice crop grow taller so he pulled at the seedlings until they all died.

I took this tale to heart in the classroom, trying not to pull too hard at the students' emerging ideas. As they told me each *chéngyǔ*, I traded a story back. Ishmael, Ahab, Jonah and Job all slipped into the conversation that way. I would tell them the Biblical stories behind these *Moby Dick* names and themes, watching them think how utterly strange the stories were. Then they would tell me another *chéngyǔ* and watch me as I had precisely the same reaction. We were all being pried—a little painfully—away from a previously unexamined sense that our own culture was ordinary and unremarkable. We were learning to read not just *Moby Dick* but each other and ourselves.

Meanwhile the book unrolled before us. Ishmael found himself in bed with the tattooed native Queequeg, and the two become fast friends, somehow establishing affection across wildly different worlds and despite language difficulties. My students and I increasingly saw how that might happen as we began to be comfortable with each other and even sometimes to laugh together.

When Father Mapple gave a sermon, I thought I might have trouble explaining exactly what a sermon was, but that proved easier than expected because they had a sense of that from Buddhist tradition. By now we had gotten used to the idea that all people create stories and look for ways in which those stories teach things. We talked about how Herman Melville's description of Ishmael's experience of Father Mapple's retelling of the story of Jonah and the whale was a story within a story within a story, each tale resonating with the others. Then there was the layer of stories that we readers brought to the book. Stories from the modern world and from an Eastern tradition that Melville did not know created yet more possible connections, swelling into an ocean of stories. Somewhere in those depths swims elusive meaning, a white leviathan.

The days and weeks on shipboard were slow going. The students nearly rebelled when Melville broke off the action and spent many chapters talking about whales, their habits and their mythos. Then one day one a student came rushing into the classroom very excited. She had opened Google that morning and found as its doodle a cartoon of Captain Ahab in a boat with the white whale in the background, Google's way of commemorating the one hundred and sixty-first anniversary of the first edition of *Moby Dick*. She was amazed. This book was famous! Google had heard of it! The great white whale was swimming in the internet, this new, yet more fathomless ocean of stories.

As my students and I sought meaning in each other's stories I remembered one of the last conversations I had had with my mother. We talked about *Moby Dick*. Facing death as she was, she reported that she understood Captain Ahab's fierce rage at the huge inscrutable white whale. "It is monstrous," she said, "that life seems shot through with meaning, magnificence and pain but the point of it is never made clear." Depressions, wars, tangled relationships, alcoholism or cancer rise suddenly, without warning, from unknown depths. They seem to mean everything, are overwhelming, but do not explain themselves. They are blankness. Being tossed about by frustrating mystery would madden a fierce spirit like the Captain's and she could understand his desire to fight back against all the unknowing, to insist on making a battle of it, to force meaning on such encounters at any cost. She did not share the captain's rage, though, because of the book. The effect of the book was to allow her to step outside herself and reflect on the rage. *Moby Dick*, showing her anger, gave her freedom from it in the face of a last blankness.

Even when I feared that my students were floundering as they read *Moby Dick*, I could hope that they would react the way my mother had first in high school and then upon reading it again at the other end of her life. In high school, people can't yet hear all the questions that may someday matter immensely to them. My students could hear the Greek philosophical question, "what is the best life?" and they knew that they would be required to decide on an answer as they chose colleges, majors, and careers. *Moby Dick* asks a different philosophical question that comes later in most lives: "Is there meaning in our pain?" For most people, the urgency of that second question will not be felt until the first choices are made and early hopes are knocked awry in some unexpected way. Then *Moby Dick* comes into its own. Like my mother the students might think themselves unimpressed by the book in their high school days, but I hoped that it would ripen in them as it had in her.

From time to time during the semester, the sheer difficulty of getting second language learners through *Moby Dick* became discouraging. At those times, I wished that, when H had asked me about my favorite book, I had understood "favorite" to mean clearest or simplest or easiest to teach. A different choice would have saved me many hours explaining Bible stories, nineteenth century vocabulary and the technical jargon of whaling. By the end of our classes on *Moby Dick*, however, it seemed like a wonderful choice, a perfect example of how the greatest books enter into our lives and help us to see our experience in richer ways. Captain Ahab's passionate determination to chase down and harpoon meaning in a maddeningly ambiguous world had first become important to me in trying to come to terms with my mother's illness and death. Seeing it through the eyes of Chinese students widened its importance for me. *Moby Dick* seemed to me to speak to the broad goal of trying to read the world and understand it. Then, still voyaging no matter what shipwrecks there may be, to keep re-reading it, keep reflecting on it and so come to be as free as Ishmael afloat on the open ocean with a story to tell.

I had this lesson from the *Moby Dick* class in mind when, toward the end of our first year in China, we decided to stay for a second year and to join in planning a curriculum for the Dalton Academy. Grant, teaching Plato, had also loved the feeling of learning to read again, as he conversed about these familiar Western books in China, with Chinese students. A voyage half way around the globe was well worth it, in pursuit of the new meanings we were finding. It was because of our own such reactions that I first began to entertain grandiose hopes about global conversation—I wanted to be part of trying to make it happen for our Chinese students, as well.

The faculty held a retreat to discuss and create a comprehensive curriculum plan for our second year at the Dalton Academy. It had been a great pleasure in the first year to set sail impulsively and to teach only from the heart, but for the second year, with the blankness somewhat filled in and a clearer picture of what the classroom experience could be like, it seemed a good idea to plan.

During two long meetings the faculty brainstormed, with H acting as interpreter for complicated ideas. We got used to being translated in China, of waiting after something had been said while it was rendered into the other language. It was a nice thing sometimes to slow down conversation a little and try to listen for how something has been expressed differently through a different framework of understanding. Everyone knew a little English or a little Chinese and thought they might have understood the first time something was said, but were uncertain. As H translated and the thing was said a second time, puzzled, earnest faces would clear as people nodded, relieved to feel sure.

After the manner of meetings all over the globe, we covered sheets of newsprint with magic-markered ideas. Grant and I pitched the value of the kind of education offered at St. John's College, where great books are explored through discussion and H was receptive, I think partly because the students had been reporting to him that they liked our classes very much. I even mentioned my hopes for global conversations through the foundational books of different cultures. The mathematics teacher Q, among others of our colleagues, was doubtful, especially when it came to math and science. She proffered, diffidently, that it was not possible to have philosophical discussions about those topics, which simply had to be mastered. We tried to persuade the group otherwise but without success. Defiantly, Grant resolved on the spot to teach a class in the coming semester on mathematics as a liberal art. Q gamely said she looked forward to his success.

In the end, the new curriculum we produced was focused on fundamental questions. The goal of spurring creative and critical thinking across disciplines in both the humanities and the sciences would be approached through a single organizing question for each high school year to be asked in every classroom.

For the 高一 (gāo yī)[4] year, which corresponds to tenth grade in an American high school, the question chosen was "what is knowledge?" It is an entryway question into philosophy but also into many topics. Helping students wonder how they know things is a step of self-conscious curiosity. In every class, gāo yī students would be asked to think clearly about the kind of knowing that is being addressed in that subject. In philosophy, the question can be asked in the abstract, directly. In literature, it could be asked in connection with a sense of character and plot. In history, it embraces what counts as reliable historical evidence. In science, it relates to the proper conclusions to be drawn from experiment and observation. In mathematics, the question can circle back to the abstract and philosophical, with students thinking about what constitutes the proof of a mathematical proposition and what such a proof means. Grant, who had enjoyed teaching Plato's *Meno* in our first year, undertook to teach a required humanities seminar around the question: what is knowledge?

---

4   *Gāo* means "great" or "big." Here it is being used to mean high school, in contrast to middle and grammar school.

Lots of possible organizing questions were proposed for the 高
二 (*gāo 'èr*) year (eleventh grade in America). Finally we settled on
the question: "what is change?" on the grounds that the pace of
change seems to have quickened in the world, perhaps especially
in China. Further, the *gāo 'èr* year is one of extraordinary change
in the personal lives of high school students who are beginning to
look outward to a wider circle, and to imagine themselves in new
settings. It was easy to see how this question too could be differently approached in from different subjects. Calculus in mathematics, for example, the evolution of species in biology, and movements in history are all issues of change. I volunteered to teach the
seminar on change that began with Homer's *Iliad*.

For the 高三 (*gāo sān*) year, corresponding to the senior year of
American high school, our committee tentatively chose the question "What is Humanity?" The notion was that in this year students are getting ready to make lives outside their families of origin, in the broader human community, so that the issue of human
nature would be important to them. In the first year of this new
curriculum, however, because the Dalton Academy itself was so
new, there were very few *gāo sān* students. It was decided to put
them in with the *gāo 'èr* students to look at the nature of change.

The faculty retreat drew to a close with high hopes about these
ambitious plans. For the next year, Grant and I would study classic
books with our students and talk about knowledge and change,
trying to offer our vision of how to read in such a way as to both
hear and add to the stories of the world. Our students' lives would
no doubt be lived in an increasingly global consciousness of
humanity's stories, so that helping them to read in this way would,
we hoped, prepare them for the new conversation they would meet
and perhaps create.

Justice　正义

Chapter 3

The *Oresteia* and Contemplating the State versus the Individual

After the *Iliad*, the seminar on change turned to a cycle of Greek plays called the *Oresteia*, the plot of which arises directly out of the *Iliad* story. Following the question asked in the *Iliad* of what is the best life, the *Oresteia* asks a logical next question of how that best life should be lived within a community. Great heroes, individuals with personal talent, may not do well in a community, as the first scene of the *Iliad* shows. They compete and quarrel, threatening the people around them.

History is littered with this problem: some proud person feels slighted and takes revenge by killing the offender; a champion of the dead person then takes revenge by killing the killer; a champion of the original killer then takes revenge against that champion, and on and on and on. There is no way to stop the killing as long as heroes seek justice and justice is determined subjectively.

The City of Athens found a solution, curbing the impulse to personal revenge by establishing courts of law so that justice is determined by the city or the state, not the individual. That solution, and the consequent invention of trial by jury, was a world-historical moment brought vividly to life by the playwright Aeschylus in the *Oresteia*.

It took some extra work for my Chinese students and I to find that life, though. The day we turned to *Agamemnon,* the first play in the *Oresteia* trilogy, I asked my opening question, but the students lowered their eyes and did not answer. I poked at the silence this way and that, getting nowhere. Finally someone asked, ferociously, pointing to the very first speech, "What does this mean?" Had she known just a little more English, she would have said, "What the *hell* does this mean?" After that ice-breaker, many others raised complaints that the play made no sense. It was time to retreat and offer context. Sometimes the strategy of plunging straight into a text takes a little massaging.

I made a list on the whiteboard of the characters in the *Oresteia* whom the students did not already know from the *Iliad*—Clytemnestra (Agamemnon's wife, who kills him), Orestes (Agamemnon's son, who kills her in revenge, although she is his mother), the Furies (goddesses whose job it is to revenge ill treatment of blood kin, especially mothers)—as well as places that needed explaining—Athens, the Temple at Delphi, the courtroom called the Areopagus—and other useful categories of information—Greek drama, the chorus, masks, and so forth. I asked everyone to write their name next to one of these things and be ready to tell about it during the next class. I saw this as a way of working with their tendency to look everything up on Wikipedia. They had learned in the course of our classes on the *Iliad* that Wikipedia was not going to help them much in philosophical discussions but using it for basic information seemed perfectly reasonable, and people should be allowed to stay in their comfort zone on a few things.

The next class buzzed. One by one the students reported on their characters, places, or topics, and we pieced together a little about the Greek world, as well as about the cycle of revenge and counter-revenge that drives the plot of the *Oresteia*. Sometimes I thought I could see them translating the story into issues they understood, a perfect way to use the classics of literature. It was especially fun to hear students make connections between the subjects of their reports and Chinese cultural references. "Greek drama is like Beijing opera, very formal," said Lily. "Delphi is where the gods touch the world, maybe like the Temple of Heaven," suggested Shirley. "Orestes is the son of King Agamemnon," reported Jack. "He is young, with no experience. He makes a dangerous, hurting decision without help."

The backstory for the *Oresteia* begins nine years before the *Iliad*, when the Greek army was sailing to Troy. The winds suddenly refused to blow, and the fleet was trapped in harbor for so long that quarrels arose and supplies dwindled. A prophet told Agamemnon that the only way to make the wind change was to sacrifice his eldest daughter, Iphigenia, to the gods, which Agamemnon accordingly did. He tricked his wife Clytemnestra into bringing their daughter to him by telling her that Iphigenia was to marry Achilles. Iphigenia was led to the altar, but, instead of marriage, she met death at her father's hands. Clytemnestra, understandably, got really, really, *really* angry at Agamemnon.

My students, too. There were loud complaints. People expressed outrage that a father would kill his own daughter, saying that there could not possibly be anything that could justify that. No matter what the gods say, no one should ever kill a child, especially one's own child. How could he have done it?

Surprisingly, there was a dissenting voice. Anne, a hard-headed person who was learning to enjoy being contrary, was ready to go to bat for Agamemnon. She was getting the hang of what could be fun about conversation. "Yes, it is bad," she said, "but what else could he do? Turn around and go home? Abandon the punishment of Troy? Humiliate himself and destroy his own kingship?"

"对! 对! (*duì, duì*, "Yes! Correct!")" called out many.

"Agamemnon is king," continued Anne, impressively, over the clamor. "He takes care of the army more than his family. His daughter is exchanged for the good of Greece. Kings do that. It hurts him too and is noble."

Some scorn was heaped on the claim that killing your daughter could be noble, but there was also some reflection. In China, the government had at times promoted morality tales praising children who betrayed politically subversive parents. Having grown up with such stories in the air, these students understood the notion that loyalty to the state was supposed to trump family relationships. The present status of that notion was unclear, though. In my classroom, the Marxist imperative was rarely mentioned, while the Chinese reverence for family that had long pre-dated Marx was clear. No one could easily imagine hurting a family member to support the ideals of Marxism. But the nation of China, with its long, proud, civilized history and its promise of future power on the world stage, surely deserved its people's loyalty. How far should such loyalty go? Were my students, whose families were planning to send them away from China to be educated in the West thinking about what loyalties they owed to whom?

A tension between the state's demands and the ways that students wanted to conduct their lives was an everyday part of their experience. Censorship, including censorship of social sites on the internet, was commonplace in China, among the many various rules and restrictions on Chinese life. Individual people everywhere, however, want freedom to decide for themselves what to feel, think and believe—hence my students' mostly successful efforts to find ways around the official censorship and talk to their friends on Facebook.

Our classroom was not the only place in Beijing where Greek drama was being used to look at this sort of question. In our first few months in China, Grant and I went to see the Greek poet Sophocles' *Antigone* (安提戈涅, *Ān tí gē niè*), another play in which loyalty to the community competes with loyalty to the family. The Greeks were really concerned about this problem. Judging from my students' uncertainties and the popularity of this play, the Chinese were, too.

The performance of *Antigone* was at Peking University (北大), usually called "*Běi Dà*," which has a tradition of political activism. A play about the clash between the state and the family seemed an interesting choice in this setting. As Grant and I made our way to our seats in the huge, crowded theater (the only foreigners, as far as we saw), we wondered if we were present at an incendiary use of the classics of literature that has been popular for centuries— Greek tragedies as thinly veiled commentary on current political events.

A colleague at St. John's College had once remarked to Grant that ancient Greek tragedy was written in a language sufficiently removed from the vernacular of its time that contemporary audiences understood no more of the words than an audience in modern New York would understand a theatre troupe shouting in Welsh. If that is true, then we got an authentic experience of *Antigone*. Chinese syllables washed over us for two hours. At that time in our Chinese adventure, the longest phrase in ordinary Chinese that I could recognize with assurance was "*wǒ bù zhīdào*" (我不知道), meaning "I don't know," a very useful phrase but a small linguistic base. When the First Messenger said this phrase to King Creon about seventy minutes into the play, Grant and I looked meaningfully at one another. Yes! We heard that!

When the performance was over, the young woman sitting next to me asked in English whether we had understood it. We knew the play already, I said, evasively. "Is it different in America?" she asked. Well, yes, of course. *There's a whole lot less Chinese in it, for one thing!* But then again no, not really. The *Běi Dà* production was wonderful, with both the dignity and agony of the conflict between the demands of the city and the love of family evident, no matter the language.

In the classroom, Anne underscored this conflict: "Leaders act bigger than family," she argued. "Their job to is care most for the state. The state needs that."

"Why does the state need that?" I asked her, and Mark jumped in. Mark had been learning lately to enjoy a little contrarianism too, and he saw that Anne was stirring it up. "If all people put family first," he claimed, "the state won't work. Soldiers fight and die. The families must be proud, not angry."

That took a little teasing out. States need soldiers and a soldier must be willing to die for the state, which means that a soldier must care more for the state than for life. If the soldier dies, the soldier's family must feel pride at the sacrifice, not anger at the state for taking the soldier away from them. Mark's comment might also have reflected another of our classroom conversations about *Agamemnon*. The chorus in that play speaks sadly of how King Agamemnon took away all of the beautiful, proud young men and returned them as ashes, killed in his far away Trojan War.

Sam raised a new point. "Maybe Agamemnon made a bad decision. But Clytemnestra is worse!" That got strong, unqualified agreement. Even the students who disliked Agamemnon were not prepared to defend what Clytemnestra did. On the day that her husband returned triumphant from nine years of war, she rolled out before him a blood-red carpet, lured him into his longed-for home, and then murdered him. Because of the carpet, his foot never even touched the earth of his city.

In the face of such unanimity among the students, my duty as a teacher was clear—I had to take Clytemnestra's side. I was glad that Grant was not there to hear, knowing that a husband is likely to cringe when his wife speaks sympathetically of Clytemnestra, even for pedagogically sound reasons.

I was a lawyer as well as a teacher and I called on my legal training to argue for Clytemnestra's point of view: "Didn't Agamemnon deserve death? Doesn't justice demand it? He sacrificed his own daughter! Iphigenia's mother Clytemnestra can't just forget that crime and live with him again, can she? What is she supposed to do, say 'welcome home, dear, and I'm so glad also to welcome your mistress Cassandra?'" Sarcasm does not always translate well, but they got that.

"She doesn't care about justice," Paul responded, scornfully. "She had a lover. She wanted power."

"Well, maybe she cares about both. Everybody has mixed motives," I argued, "some motives are noble and pure, and others are corrupt and selfish. Agamemnon killed his daughter at least partly because he wanted power, too—he wanted to lead the Greek army to conquer Troy and get rich. Shouldn't he be punished for it? It can't be right for him to come home and be king again as if nothing had happened! Clytemnestra seems to have ruled the kingdom well enough for a decade. Now this murderer Agamemnon is going to take over. Is it good for a kingdom if the king is willing to kill, even kill his own child, to keep power?"

Anne led the way for a faction of the class who were willing to say that it was good for a kingdom if the king was willing to do whatever it took—even the murder of children—to make the kingdom rich and safe. Others were not so sure. Kings should be examples to their people, they claimed. If the king committed murder and got away without punishment, wouldn't other people feel that they could, too? If kings are criminals then the people will be, and the society will fall apart.

Someone mentioned corruption in high places as setting the kind of example that is bad for a country. This was a provocative comment, as corruption in high places is a sensitive topic in China. Our online subscription to the *New York Times* became worthless early in our stay after the paper published an exposé of how the families of some high Chinese government officials were squirreling money away in Swiss bank accounts. Government censors swung into action, and neither we nor anyone else in China could access the site, not even to cancel our subscription. Amid China's generally growing prosperity, some people were getting especially wealthy and, it seemed, those people did not want the sources of their wealth discussed in public. Nevertheless, rumors circulated constantly. I sometimes heard it said that anger at government corruption was in a race with how satisfied people were with improvements in their own lives. Corruption in high places was tolerable as long as the government could prop up a general prosperity. Someone who expressed that opinion might go on to say, "if the general growth ever falters …" but then the sentence would trail off.

Another perhaps especially Chinese dimension to the issue of family and government was the ever-present concept of 关系(*guān xì*). *Guān xì* is hard to define. At the crudest level, it can apply to greasing palms with money, but more often it means subtler connections and social debts that help to get things done—having a cousin at a government office, being willing to sell at a discount to the business license people, allowing the friend of an uncle to jump a line, favor for favor off the books. I never saw it at work in any ugly or even obvious way, although once a chief administrator in our school came home to our apartment complex drunk and singing at four o'clock in the morning after a night out with Communist Party friends. Later that same day we got our work visas, which had been delayed for many weeks, and rumor made a connection. Is that corruption? The word seems far too strong for so human a transaction.

Rumor was always busily at work about instances of *guan xi*. Rumor often spread the names of government officials who were said to need special attention before they would do their jobs. Rumor swirled even about students at our school who might have been accepted to the Dalton Academy not on merit but because their relatives were Communist Party bigwigs. I never knew whether to believe such rumors, but they circulated as probably true and certainly the way the world worked. Even if they were all false, they made for a cynical and disbelieving atmosphere. They encouraged people to look for angles—inside advantages, *guān xì*—rather than to play it straight. Playing it straight was for chumps. I think this feeling may have contributed to our students' surprise that we wanted them to love learning rather than to strategize about how to do well on tests. Gaming tests seemed like the clever thing to do, while seeking learning directly was for chumps. Grant and I appeared to be too smart to be chumps, but we were—oddly, from the students' point of view—encouraging chump-like behavior.

All of these factors confused the question of the right connection between personal matters and duties to society. My students and I found the question confusing in the *Oresteia,* too. Agamemnon kills his daughter. Is that a kingly decision for the good of Greece, as Anne argued, or a crime that cries out for justice, as most of the class thought? We found the same ambivalences with the other characters. Clytemnestra kills Agamemnon. Is that justice finally served or a crime of hatred and ambition? Orestes, their son, after hesitating, kills his mother Clytemnestra. Is that justice, revenge, or a crime? If Orestes goes unpunished, then won't people everywhere think they can get away with murder as long as they can make some claim that the victim deserved it?

Society can't function under such conditions. If each individual gets to decide what justice means, then revenge will continue forever, perpetual warfare. A working society, therefore, cannot allow individual people to decide what justice means. Individual opinions on justice are dangerous to the state. This is also an aspect—maybe the most important aspect—of the dangers of encouraging people to think for themselves. People who start philosophizing about the best life might come up with a different view of justice than the state has, which will make everything fall apart. I imagined the reactions of worried Chinese authorities: "Stop that! Close the door on liberal education!"

As I was holding forth on these points, the door of the classroom opened and six people trooped in. They stood behind the circle of students—five men in sober suits and red ties, and one woman, somewhat more brightly dressed. The Communist Party was here.

I had been told they were coming, so I was not surprised. I imagine the students were also told in their morning assembly that the Party would be visiting, as they did not seem surprised either. But no one had said what the Party officials would do or what they wanted. I had no idea if this was an ordinary thing in China or whether it occurred because foreign teachers were offering this experimental (possibly politically dangerous) curriculum. The thought was troubling and I never found out what was true about it. Not knowing such things is one of the great discomforts of a surveillance state. People create their own fears out of not knowing.

The Party officials and I nodded at each other. The class continued.

"What the state wants must win," asserted Jack. I wondered if the presence of the Communist Party members had prompted that statement.

"Tell me why you believe that," I responded. Then I wondered if my own reaction was a little blunted for the benefit of the silent presence in the room.

"The community is more important," he responded, seemingly a little ill at ease. "The state must come first." Did he glance at one of the men? Sara tried a peace-making approach: "The state is advantaged by tranquility, so it should promote cooperation, even if the state has the power to show more strength, to compel." Suddenly Janie came in, perhaps not liking the atmosphere of caution. She said defiantly, head thrown back, "The state's justice will be for its own benefit. The state must be challenged by individuals."

There was no reaction from the still figures outside the circle. After a moment of waiting, I took the class to a place in the text and we read aloud for a while before continuing the discussion on a different point. A few minutes later, the Communist Party officials left the room.

It was impossible to tell what had been in their minds, or whether they even understood English. They might well have been completely unaware of the subject of our conversation, seeing only that Chinese students were speaking up in a second language. Nor could I be at sure that the students had reacted with the self-consciousness that my imagination had supplied. In any case, as far as I know, there was no consequence to the inspection.

Yet I didn't like the effect it had seemed to have on me or the students—the feeling that we needed to censor ourselves. In one of Grant's classes about the time of the Communist Party's inspection, a student turned in a paper proposing that the right way to resolve political questions was "we listen to those in authority, we agree and we obey." When Grant asked her about that position, she was surprised that he had taken it seriously. "That's just what you say in papers," she said. I didn't like such thinking. For my grandiose hopes of global conversation to come true, people would have to avoid that constraint and speak freely what they feel, think and believe.

Our class focused again on the *Oresteia*. Orestes, having killed his mother, is chased by the Furies, the goddesses of revenge and protection of the family, especially of mothers. They chase him all the way to Delphi, where he asks Apollo for help but Apollo, stumped, sends the whole cavalcade to Athena in Athens. Athena proposes a novel solution, a striking change in the way justice will be found. She offers to hold a trial on the issue between Orestes and the Furies in which she would be the judge and twelve citizens of her new city of Athens would be the jury.

Orestes and the Furies all agree to this new procedure. It is an extraordinary move, mythologizing the spectacularly import-ant moment in history of the invention of trial by a jury of peers, which provides a way to stop the cycle of revenge that happens when individuals decide for themselves what justice means. Under the new system established by Athena, a jury is chosen from the citizens of the city—not from the government of the state—and that jury will decide what is just, although with a judge pres-ent—who is from the government of the state—to make the sys-tem work. As a lawyer myself, I find this compromise brilliant. In the study of the humanities, philosophy and literature get all the splashy press but I secretly advocate for the proposition that it is the structures and messy compromises of law that make human progress possible.

Casting about for how to bring home to my students the importance of the invention of trial by jury, I hit upon the idea of recre-
ating Orestes' trial in class. I wasn't sure how much my students
knew about jury trials. The Chinese legal system had only in the
previous few years begun experimenting with a trial by jury system, a reform that must have been motivated by a sense that trial
by jury was a necessary part of modern law. Most people describing the new Chinese system, however, observed that the jury had
little independence, simply endorsing the guilty verdict that the
state made clear was expected. In any event, there was no reason
to think that my students would be following this development.
Fortunately, they had watched a lot of American movies, and they
liked the drama of courtroom clashes they had seen there. When
I asked for volunteers to be lawyers for the characters in the play I
saw plenty of raised hands.

Anne, who had a weakness for Agamemnon, volunteered to
be his lawyer and present his case for Orestes' innocence. Mark
bravely decided to take on Clytemnestra as a client, arguing that
Orestes was guilty. Then one of the quietest members of the class,
Cindy, unexpectedly offered to represent Iphigenia, who is not a
party to the case in the original plays. I asked her whether she
was for Orestes or against him, and she wasn't sure how to answer.
Probably against Orestes, but it took some thinking out. "So be it,"
I said, "everyone gets a lawyer." Each lawyer had to offer at least
two arguments in the case. The remainder of the class would con-
stitute the jury and would vote anonymously.

Despite having seen so many American movies, many of my
students were shaky on the idea of advocacy. They hesitated to
push zealously for their client, uncomfortable with the lawyer's job
of presenting the most advantageous case for one side only. The
exception was Anne, who was suitably forceful on Agamemnon's
behalf, arguing that he was a statesman and a seeker of justice.
Most of the others, however, wanted to try to be neutral, offering both sides of the issue and trying to appear statesmanlike

themselves—on the one hand Clytemnestra was understandably angry at Agamemnon for killing her daughter; on the other hand, she was wrong to deceive and murder her husband. My students didn't like being jurors, either, since jurors don't get to argue. What they really wanted to do was to be the judge and make a unilateral decision. Maybe this reflected their upbringing under a centralized governmental authority, or maybe it only reflected that peremptory authority tempts us all.

The most remarkable thing about our experiment with the trial of Orestes was how the jury voted. In the *Oresteia*, the twelve-person jury is evenly split, six for Orestes, six for the Furies. Athena, the judge, breaks the tie in favor of Orestes. To me, the jury's even split always seemed contrived, a literary artifice created by the playwright to make Athena's vote necessary. Very few juries in real life have a hard time deciding one way or another, *Twelve Angry Men* notwithstanding. But I had not given Aeschylus enough credit for having set up the circumstances of the case in perfect balance. After arguments from all parties, the jury in my classroom was also evenly split, just like the Athenian jury of so many centuries before. I could hardly believe it. Because the votes were anonymous, no one could be manipulating this result. Moreover, it was repeated. In two out of three sections of the class I taught, the split was perfect, while in the third it was six to five that Orestes was guilty. Across three millennia and across a wide cultural and geographical gap, there was *still* no agreement on the justice of Orestes' actions. Taking the philosophical issues of the *Oresteia* seriously, such a result implies that, on the abstract question of what each person owes to a personal sense of justice versus what each citizen owes to the need to maintain an orderly state, the human jury is still deadlocked.

The *Oresteia* does not end with the verdict. There remains the problem of the Furies, the losing side. Despite their agreement to the trial, the Furies at first refuse to accept the verdict. They are furious (it's their signature attitude). They mourn their humiliation and the loss of their power and threaten to transfer their thirst for revenge from Orestes to the new city of Athens. It looks for a moment as if Athena's invention of trial by jury has failed to tamp down the conflict, that the cycle of revenge will start again and that the Furies' passion of disappointed rage will destroy the city.

Athena sets to work to talk the Furies out of their anger. She calls upon the goddess Persuasion and offers the Furies gifts and status. Three times she tries to persuade them, with different arguments and different gifts. Twice they refuse, repeating their chorus of fury. On the third attempt, Athena mentions glancingly that she is stronger than them—she could simply overpower them—then immediately returns to persuasion. This time, the Furies listen to Athena's invitation to change their character from being gods of revenge to being gods that support the city, agreeing to live beneath the city and watch to make sure that due ceremony, especially toward mothers, is observed. Their power is still terrifying, but it now upholds the obligations of Athenian citizens towards each other. The Furies are renamed Eumenides, which means "blessings."

Persuasion is in the end what that holds a city or a state together and protects it from the destructive cycle of revenge. It was not enough to invent the brilliant compromise of trial by jury, in which individual citizens vote and the state adopts their decision. Respectful persuasion is needed to make that decision stick. Drawing on my experience as a lawyer, I told my students that I saw this at work in modern courtrooms all the time. When losing parties are offered respect from the judge, they accept the decision against them. Perhaps the need for honor is stronger than the need for prizes.

As with the *Iliad* and with *Moby Dick*, reading the *Oresteia* in a Chinese classroom opened the book for me in a new way. The question of the proper relationship between the state and the individual is considered and answered differently in a society that has been acculturated to centralized governmental power for millennia. That setting brought out new meanings to the dead-locked jury. On the one hand, the split jury verdict might suggest that the trial by jury process was pointless as a practical matter; what actually ended the conflict was the power of Athena. Does that imply that a centralized state will inevitably do what it wants, regardless of trials or individual opinions? On the other hand, Athena's judgment was for Orestes, the avenging son who defied custom and the Furies to assert his own individual ideas of justice. Does that imply that an individual view of justice can sometimes be vindicated? Also, Athena's power was not exercised until the jury had been given the first chance to decide the issue. She only steps in when they cannot agree. Presumably, in less difficult cases, the jury would have the last word, although only because the state says so. The whole question was beginning to feel like hands topping each other on a baseball bat. I could not tell for sure which hand would end up on top and get to swing the bat, although on days when surveillance felt heavy on us it seemed like the smart money was on the (Chinese) state.

One of the hardest things about teaching through reading and conversation is obeying the duty to allow the conversation to go where it wants to—as long as it is rooted in the text—instead of where the teacher would prefer to steer it. I discipline myself not to have plans for what my students will conclude from a work and to confine myself to seeking out where the interest lies in discussion. My experience is that the classic works speak better for themselves than I could anyway. Even so, privately, I hoped that my students would consider the idea that, while justice is important, the stability of government finally rests on respectful persuasion, subtly backed by power, resulting in consent. I hoped for this conclusion because it leads to the practice of persuasion as a solution to conflict. Persuasion is related to conversation. Seeking to persuade each other, we will converse passionately, as if it mattered.

Curiosity 好奇心

Chapter 4

Carp Week and the Light of Knowledge

Besides the seminars on knowledge, change and humanity, the new curriculum for our second year in China included an innovation that we called Carp Week, during which ordinary classes were replaced by special projects related to a theme chosen by students and faculty. The name had an East-West origin. On the Western side, it derived from the Latin phrase *carpe diem*, meaning "seize the day," while on the Eastern side, the carp is a familiar Chinese symbol for success in education which springs from the saying—"鲤鱼跳龙门" *(lǐyú tiào lóng mén),* "carp leaping the dragon's gate." According to myth, carp swimming upstream to spawn encounter a waterfall. If they can leap high enough to clear this obstacle they become dragons.

The traditional meaning of this image didn't quite fit our agenda. Originally, H informed us, it meant that hard work can lead to success in the imperial exams that had for centuries shaped China's state bureaucracy. In our effort to deemphasize tests, we proposed a different meaning, casting the change from a carp to a dragon as the transformation from learning by rote memorization to learning through a desire to understand. Such understanding happens most easily when students are free to seek knowledge because of curiosity rather than because of obligation forced on them by school administrators. The goal of Carp Week was to offer choices to tempt curiosity in the hope of giving students an experience of learning for love of it. When people pursue learning for its own sake, the results are magnificent, powerful, and even fire-breathing.

The idea behind Carp Week was born early in our first year at BDFZ when about two-thirds of the upper classes suddenly went away on various international field trips, together with most of their teachers. In the rush of planning for the trips, nobody had made any provision for what the rest of the students in those classes would do during that week. Left to their own devices they would fill up that time with nothing but SAT and TOEFL preparation.

Grant and I felt called to offer an alternative to that bleak prospect, in line with our ideas about learning because of curiosity rather than because of test pressure. Our alternative had to be something that could be finished within a week and also had to be appropriate for students from many different classes. Ideally, it would be something that the students left behind could brag about as more fun and better than the field trips.

We devised a course of seminars, projects, movies, and games, mostly focused on the first half of the Twentieth Century, which was where their history classes were. We picked the year 1936 and asked teams of students to tell us what was going on in particular places all over the world in that year. Each team made posters and presentations about those events in whatever style they chose. We settled on 1936 partly because there was an impressively wide range of movies to see that had been made in or about that year. In the course of a single week we screened: *The Grapes of Wrath*, *Top Hat*, *The King's Speech*, and *Triumph of the Will*. The favorite was *Top Hat*, the leisurely pace of which made lighter demands on viewers for whom English was a second language. Besides, people love ballroom dancing in China. On every warm evening couples twirl together in public parks in Beijing.

As a seminar class we assigned *The Great Gatsby*, which worked well because a movie version starring Leonardo DiCaprio was about to come out—beautiful people together with capitalistic excess was a winning combination. Then, for pure fun, we also asked the students to read at least a chapter of either *Alice in Wonderland* or *Through the Looking Glass,* books that had nothing to do with the early twentieth century, but are classics that they might hear referred to at an American university. We invented *Alice*-themed games for all to play. This led to a wonderful, giggly afternoon of tea party races, human card games and the design of absurd new animals. One game was based on the declaration of the White Queen in *Through the Looking Glass* that she "sometimes believed six impossible things before breakfast." We split the students into two teams and asked each team to propose impossible things for the other team to try to believe. It was a silly game since anyone could *claim* to believe anything, but the students were very earnest and honest. They made surprising proposals: "in five years, North Korea will be a great power." Despite their competitiveness, the other team was unable even to pretend to believe that.

The impromptu week's program, all of which was ungraded and voluntary, went over well. It was good for these earnest, hardworking students to do some laughing and creative work, while as teachers we were pleased to have smuggled books and ideas into so much unpressured enjoyment. We brought up this experience during our faculty retreat to plan a curriculum for our second year at BDFZ and made a pitch that, although perhaps most of a student's time should be dedicated to serious, graded work, there should be breaks in the course of an academic year when students are encouraged to pursue things they find simply interesting and fun, without regard for what looks good on a college application. Our colleagues were willing to try this experiment, and so we developed the idea of Carp Week, which we tried out in our second year, the year in which I was teaching my seminar on change.

Planning for Carp Week started while regular classes were still going on. One morning the students arrived in the classroom building to find a large new poster in the central hall that I had stayed up late the night before to make. "Leap into Light!" it said.

We had chosen light as an organizing theme for Carp Week because there were so many possible angles from which to approach it, scientific as well as humanistic. Teachers had been asked to offer workshops that could be literary, scientific, mathematical, philosophical or any combination, as long as they related to light. In the end, the poster had sign-up sheets for nine workshops to meet every morning for a week. In the afternoons of Carp Week there would other activities, including games, movies and an all-school seminar on Isaac Asimov's story "Nightfall."

The students crowded around the poster, reading the workshop descriptions and consulting each other about what to think. There was considerable laughter and some wonderment. Friends negotiated about which workshop to take together, while other students tried to guess which topics would be easier. Some were unsure what they were supposed to do, and, seeing me standing nearby, came up with questions.

"How do I choose?" someone wanted to know.

"Choose what looks interesting," I answered. "Choose something you have never done before. Choose something that makes you curious."

"Why is it called 'Carp Week?'" asked another.

The complicated series of accidents involving Latin and dragons was too much to explain in the excitement. So I said, lamely, "Because we are fishing for wisdom."

"Why do this? Will it be graded?" a particularly serious student wondered. She seemed concerned that her concentration would slip and her studies get off track.

"No, it won't—just pass/fail. All you have to do is be there. Don't worry about it," I told her, "we will talk afterward about whether it was a good thing. Go, sign up!" I shoo'd them toward the poster. Another little knot of students scurried up to me with the same sorts of questions.

By the end of the day, most of the students had signed up for something. I offered an ambitious workshop on Sophocles' *Oedipus Rex*. Light is a big theme in that play, a symbol for knowledge that transcends even physical blindness—it is the blind people in that play who can see. I got twelve takers.

My plan was to put on a short version of the play on the Friday afternoon of Carp Week, when at a schoolwide assembly each workshop was to give a presentation on what it had done and learned. We had a week, therefore, within which we had to read the play, discuss the play, edit the play, assign roles, memorize lines, create costumes and rehearse. I could feel the ghost of Sophocles peering doubtfully over my shoulder at this undertaking. Looking back on it now, I see that the thing should have been impossible— the gods must have driven me mad with hubris.

Luckily, I got an unexpected partner to help me. S was an American, a scientist, and was inclined to think that literature and philosophy are rather soft-headed and pointless. Nevertheless, when his workshop was cancelled due to insufficient students signing up, he deliberately decided to get himself involved with *Oedipus Rex* as a tribute to the interdisciplinary spirit behind Carp Week. He took home the play to read.

The next morning S strode into our office and slapped his copy of Sophocles' play on my desk. He had read it through the night before, he announced, and found it boring, impossible to under-stand and, to the extent that anyone could understand it, pomp-ous and dumb. Aware that he was disagreeing with twenty-five centuries of opinion that *Oedipus Rex* was one of the great works of the human spirit, he said he was open to persuasion—perhaps, he conceded, his understanding was not yet complete, although it was clear he didn't really think so. Humanity had been dead wrong about science for a good deal longer than twenty-five centuries, after all, and it seemed perfectly plausible to him that a scientist's keen eye could spot that Sophocles was a fraud. Western culture needs selling even to Westerners, apparently, and I noted that down as one of the many ambitious hopes for the week.

Despite its seeming impossibility, the *Oedipus Rex* workshop went wonderfully. A drama workshop held in a theater has the great advantage of starting every day with performance exercises, which the students loved. They arrived cautious, but by the time I had made them run around, do poses, exaggerate emotional responses, play charades and interpret situations, they were giggling and energetic. When we settled down to do some reading together, the effects of the preliminary hamming up were reflected in the way they delivered lines and spoke up easily with jokes and questions. There are strategies to encouraging curiosity.

Many of these students were also in my change seminar, so, as the group read through the play, they were able to demonstrate the habits we had formed in the seminar of how to talk about a text. The other students quickly learned to follow their example and by the time we got to performance day, the student-actors understood the issues at stake in *Oedipus Rex*. They saw how the play displayed the costs of knowledge. When we first meet him, Oedipus is a strong, confident ruler facing a straightforward problem. A plague has descended on his city and oracles have announced that it will disperse only when the man who killed the previous king is found and punished. Oedipus resolves to seek out the murderer, despite the prophet Teiresias' warning that finding the truth about the previous king's death will destroy him. Other dark prophecies lurk in Oedipus's past—that he would kill his father and marry his mother—but he believes he has avoided their fulfillment, so he brushes off Tiresias' prophesies, too. As a result of his inquiry, however, he uncovers the horrifying reality of his own position. He finds that he himself is guilty of killing the previous king and that this previous king was his own father, meaning that the widow he had married was his own mother. All of the prophecies have come true. Faced with this dreadful knowledge he blinds himself and stumbles away into exile.

The students were amazed and embarrassed when they learned that Oedipus had children with his own mother. They tried to hide behind a pretense of sophistication, but Oedipus's family situation left them bewildered. Was this accepted in Western society, or Greek society, or ancient society? They wondered. I told them that it had been just as shocking to the people in Sophocles' first audiences as it was to them, but they remained doubtful.

We had long discussions about whether Oedipus should have taken the prophet Teiresias' advice to remain ignorant. Knowledge is dangerous; it can undermine comfortable assumptions. S brought up Charles Darwin's discovery that humanity descended from animals, suggesting that if you look too hard at your origins you might find out something that could seem ugly and bring down your spiritual and intellectual status—should you refuse to look? We also talked of how Freud had used the Oedipus story. In the most ordinary family it makes people uncomfortable, even repulsed, to think too hard about their parents and where they came from.

One student, hastily changing the subject, made another point about the dangers of knowledge: "Maybe people were happier in villages before they knew what cities were like. That old happiness is ruined when they know." Others agreed. Before China was open to the West, before people knew what prosperity could look like, many more people lived in small villages surrounded by close families. Now everyone wanted to come to the big cities to make their fortunes, and family life was weakened. Someone added that, in a similar way, these students would be going to America to try to make their fortunes. On the whole, they were confident that this would be a good thing, but they were aware that gaining knowledge of the world would forever change their view of

China. I sympathized, as I was going through the same thing from the opposite direction. China had given me new lenses through which to see my old life, and, as a result, some of my unquestioned notions had been exposed as questionable. In voyaging, there are losses as well as gains.

Oedipus Rex has other themes besides knowledge. Many readers get interested in the question of fate and Oedipus' unavailing effort to avoid the prophecies against him. My Chinese students were not attracted by that question. They cared more about the way the play pointed to a different direction for knowledge. When Oedipus finds out the devastating circumstances of his life he does not do the obvious thing—as his wife/mother Jocasta does—and kill himself. Instead he blinds himself and exiles himself from the city. When we wondered about why Oedipus chooses to live, the students suggested that he was experimenting with seeing by another light than the light we see with our eyes. Even after this horrifying discovery about himself, he still insists on seeking knowledge, this time guided by an internal light. His hope, from the beginning of the play to the end, is to see with the light of knowledge no matter what it revealed. I was especially satisfied with this interpretation because it matched my own deeply felt conviction that curiosity leading to knowledge, while dangerous sometimes, should always be pursued.

When S said he was impressed by these discussions and no longer thought the play was stupid, my satisfaction was complete. He still believed the play was clumsily written, however, and warned that it needed a lot of "dragging into the light" to be understood. Thus, S and I stayed up most of one night chopping down the play for a twenty-minute performance. Several major characters were left forlorn on the cutting room floor as we gave their stories to the chorus to narrate. I thought I could hear the ghost of Sophocles screaming in protest by the time we were done.

As for casting, we decided that with such a short time to memorize lines we had to divide up the big parts. In the end, there were five Oedipus the Kings, of all shapes and sizes. We made a shiny crown for each to wear so the audience could always tell who was the king. The last Oedipus got to pull it off and toss it into the theater seats, as if it were a bridal bouquet. There were two Jocastas (Oedipus' wife/mother). Although she dies offstage in the script we had her come on and act out her death while it was being described. This was fun for all concerned, although there was perhaps too much laughter for high tragedy. One student volunteered to play all of the small mime parts, including the Sphinx, whose battle with Oedipus we acted out, even though in Sophocles' script it occurs before the action of the play. This student was, in his own words, the "路 人 (lù rén)," the all-around useful anonymous person. His mask was blank, except for the words "lù rén."

The students had a great time with dressing up, of course. A bedsheet over black clothing was the basic costume, which could be draped in various ways and subtly accessorized. Creating the masks that are characteristic of Greek drama was surprisingly personal and expressive. The five Oedipus the Kings each had a different look for their different places in the play, although the beard was constant. A breakthrough moment came when it occurred to S that lines could be written on the inside of the masks to help the actors remember them. Had the ancient Greeks had invented that dodge? Maybe that's why the custom of masks continued for so long. A brilliant people, the Greeks.

Carp Week games were in a place called the Black Box, so named because it could be reduced to absolute darkness, which was useful for hiding and surprises. Within a theme and a few props related to Isaac Asimov's story "Nightfall," which is about a civilization destroyed when its people see the stars for the first time, we held various mostly ridiculous contests. Winners received liberal rewards of candy, as did those who came in second—or third, or fourth, or eighteenth. China's traditional cuisine does not have much in the way of sweets and candy is a relatively new, Westernized experience, so it was well received. The judging was arbitrary and unserious. Anyone who complained was pelted with candy. Even under these circumstances, there was still some Chinese student-warrior culture affecting the games and the students competed hard to win. I hoped that the essential frivolity of the games made that impulse to compete a look little silly.

The seminars on "Nightfall" were only partly successful. For some of the faculty, this was their first time in a discussion setting, and they did not know how to carry it off. I have led seminars on texts for so many years that I tend to forget that conversation is a learned skill that takes time and practice to acquire. There are obvious rules—don't interrupt, don't monopolize, don't get mad—and even these rules don't come easily for some. The subtler rules are related to being genuinely interested in what is being said, as well as in what is at stake for the person speaking. Conversation also requires having a sense for where the most fruitful questions are and a willingness to let the conversation go where living curiosity takes it. That last one is especially hard for teachers, who often feel a duty to hijack the conversation to make sure that important substantive ideas are covered. I feel the temptation too, but living curiosity will, with a little help from a person experienced in conversation, find for itself those important ideas.

"Possibly," my skeptical colleagues might reply, "but why not just explain the material rather than listening to the uninformed opinions of students who are reading it for the first time?" The answer to this question is at the heart of liberal arts teaching. Listening to students with respect and interest offers a model for sincere inquiry that the students will imitate with each other and in their later lives, so that this indirect approach to teaching is more effective in the end. When people get to what matters in a text through their own curiosity, encouraged by a teacher who demonstrates what it means to be interested in a subject for its own sake, the substance of a text comes alive for them. In addition, they have developed the confidence to use that substance as a resource for new ideas. Because these first Carp Week seminars had not fully succeeded, I made a note that preparations for Carp Week should include practice seminars for the faculty so that we could help each other acquire the conversational skill to encourage this creative process.

As I worked to make other aspects of Carp Week run smoothly, S took over rehearsals for the play. He brought some scientific discipline to the need for clear speech and volume, so that the farthest seats would be able to hear. For second language students, this was a particular challenge, as I knew from my own tendency to swallow my shy and rudimentary Chinese. I would catch glimpses of people in bedsheets in the corners of classrooms, declaiming to each other at the tops of their voices, S looking sternly on. Once, late at night in the library, I ran into the chorus hard at work, with a strong-minded student leader taking S for her model and choreographing without mercy. Well done!

The Friday afternoon of the performance came before anyone was ready for it. Only that morning we had had our first full run-through, discovering problems we had not anticipated—unclear entrances, awkward blocking, inadequate lighting—as well as missed cues and forgotten lines. Students, now fully inhabiting the role of actors, had all sorts of thoughts about how to showcase their own parts to the audience. The chorus leader fought masterfully to increase the dramatic effect of the chorus' unity and also to give each chorus member a solo moment. The Messenger, who is the only cheerful character in the play, had made a mask with a giant smile and wanted to peek out from behind the back curtains and to flirt with the audience. Great idea. The Sphinx and Oedipus No. 1 had created a brief fight scene, which I liked, although I nixed the fake blood. I was operating in director mode, which meant swift clear decisions, regardless of whether they were the best ones; at such times the appearance of knowledge is required, even if actual knowledge is not there. The ghost of Sophocles whispered (pompously) that the appearance of knowledge might be the best we could ever hope for. "So act with confidence," the old dramatist advised.

Curtain time for Oedipus the King. My actors launched, I hid behind the scenes, not wanting to watch. I was able to hear everything, however, so I could monitor the audience reactions. There was silence at first, with a little puzzlement. Then came giggles when the Sphinx came lumbering monstrously onstage to struggle with Oedipus and be conquered. From that moment forward, the audience was ready to see comedy. The blind prophet Teiresias entered, creaking with age, tapping with a cane, and they laughed. Tiresias and Oedipus shouted at each other and they laughed harder. Things calmed down a little during the chorus' speeches, as the audience seemed unsure how to take them. Oedipus' gradual discovery of his dreadful situation unfolded fairly seriously, although the Messenger kept the comedy alive. There was much the audience did not understand, a consequence both of the second language situation and the chopping up of Sophocles' text. To the extent that they did understand the story, however, they were thrown off by its strange unspeakable themes and had no other response but laughter. I reassured the actors backstage that laughter was engagement and that engagement, in the theater, was the same thing as success. I need not have worried. They were having a great time. The last Oedipus in particular orated with powerful emotion as he plunged the needles of his wife/mother's brooches bloodily into his eyes, shutting off the light of the world, leaving him blind. The audience enjoyed it immensely and applauded at length. For the rest of our time at the Dalton Academy, the performance of *Oedipus Rex* was celebrated. "I loved it," one of my students remarked later. "That play is *funny.*" That wasn't quite the reaction I was hoping for, but I'll take it.

One reason I had chosen to teach a workshop on *Oedipus Rex* was that I wanted the students in my change seminar, who had just read the *Oresteia,* to get a living picture of Greek tragedy. As it turned out, the picture they got was of what it looks like when a truncated Greek tragedy is performed by Chinese students, in English, in bedsheets, at high speeds, in front of a laughing audience—perhaps not an authentic experience. In my ongoing conversations with the ghost of Sophocles I had an impulse to apologize but I never quite did so. The classics can take a lot of pummeling and still stand. That's what makes them great—magnificent ideas come through, no matter how roughly they are treated. Because of our work with *Oedipus Rex*, questions about the value and danger of knowledge now lived in my students' minds. They have the basis for conversation with those questions for the rest of their lives, as they make their own voyages. I thanked Sophocles and sent him back home to Greece.

As for the success of Carp Week, who can know? There was no test. Yet I am convinced that it offered something valuable. At the very least we filled the poster with ideas and reflections of the students' experience (my student actors' masks are on the upper right):

In addition, the students' experience of being encouraged to follow their own curiosity was new enough to many that by itself it might cause shoots to grow—that counts as learning, that opening of perspective. Besides, they had a great time talking about a book! A Western classic, too, that anyone might have thought would be boring or too weirdly foreign to be interesting. Instead of being bored they were engaged, and engagement, in the liberal arts, is the same thing as success.

Identity 身份

Chapter 5

Livy, Plutarch, Empire, and Identity

The next stop for our class was Rome. "All roads lead to Rome" we say in the West, and Rome sits at the heart of many paths of memory and thought. Politically, it reflected the next step up from the Greek city-state to a multicultural domain. Thus, in our approach to Western literature and philosophy, we had followed a clear progression from the individual hero—Achilles—to the city of Athens, established around the issue of how the individual relates to a community, and now to the assembly of diverse cities and people, an empire. As imperial China certainly knew, empire presents a new problem, the issue of how a centralized state can govern effectively a far-flung range of people who speak different languages and have different cultures, stories, and ideas of truth.

Many empires in history have responded to this issue of diversity by oppressing or marginalizing foreign cultures. Rome, by contrast, demonstrated a relative tolerance, overlaying existing cultures with Roman law but otherwise allowing them to continue. The Chinese empire approached the same issue in a different way, by creating a common written language. There may be other strategies, as yet untried. In any event, I wanted my students to think about the decisions made by nations and people about whether to fend off differences and changes or to take them in. As our modern world globalizes, such issues are as urgent as they ever were. My Chinese students would encounter them personally when they went to America. It is a matter of identity.

To establish Rome's vision of its identity before it rose to rule the Western world, we read the Roman historian Livy's description of the founding of the Roman Republic. According to Livy, the central principle of early Rome was the cry of "no kings!" The Roman Republic founded its identity on the defiant attitude that Rome would not suffer the tyranny of royal rule. The greatest hero of the early city was Lucius Junius Brutus, who executed his own sons when he discovered that they were plotting to invite kings back into the city. For the next four hundred years after that heroic founding, Roman politics was shaped by the rejection of kings and the hatred of tyranny.

The Roman Republic's rejection of kingly rule left my Chinese students cold. Almost nothing in the five thousand years of Chinese civilized history corresponds to the Roman repudiation of royal power. Most students were horrified rather than inspired by Lucius Junius Brutus' execution of his king-loving sons. Only the stubbornly independent Anne defended it, while others shook their heads at her.

"Why do so many Western people kill their children?" Sam asked, harking back to Agamemnon's murder of his daughter. It was my first encounter with an aspect of my teaching in China that I had not expected, although perhaps I should have. My students were constantly comparing Western ideas, as learned from me, with the Chinese ideas that they already knew. I had not really understood that I would be airing dirty Western laundry by assigning these books. Despite my effort to tamp down a defensive reaction, they sensed my temptation to feel insulted on behalf of the West in response to Sam's question. Seeking harmony, students politely told some ugly stories from ancient Chinese history. The discussion reached a mutual acknowledgment that human beings everywhere have stories of horrible violence, in which famous people betray even the most intimate relationships.

The wheels of comparison kept privately turning, though, for all of us. For the first time I appreciated that the cross-cultural comparisons we all made might not be entirely comfortable for me, might not always confirm my Western biases. Aspiring grandly to a globalizing conversation, I had not quite faced in those gauzy dreams that there would be harsh judgments. Yet this is the risk of genuine conversation, that someone might have to change her mind or be changed in other ways. Identities might shift.

This classroom discussion also impressed on me my own need to read Chinese classic texts more deeply. Consequently, after work that day, Grant and I went to *Xīnhuá* (新华), the official state-run bookstore, which had a diverse selection of English language books and movies. Early in our stay in China, we had bought there a deceptively labeled collection of "Oscar-winning" movies—many titles had won their Oscars in obscure categories like make-up and set design—because the collection included a free globe of the world, which I had used in my *Moby Dick* class to trace the voyage of the *Pequod*. Now I bought English translations of some of the foundational works of Chinese history and literature, the *Records of the Grand Historian* by *Sīmǎ Qiān* and the four great novels of China: *The Romance of the Three Kingdoms*, a fourteenth century work attributed to *Luó Guànzhōng*; *A Dream of Red Mansions (or The Story of the Stone)*, by *Cáo Xuěqín*, dating from the eighteenth century; *Outlaws of the Marsh*, attributed to *Shī Nàiān* and of uncertain date, though probably between the fourteenth and sixteenth centuries; and *The Journey to the West*, attributed to *Wú Chéngěn* in the sixteenth century. All of these books are great not just because of their literary merit but also in the literal sense: they are enormous, consisting of four fat volumes each. It was rather a slog home.

Back in my seminar on change, we spent time with the Roman Republic's identity as the city with no kings. The Roman principle of "no kings" has shaped Western political development, persisting despite and alongside its centuries of monarchical government. Livy has been in the memory of all great Western political writers. Certainly the American founding fathers at the time of the American Revolutionary War were reading Livy and think-ing of Rome. The United States Constitution re-creates the Roman Senate and copies from Rome the concept of sharing power under a rule of law. Except for a few years in the early twentieth century, China has never experimented with any such form of government.

I asked my students how they understood Chinese identity.

"Five thousand years of civilization!" Jack said, proudly.

"中国" (*Zhōng guó*) added someone else, more softly, but with satisfaction. "中国" means "Middle Kingdom." I was astonished one day when a Chinese colleague of ours asked "Why do you call our country China?" When I researched the origin of that name I found that no one is sure why the country is called that. Theories range from an early dynasty called the Qin to a Sanskrit word used by the Italian explorer Marco Polo. It is not entirely fair, though, to suggest the name is simply a Western imposition, since the Chinese government has adopted the appellation "People's Republic of China" as the official English language designation for itself. Day to day, however, the "Middle Kingdom" is the unofficial but most common way that the Chinese think of their country, as occupying the center of the world.

So, according to my students, Chinese identity was not based on a form of government as was the Roman Republic and as is America today. For the Chinese, China is the literal, geographic midpoint of its region, and, much more importantly, the epicen-ter of civilization. The splendors and accomplishments of Chinese culture—philosophy, poetry, painting, porcelain and calligraphy, among others—are overwhelming. This view of the superiority of Chinese culture has apparently been shared by at least some of the surrounding nations. The great eleventh century Japanese classic, Murasaki Shikibu's *The Tale of Genji,* admires the excellences of China at the center, accepting that her own Japan is distant from that center.

The Romans, by contrast, were oddly humble about their cul-tural accomplishments, tending to believe that all the truly brilliant refinements came from other nations. In the Roman world, Greeks were revered for their philosophy and art; Jews were respected for their intellectual spirituality; and Egyptians were admired for their building and their antique learning. As the Roman poet Virgil wrote in his epic poem the *Aeneid,* Romans believed that their own contribution to the world was law and the skill to govern others:

> Others [that is, other nations] will cast more tenderly in bronze
> their breathing figures, I can well believe,
> and bring more life-like portraits out of marble;
> argue more eloquently, use the pointer
> to trace the paths of heaven accurately
> and accurately foretell the rising stars.
> Roman, remember by your strength to rule
> earth's peoples — for your arts are to be these:
> to pacify, to impose the Rule of Law,
> to spare the conquered, battle down the proud.[5]

Thus, Rome's centrality was not based on a claim of general superiority but on Rome's invention of the rule of law. Although it is a little self-serving for a nation to assert that it has some special gift for ruling others, Rome's claim to that status was founded on a genuinely great achievement. The Roman system of law, starting with the Twelve Tables of Law described by Livy, was a plausible source for national pride and a lasting accomplishment. Compiled into the Code of Justinian, Roman law is the foundation for much existing European and American law. The American system was created under the rule of law with Rome in mind.

As Rome bound its empire together with law, Chinese emperors unified their far-flung dominions with a common written language. Not, please note, a common *spoken* language. The Chinese writing system was intentionally developed to avoid any phonetic connection between the way a character looks and how it sounds.

---

5   Robert Fitzgerald, trans., *Virgil's Aeneid* (New York: Knopf Doubleday Publishing Group 1990), book 6, lines 1145-54.

It seems crazy to Westerners that the shapes of Chinese characters provide no clue to the sound of words, but the system worked well in an empire as extended as ancient China, where there were lots of languages. A common written language that was separate from speech meant that people from widely different parts of the empire, even though they spoke mutually unintelligible dialects, could all read the same imperial decrees. This allowed for a bureaucracy that could expand further than any single spoken language. Written Chinese continues to serve this purpose today. Every television show—all TV stations are owned by the Communist Party—has character subtitles so that, no matter what language people speak, if they can read simplified Chinese characters they can understand the Party's programming.[6]

Both Roman and Chinese imperial strategies are present in our globalizing world. Schemes for international law are developing in response to the needs of trade, just as analogous schemes developed in Rome. At the same time, because of the reach of the internet and increasingly effective translation programs, barriers of language are falling down. These developments appear, based on the histories of Rome and China, to tend toward political unity. Maybe these Chinese students (and my own children, too) will see a world in which identity is at a planetary scale, the empire of the Earth.

My Chinese students might have been puzzled by the "no kings" principle at the beginning of the Roman Republic, but the events that marked its end, and the change to the Roman Empire, made perfect sense to them. In the four centuries between the founding

---

6   Although it may have been useful for the administration of the empire, the disconnection of Chinese characters from pronunciation magnifies the difficulties that foreigners have in learning the language. Grant and I never got very far in our efforts to learn Chinese, partly because of our age, partly due to not having the necessary time or discipline, partly from the hugeness of the vocabulary task (there are no cognates between Chinese and English as there are between, say, English and French), and partly because each Chinese word has to be separately learned as a sound and as characters, more than doubling the difficulty involved.

of the Roman Republic and the beginning of the Roman Empire, the Republic had risen to dominate the Mediterranean world, so that the rulership of Rome had become a prize worth hunting down. It was a familiar story to my Chinese students that, once there is a center of power, great warriors seek to possess it at all costs. Writing of the end of the Qin dynasty that had unified China, the Chinese Grand Historian *Sīmǎ Qiān* (司马迁) (146-86 BCE) explains how power becomes the prey sought by everyone:

> The web of [the old] government had rotted away and the strands of its rule grew slack... The empire slipped from [the old government] like a fleeing deer and all the world joined in its pursuit. As it happened, he with the tallest stature and the swiftest feet seized it first.[7]

As the Roman Republic faltered and the strands of its rule grew slack, power slipped from the Senate like a fleeing deer. Great warriors began to contend for its vast holdings, and Rome suffered a devastating civil war.

To get a feel for the personalities in that conflict, our class read some of Plutarch's *Lives of the Noble Greeks and Romans*. *Sīmǎ Qiān* and the Greek historian Plutarch (46 CE to 120 CE) were not far apart in time and they both surveyed history on a grand scale, approaching their subject matter by writing about individual lives and characters. It is remarkable that these two authors, so far separated geographically, each invented the same new art form, the biography. Perhaps the astonishing synchronicity of the Axial Age continues to operate. Or perhaps it is inevitable that there would be a special attention paid to biography during the establishment of empires when so much depends on the character of the emperor, whose single personality can stamp an entire civilization. Historians of such times might naturally begin to

---

7   Burton Watson, trans., Records of the Grand Historian, Han Dynasty I, (New York: Columbia University Press 1961), part 5, 183.

meditate on personal identity and want to know what it is and where it comes from.

We read Plutarch's life of Julius Caesar, a figure notoriously ambitious for supremacy in Rome, who was assassinated because of this ambition. Marcus Brutus, who claimed to be a descendant of Lucius Junius Brutus,[8] accused Caesar of wanting to be a king and killed him, hoping to return to the principle of "no kings." Alas, the days of the Republic were over. Royal power was inevitably coming to Rome, and Marcus Brutus was defeated at the Battle of Philippi. The person who came out on top of the chaotic struggle that followed, who successfully hunted down the deer, was Julius Caesar's heir, who named himself Augustus Caesar and became the holder of all power in Rome. The tradition of "no kings" was still strong enough, though, that Augustus bowed to it by continuing the forms of the Republic—he pretended he wasn't a king. For all of the long years of his successful reign he attended the Senate and coyly behaved as if he were just another senator, nothing special, even though everybody knew that he had absolute authority. It's hard to tell whether such a show is a polite saving-of-face or a mockery. Either way, there is a hollowness at the center of power.

I asked my students about their own identity: "Are you still the same person you were when you were seven years old?"

"Yes," said David, quickly. "Same name, same family."

"Some things are different, though. You are taller, probably," I asserted. What else?"

"Lots of body changes," added someone, after a minute, and got a few sly grins.

"I know more; I've seen more," someone else cut in, repressively.

"Do you like different things?" I asked.

---

8   Plutarch suggests that Marcus Brutus was actually Julius Caesar's son, as Caesar was the lover of Marcus Brutus' mother. One can only imagine the complicated father issues that would have driven Marcus Brutus to try to establish his legitimate descent from Lucius Junius by killing the man who was rumored to be his real father. These were racy times in ancient Rome.

"Pizza!" another student called out, to general laughter.

"Music is different," said Allen. "When I heard rock music for the first time it made me see and feel differently."

"Okay, so what is the same about you from when you were seven years old, besides your name and family?" I asked.

"I remember the same things," said Helena, wistful as she looked into her past. "I have more things to remember now, but I still have the first things to remember."

I pushed on this: "Maybe you might understand them better now, though, do you think? You remember playing somewhere, perhaps, and now you can guess where it was or who was with you in a way that you couldn't as a child." She agreed. "Does that change the memory? Is it the same memory?"

"As I grow older, I combine first reminiscences and newfangled ones together to make a fluctuating self." Sara, an imaginative thinker, had done considerable work on English vocabulary words, and enjoyed expressing herself in unusual ways. I learned a lot from her about how my own use of English words relied unconsciously on custom rather than rules. She would create sentences with English words that sounded wrong or funny to me, but when I thought about the grammar of them it turned out she was almost always right, or at least so close that it was difficult to pin down what exactly was wrong. The differences between "memories" and "reminiscences," or "new" and "newfangled," are hard to explain.

I asked a generalizing question: "Are you saying that you are creating a changing self when you add new memories and experiences?"

That was too airy and philosophical for several students, who shook their heads. "No," said Tyler, impatient with abstract, artsy notions, "we are bodies, genes, and history."

Sara and Helena both objected to that, and we tried to decide what it is that most defines identity, the constant self that we remember from our earliest years. Some thought that identity is defined by unchanging things like DNA or country of birth, things over which a person has no control. Others argued the opposite, that it is what we can control that makes up our identity—our choices define who we are. Choosing to go to America for college, Sara was sure, would change all of their identities. This observation caused uncomfortable glances around the table, and Sara faltered in the full flow of her ideas, seeing that she had stumbled into strong feelings in her classmates.

I left that for a moment and went back to Rome, trying to get my students interested in the issue of identity as it related to Rome by asking, "Suppose you are a small kingdom. One day Roman legions, with their famous invincibility in battle, invade, conquer, and threaten to destroy you. Before doing so, they offer the following deal: 'Pay us tribute, submit to having a Roman governor, and put a statue of the emperor among the other gods in all of your temples. In exchange, even though we can destroy you anytime we want, we will hold off. As long as you keep up your end of the bargain, you can maintain your day-to-day culture, worship your own gods—plus the emperor—and even have a local king. In addition, we will build roads and aqueducts in your territory and allow you to be part of the great, prospering Roman trade system that is unifying the world.' Would you take that deal?"

"No!" said a few. "Maybe" said others. "Why not?" said Anne, in a practical spirit. "Perhaps it felt like being asked to join civilization."

"What about the small country's own civilization, pride, and history?" Jack asserted, indignantly.

Mark asked a shrewd question: "Who makes the decision to accept the deal? The king? The people?"

Then, thinking of Sara's observation, I offered a twist to personalize the issue of identity. "Now imagine that you have arrived in the United States for college, as you are going to do in a year or two. How much of your present identity will you be careful to keep, and how much will you be willing to let go in order to get your education? Will you merge into American culture and become as American as you can? Or will you find other Chinese people and create a small China around yourself?" It seemed both appropriate to the conversation and, I hoped, helpful to the students to ask them to think explicitly and in the general case about what was causing them to feel so strongly. This is one of the uses of the liberal arts.

Several people objected that the analogy between the two situations didn't quite work. When they arrived in the United States they would not be a conquering country, nor would they be a conquered one. After discussion we concluded that the point was that when different cultures encountered each other, there were questions about identity. Historically, this is the great issue of empire. From the point of view of the dominant power, it is a question of how to administer a variety of languages and cultures without losing its own culture. From the point of view of the submitting powers, it is a question of how much sovereignty and culture to give up without a fight. The same issues of identity are part of our personal lives, as well. For each person encountering a new culture, both of these aspects of the question are involved—how do we accept new ideas while retaining our identities in a way that honors what has shaped our identity from our beginnings? It is, in a way, also the problem—or perhaps the delight—of gaining knowledge in a globalizing world. We all get a newfangled identity.

Stories 故事

Chapter 6

Ovid's *Metamorphoses* and Stories

Our classroom discussions about Roman history had gotten us to the point where we were ready to read a classic text that was central to our seminar's theme of change—Ovid's *Metamorphoses* ("Changes," in English). Ovid, like Virgil, wrote just after the change from Roman Republic to the Roman Empire. Both writers were trying, I think, to understand the concept of identity. Was Rome still Rome, now that its central principle of "no kings" had been left behind? Virgil wrote directly for the first emperor, Augustus, and answered the question by making Augustus the culmination of a retold Roman history, the unfolding of which had been intended by the gods. He asserted that Rome was still Rome, even though under Augustus' new rule the four-centuries-old Senate and Republic were only a show.

Ovid, more subversively, tells stories in which there is both gain and loss in changing identities. Fleeing from the god Apollo, Daphne is rescued by being changed into a tree. Is she still Daphne? Io becomes a cow, Zeus a shower of gold, Philemon and Baucis become intertwining vines. People and things flow in and out of each other. Ovid retells the story of the Trojan War in a way very different from the *Iliad*, with backstories and satisfying endings to the tales that Homer only half told. Do Ovid's characters have the same identity as Homer's heroes? There is no real answer.

I arrived at the next class planning to ask the students to talk about the stories in the *Metamorphoses*, exploring from this angle the life-shaping role of stories that had been so much a part of my *Moby Dick* class the previous year. My change seminar students, though, were not yet done with our conversation about how they would react to America. There was an intense discussion in Chinese already going on in the hallway as I opened the door. Switching to English, Alice began to ask me questions, a reversal of roles that seemed fair.

"Does everybody in America have a gun? Does the U.S. Constitution make you get a gun?" She sounded worried. The rest of the class turned expectantly to me; I was being asked to settle an argument.

"No," I assured her. "I know that there is lots of talk about guns in the news, but they have never been a part of my life. They aren't everywhere. The government certainly does not force you to own one." The students weighed what they thought of this. It seemed that American gun culture felt strange, frightening, and even uncivilized to them. It was a part of the American identity for which my students had no empathy.

I went on: "Some people interpret the U. S. Constitution to say that everyone has an unrestricted right to own a gun. Others disagree. At any rate, there are lots of people who don't own guns."

"I hear America is dangerous;" someone added, "that the streets are not safe." At that, several students looked anxious. Apparently, their ambition to go to the United States for college carried some fears with it.

"There are places in American cities where I don't go at night, I guess, just like in cities anywhere in the world," I answered. "But your college campuses will be safe. People will be there to help you." They still looked troubled.

"Is everyone in America religious?" asked Janie, abruptly. In our discussions of both the *Iliad* and *Oresteia* she had shown herself to be wary and scornful of religion. Religion was for most of the students another aspect of American culture that felt odd.

"No, not everyone. Many people are religious, and you will see lots of churches, as well as some synagogues and mosques. There will probably be religious groups on campus, just as there will be other types of groups. Some people might ask you about religion and want to talk to you about theirs." I tried to give them confidence: "You will figure out how to deal with it."

"What do Americans think of Chinese people?" asked Tracy, who seldom spoke up. Seeing that the concerns the students were raising about America were important to them, I decided to delay my lesson plan and continue this conversation. Everyone in the class was sitting up and paying attention, ready to see me as an inside line on what their lives would be like when they went to college in America. Such engagement needed to be treated respectfully.

Tracy's question was a tricky one. I answered slowly: "I don't like to think about people in groups. There are all kinds of Americans, just like there are all kinds of Chinese. Different Americans will feel differently."

They sat back a little, disappointed in this reply. I could see that I would lose the moment if I didn't offer something more. "There are some general things that many Americans might have in their minds when meeting a Chinese person. Your fellow students are likely to assume you are all very focused on studying, for example, and good at math."

They groaned, clearly disliking the stereotype of Chinese people implied by such a reaction. I added, wanting to meet their fears directly and truthfully: "Some people think of China as a threat to the United States, and you might possibly meet some resentment, though I certainly hope not."

"Resentment because of politics or because of us?" Paul asked, a little obscurely. I took him to be asking whether people would resent them as a symbol of China's rising place in the world, or whether they would resent them personally.

"Well, that's the whole problem with stereotypes." I answered. "People take general opinions and use them to pre-judge particular persons. If they are angry at China for something they see in a newspaper, it's possible that they could take out that anger on a particular Chinese person. It would be very unfair. I like to think that you won't find very much of that in America, but I can't guarantee it won't happen."

The students' questions about life in America turned more and more to race, and then slowly trailed away. Feelings were still high, but race was, it appeared, a hard topic to discuss. The students knew that there were big tensions around race in America. Most of them believed that race was not a problem for China, where 90% of the population were racially homogenous Han Chinese.[9] This contrast between the two countries was a big part of what was driving their worries about what their lives would be like in America. The biggest concern wasn't so much that they would they have to face racial minorities in America but that they would, for the first time in their lives, be *members* of a racial minority. They were reticent to ask about this.

During the silence that settled on the class in this reticence, I thought about an incident that had happened a few nights before, which had invoked my own confusion about being a racial minority in China. As Grant and I sat down to dinner with some of our Chinese colleagues in the faculty dining room, one of them remarked cheerfully, "I hate the Japanese, don't you?"

Whew. I had no idea how to reply. There is plenty of racism in America, as everywhere, but it is rare to hear it out loud and unembarrassed. I mumbled something like what I had said to my students, that I was sure there were all kinds of Japanese people. This person half-accepted this but in a disconcerting way. "Yes," she said, "You are a typical American woman, but ...[she named another colleague] ...is not at all a typical American man." I had no idea what she meant, although she seemed to expect all of us to agree happily. What was a typical American woman? Had I been

---

9 Once or twice I heard some amazement at the election of Barak Obama to the American presidency, as it was unimaginable that a non-Han would ever lead China.

insulted? It felt like it, but the insult did not seem to be intended. Very puzzling.

Back in the classroom, I tried to shift the discussion to the connection between identity and stories, a connection that I saw in the *Metamorphoses*. "We have been talking about identity," I offered, "but now I want to talk about stories. A lot of your identity comes from the stories that you hear told and that you tell about yourself."

They were still distracted, but I pressed on. "Some Americans, for example, hear stories all their lives that American identity is connected to being ready to rebel against oppression. Some of these people tell themselves a story that claims owning guns is a part of an American identity."

That was a mistake. Worry clouded their faces once more. "Just a few people are like that," I assured them quickly and hurried to a new topic. "Many people grow up with religious stories that tell them who they are." Janie shook her head rejectingly, and I took refuge in a general assertion, saying "Everyone has stories of some kind that help make sense of the world." The reaction to this was more receptive. I asked them if they thought *chéngyǔ* helped them make sense of their world.

With a little prompting, the students admitted that *chéngyǔ* shaped the way they spoke. They were less sure that having those stories embedded in the language shaped the way they thought. They preferred to believe that they thought with objective truth unaffected by how the thoughts were later expressed. I let that belief go unchallenged for the moment and we began to talk about Ovid's stories.

Ovid's *Metamorphoses* is the book from which a lot of Western stories come. Only the Bible provides more of the foundational stories of the West. Most of the myths about the Greek and Roman gods are in it, as are creation stories, stories about the Trojan War, and stories about love. As we read and talked about the book a picture arose in my mind of all sorts of different stories from different peoples of the Mediterranean world pouring down all the roads leading into Rome. Ovid took them and rendered them into poetry, making of them in the *Metamorphoses* one story. I remembered when, in my *Moby Dick* class, the students and I had told each other our foundational stories, then folded them into Melville's great story that we were studying, as well as the personal stories we were all and each making out of our time together. This range of stories joins the stories of the entire world that are pouring down the roads and airways among countries and through the virtual highways of the global net.

Metamorphoses begins with the creation of the world, order from chaos, and describes a decline from a golden age to later degenerate times, when the sins of the giants drove the gods to flood the world. A single virtuous human couple re-peoples the Earth. The resonance with the Biblical story of Noah was one example of the mixing of Western stories that had poured into Rome. I wondered if there was anything like these stories in China.

At my request, the students looked up Chinese creation stories, which often described the development of opposites in balance called the *yīn yáng* (陰陽). There was one involving a cosmic egg, too, in which human beings arose from the dismembered corpse of the giant *Pán gǔ* (盘古). We got so interested in creation stories that I gave them some selections from Genesis, asking questions about how the stories from all of these sources were the same or different. It was a good exercise in the close reading of texts, and also allowed us to approach God in a dispassionate spirit. Wanting my students to think more about creation, I asked them to write their own creation stories, and got spectacular results. They had a great time rebuilding the heavens and the Earth.

"Do you think," I asked, pressing once more in the issue of whether stories shape the way a person thinks, "that it makes a difference in your feeling of identity if you believe that you were intentionally made by God rather than arising by accident?"

Unlike our analytical approach to Genesis, this direct question did not seem to permit any way for them to distance themselves from the topic of religion. I should have put the question in terms of the difference between being created in a universe of balance ruled by the principles of the 陰陽 (*yīn yáng*) and being created from the corpse of the giant *Pán gǔ*. I had missed a trick.

For a while, we just enjoyed the stories in the *Metamorphoses*. Greek and Roman myths are great to teach because no one has any stake in believing them anymore, so that they could simply be appreciated as good stories. It was fun to revisit the Trojan War and meet all the characters they already knew from a different angle. Also, the students liked the fact that Ovid makes even the most powerful people ridiculous when it comes to love. I was glad to drop my agenda and simply read a great book for pleasure. Quite possibly none of my little self-told stories about what the students were learning from our discussions were right, but as long as they were getting a taste of the delights of these books the class was a success.

I kept thinking about stories and empire. China sometimes seemed to me a great sea of competing stories, each clamoring to be the dominant one that would shape the society. Competing stories showed up in many settings in China, including during our several trips to Tiananmen Square, the ancient city center of Beijing, where symbols of Chinese identities and stories from many centuries stand side by side. The Great Hall of the People, the present seat of government, stands on the west side of the Square near a magnificent gate through which the Chinese emperors walked on their way to the Temple of Heaven to make their privileged contact with the skies. The National Museum on the east provides a home for the artifacts of five thousand years of various Chinese stories, and the Forbidden City, built in the 明 (*Míng*) dynasty, is on the north side of the vast space. A forty-foot photographic image of Chairman *Máo* hangs above the door to the Forbidden City, where he stood on a balcony in 1949 to declare the founding of the People's Republic of China, superimposing his new story of Marxism over the stories of China's past. On that day,

Máo faced south from that balcony. In the imperial councils of ancient China, the ministers sat in a square representing the four cardinal directions of the world, with the emperor sitting in the north side of the square facing south. To "face south," therefore, is the Chinese expression used by the Grand Historian *Sīmǎ Qiān* for becoming the emperor. When *Máo* stood on that balcony in Tiananmen Square he was inhabiting the idiom of *Sīmǎ Qiān*'s stories of China's past. Those stories still had life for him and still have life now.

Stories of political power are part of the tile and scaffolding of the Forbidden City. Grant and I had learned a little about these stories from a Smithsonian Institution DVD that we had bought in Washington, D.C. before coming to Beijing. The DVD had two parts, the first of which focused on the *Míng* dynasty emperor 朱棣 (*Zhū Dì*). Having seized power in an epic intra-familial struggle in about 1400 CE, *Zhū Dì* decided to impress everyone by building the biggest palace that anyone had ever seen. He was dissatisfied with the plans offered to him and told the architect that he would lose his head if he didn't come up with something better by dawn the next day. The architect despaired. Resigned to his imminent death, he spent the night designing a cricket cage for his pet cricket. When the morning came, *Zhū Dì* liked the cricket cage so well that he scaled it up a thousand percent or so and spared the architect. The stories around *Zhū Dì* were all like this, reflecting cruel, capricious authoritarianism, leavened by occasional quirky mercy. Government depended on the personality of the ruler, who could be cruel or sparing as he chose, without any accounting— raw, open and arbitrary.

The second segment on our Smithsonian DVD was about imperial history in the nineteenth century, especially the life of the Empress Dowager *Cíxǐ* (慈禧). Empress *Cíxǐ*'s story began when at age fifteen when she was a candidate to be a concubine. She filed through the archway over which the *Máo* portrait now hangs with other concubine wannabes, expecting to be imprisoned for life amidst jealous rivals and eunuchs. Imperial life in the palace had changed from the free-wheeling days when *Zhū Dì* could do exactly as he pleased. It had become a strange mix of intrigue and ritual under a code of 風水 (*fēng shuǐ*). *Fēng shuǐ* sounds attractive when all that's involved is which direction your television should face in your living room, but for the Chinese imperial family at the time of *Cíxǐ* it was stiflingly intrusive and constricting. Despite their political power, the emperor and his family were trapped in a set of *fēng shuǐ* rituals that defined even their most intimate actions in accordance with cosmic orientation meridians and the rotation of the celestial spheres. Every movement they made risked disordering heaven and Earth. According to this code, when the young *Cíxǐ* managed to intrigue herself into the emperor's bed, she was ritually placed on the imperial copulation platform in the Hall of Union between the Palace of Earthly Tranquility (*Yīn*, to the North), and the Palace of Heavenly Purity (*Yáng*, to the South), while a eunuch dutifully sat by to record all relevant details of the coupling—not the romantic setting one might like. *Cíxǐ* triumphed by conceiving a son under these trying circumstances and rose from the status of concubine to the Dragon-Lady-Behind-the-Throne, presiding over forty-seven increasingly dismal years of decline for the last imperial dynasty. The stories around *Cíxǐ*, who resisted new ideas for China, were about the subtle manipulations of power through others, in stark contrast to *Zhū Dì's* unbridled boldness. Adding to that, the enormous portrait of *Máo* on the entryway to the Forbidden City layers Marxist ideology, with its materialist-determinist narrative, on those old imperial stories.

An American colleague at BDFZ kindly offered to guide our initial visit to the Forbidden City, where she had worked as an intern. She took us through the massive red walls of the complex by way of the tunnel that the young *Cíxǐ* entered as a young girl while I tried to imagine expecting to spend the rest of my life in this enclosed place. In the first courtyard, there are now ticket booths on the right and basketball courts on the left, installed for the use of the People's Liberation Army detachment that lives in the city. Entry to the palace complex and museums was 60 rmb (a little over $10). Grant quipped that the Forbidden City is no longer forbidden, just expensive. I usually like Grant's jokes, but this one died a sad death. The Chinese don't call it "Forbidden City" but "故 宫"(*gù gōng*"), or "former palace."

Within the palace, a great many ancient Chinese stories are reflected in items on display. There is a Museum of Porcelain, for example, an essential aspect of Chinese sensibility. Grant remarked that until that moment he had encountered the *Míng* vase mostly as a fragile and expensive item that occupied centerstage in slapstick comedy routines, waiting to be broken. I suppose there are many wonderful things that we meet first in parody. It was good to see it in a serious setting and get a sense of the beauty and elegance that makes these porcelain works so storied.

The Forbidden City also has a Museum of Calligraphy and Painting. In China, calligraphy is considered a measure of leadership qualities. Thus, the museum contains a transcription of the "Thousand Character Classic," which consists of a thousand different characters done in the hand of the *Qiánlóng* emperor (乾隆, *Lasting Eminence*, 1735-1796). Political leaders in China offer samples of their calligraphy to favored followers, a custom that has continued into the modern age. Near the gate of BDFZ there is an enormous rock inscribed with the name of the school in characters as drawn by *Máo*. Western political leaders, by contrast, don't spend substantial time improving their handwriting, and in the age of Twitter there are few occasions in which they use one thousand words together.

Our second trip to the Forbidden City was to show it to our children, who came to China for a visit almost a year later. This time we were the guides, posing as experts (partly habit from parenthood) explaining Chinese history, which we had learned a little more about since those first days. With a self-confidence that was absurd given the shallowness of our actual knowledge about the deep history of China, Grant and I told all the stories, from the Smithsonian DVD, from our previous guide and from the books we had read, as well as ones we had heard from friends. We answered questions and made comparisons to stories my children knew from being raised in the West.

This experience reflected the vision I had of Rome and also of education, that the challenges to identity are invoked when there is an effort to stretch a human community—or perhaps even a single person—to embrace more and more diverse stories from widely different origins. All kinds of stories had come pouring down the roads that led to Rome, and the same thing had happened when stories had poured into the Forbidden City. I had been pouring such stories into my students in the classroom at the same time that stories had poured into me from both West and East. And now here I was playing Ovid to my children, telling the stories and watching those stories shift and overlap. No doubt they would metamorphose and take on same/different identities yet again.

The existence of so many conflicting stories invited opposite reactions. On the one hand, the situation contributed to a sense that all stories belong to all people in a globalizing world, resulting in a pleasing sentiment of sharing. On the other hand, it highlighted a sense that entertaining so many stories might lead to an empty feeling and a loss of complexity. We might never do justice to the beauty and meaning of stories that we collect carelessly, trading broad knowledge for depth. Also, we could become unmoored from our own original stories, seeing how others, who started with other stories, believe them as strongly as we believe what we thought was ours. This, I guessed, was one thing that the Chinese government could be worried about with the Dalton Academy students going to America. They might lose their appreciation for, and their connection to, the stories that identify them as Chinese. I considered again how identity is both a personal and state issue. Human global interaction and the mixture of stories can not only cause a nation to fear loss of identity, but individual people can also feel lost when belief in personal truths are diluted. If there is only an ocean of stories, each with as much claim on truth as any other, it might seem that none of them matter much. No one story can explain the world and guide our choices if all of them claim to do so with equal force.

Rome faced this problem, too. By the time of the establishment of the Roman Empire, so many stories of so many gods had traveled down the Roman roads that many people must have found it hard to take any gods seriously, including the original gods of Rome. Once sophisticated Romans had loosened their ties to their own gods, there would be no obvious reason to believe in any of the other stories that surrounded them, leaving them lost in an ocean of stories, none of which had much of a claim to be true. Ovid saw the issue and consequently ended his book with a speech by someone he called the Philosopher, who argued that the fact of unceasing change was a kind of truth. This was a clever dodge, but not very persuasive.

"It's a trick," said Mark. "Gods are more interesting."

Whatever its merits, Ovid's story about unceasing change being the truth did not take hold of the Roman public's imagination. Another story did instead. The ideology with a claim of truth that ultimately took over the Roman Empire was Christianity. In the light of that inescapable feature of Western history, our class would have to tackle the deferred topic of religion.

Religion 宗教

Chapter 7

Conversion Stories and Religion in China

I eased the way for class discussions on religion by first discussing in the abstract how an empire might deal with the convergence of the many religions that flowed into it. Different religions can be seen as different stories about the world. The choices for dealing with these different stories ranged from embracing them to tolerating them to suppressing them. Rome, which by the time of the Empire was no longer very attached to its own gods, leaned toward tolerance with regard to religion, a practical, cosmopolitan attitude that allowed for some people to worship Zeus, others Jupiter, Osiris, Mithras, Zoroaster; or to follow the practices of the Manichees, the Cynics, or the Peripatetics. A cosmopolitan Roman like Ovid might say, broad-mindedly, that there were many approaches to understanding the world.

The students embraced this view. "That's true!" Janie asserted. "It's bad and useless to argue beliefs." No one disagreed.

One consequence of Rome's tolerant approach to religion, I suggested, was to drain it of passion, urgency and identifying power. Rome's own homegrown philosophy was stoicism, according to which the chief way to be at peace was not to care about the circumstances of the world. The world could not be controlled, so the most important skill to develop was control over your passions, which were yours to manage. If you could contain your passions, then nothing that the world could throw at you would cause you to suffer. I tried to impress my students with the fact that the two most famous stoic thinkers were at the extreme opposite ends of the social scale. Epictetus was a slave, while Marcus Aurelius was a Roman Emperor. Both professed indifference to their worldly positions of political power or lack of it. The pair were an interesting contrast to *Zhū Dì* and *Cíxǐ*, who were also from the extremes of a social scale but neither of whom were indifferent to power.

My students liked stoicism, as many high school and college students do. It is appealingly sophisticated and tolerant, as it seeks to rise above all the destructive disagreements of the those who champion their own parochial stories. I reflected on how it is relatively cheap to renounce attachments when you are young and haven't developed many serious ones yet, and how passions can be scary, especially for the young, feeling them for the first time.

Next, appealing to their fairness and willingness to hear all stories, I gave an example of the opposite view. I related how the Roman province of Judea, present day Israel, insisted on maintaining for its people the truth of a single story, its own story of Judaism.

Rome, in its cosmopolitan, passionless way, offered the province of Judea its usual deal: in exchange for roads and aqueducts and the chance to trade with the imperial community, all the Jews had to do was what other provinces in the Roman Empire were doing: pay tribute, accept a governorship, and put a statue of the emperor in their temple. Religiously tolerant Rome was no doubt astonished when the people of Judea accepted the first two conditions but absolutely refused the third, viewing the Second Temple (which had replaced the First Temple built by the biblical King Solomon) as a place where only the true God could be. For a period of time—during which Jesus lived—Rome put up with this peculiarity. Finally, however, it responded to Judea's religious stubbornness with violence, oppression and, at last, the reduction by siege of the city of Jerusalem and the destruction of the Second Temple, all but one wall. Rome crushed Judea.

After telling this story, I asked if they felt any sympathy with Judea's underdog battle for truth against the world-weary power of

Rome. Cindy said, politely, "It's a noble stand. It deserves respect." Paul snorted. Janie laughed. These two were not buying it.

Alice, however, spoke in support of Cindy. "I wish I was sure like that about anything," she said, pensively. "I agree, it deserves respect." A few students picked this up, experimenting with the notion that it might be enviable to feel that you knew the truth, and wondering what it would be like to believe in truth so absolutely.

Helena had a different kind of thought about the situation between Rome and Judea. "Maybe because Rome had many gods it could accept many stories," said Helena. "One God means one story."

Sara responded, "A single narrative elucidates. It can arrange thinking patently."

We spent some time sorting out these ideas. If there was only one God whose story was the only true story, then things would be less confusing, we concluded. Perhaps, I thought, this sort of insight is explicitly behind the creation of an official Party line in Communist countries. And perhaps Cindy and Alice's wish to be able to believe in truth related to how hard it was in present day entrepreneurial China to adhere to the austere Marxist assertion of truth about the inevitable end of capitalism that had moved these students' parents and grandparents to great deeds.

Hopeful that these ideas might help make discussions of religion possible, I decided that the kind of change appropriate for this topic was conversion. I assigned them three famous conversion stories: St. Paul's conversion on the road to Damascus; part of St. Augustine's *Confessions* in which he describes his dramatic conversion in a garden in Milan; and an account of the conversion of the Emperor Constantine, the moment when Christianity became the *de facto* state religion of Rome.

By way of opening a class discussion, I asked: "What exactly is different in a person after an experience like the ones described in these stories?"

There was silence, as deep as the silences in our first classes together.

I tried to personalize: "Has anyone ever had a moment when they made a sudden, radical change in what they believed?"

The silence continued.

My experiences with religion in China often included silence and hiddenness. A colleague at the Dalton Academy was a member of an American Lutheran sect and was connected to a Lutheran missionary group operating in China. He took me one Sunday morning to a highly illegal "house church." There were only a few Chinese people there; this service was mostly the missionaries themselves, providing support for each other. During the part of the service when announcements were made and prayers requested, someone reported that another house church had been raided by the authorities and all of its prayer books and Bibles confiscated. People shook their heads sadly, and a collection was taken up for replacements.

The service itself had a sentimental sweetness that I recognized. The congregation sang songs and repeated words from memories of times and places where they had felt loved, and in the presence of earnest sincerity. I didn't know any of the songs, but I could tell that they were the kind of songs that could sink into your heart as a child and seem for the rest of your life to mean something central to safety and goodness, like a comforting and familiar story. These missionaries had traveled 12,000 miles to offer that experience of goodness to others, a project that seemed like it should be admired. Afterwards someone handed out a little pamphlet with a short theological reading and some discussion questions. The discussion was mostly carried on by the young men of the group and was a genuine conversation about some of the challenges of faith in the modern world. One man made a comment about Kierkegaard, and a woman leaned over to me and whispered, "I never understand what John is talking about." It seemed to me that she was trying to make me feel comfortable by assuring me that the group generally wasn't too intellectual. I did my best to accept her kind intention.

After the discussion people stood about drinking coffee and talking. There was much congratulatory buzz and flutter over the news that the leader's wife was pregnant, and some exchange of hopes and fears about new assignments, possible progress, and plans for the future. It was all lovely and warm. Then I made a foolish mistake. Chatting with a friendly young woman, I asked if she was intending to be ordained as a minister in the Lutheran church. Her face froze and she informed me that her church did not ordain women. We retreated from each other hastily and struck up different conversations with other people. She did not want to discuss the matter, and neither did I. Silence.

There was a state-sponsored Christian church not too far from the BDFZ campus that had a steeple lit with neon signs. Every Sunday morning it played Beethoven's *Ode to Joy* loudly over the streets of Beijing, competing with the explosions of fireworks that celebrated the opening of new businesses. I never went there, feeling bewildered by what I imagined must be the complicated motives of the people in such an institution and unsure how to trust anyone. I would have to keep silent.

One hot summer day we visited a Jesuit church that had been built near the center of the city in 1909, just before the fall of the last imperial dynasty. The church now stood at the end of a high-end downtown shopping district called *Wángfǔjǐng* (王府井). After being shocked and overwhelmed at how glitzy and expensive it was in the heart of the capital of the People's Republic of China, the cool of the church was welcome. Other tired shoppers were there, some with fancy shopping bags, sitting in the pews and resting or watching the many televisions that were mounted on stone pillars throughout the nave showing some version of the life of Christ. The show and its audience felt like a parfait had been put in a blender: modern Europeans pretended to be ancient Palestinians while their voices were dubbed into Chinese for the benefit of exhausted former communists resting up from their extravagantly capitalist shopping sprees—layered human history mixed up to near-incoherence. No one was talking.

We also experienced a mixture of ideologies and customs of East and West during the two Christmases we spent in China. Beginning in November, Christmas decorations went up every-where, including on the conical pine tree beneath the flagpole in the main school quadrangle at our school. Although China is not a predominantly Christian country it has quite a few Christians and even more Christmas lights, since most of the world's supply of them are manufactured in China. The lights glittered handsomely beneath the red and yellow People's Republic of China flag, while across the street from the school, the shopping center sprouted dozens of Santa Claus figures, including, for some reason we could not guess, a number of Santa Claus mannikins carrying or play-ing saxophones. There were no religious icons, even cheesy ones made in China, like nativity scenes with lightbulbs in the manger or plastic menorahs.

Such enthusiastic adoption of the forms of the celebration cou-pled with total silence about its history and meaning pulled at me a little. Hopes for Christmas were entirely mercantile in China, with no countervailing admonitions to remember the "true spirit of the holidays," as if Christmas should mean something power-ful or cosmic in scope. In the Carrefour market across the street, "Rudolf the Red Nosed Reindeer" played as we bought our weekly rations of tea and soy milk.

A colleague told us that he once heard a little Chinese girl singing along to Christmas music. The song was "We Wish You a Merry Christmas." The little girl knew scarcely any English, so she imitated the sounds as best she could - "啊 为什么 Merry Christmas," she sang, which in Pinyin transliteration is "*a wèi shén me* Merry Christmas" translated "Ah! Why Merry Christmas?"

I called on my cosmopolitanism to rebuke my naïve longings for meaning in the face of so much consumerism. There was nothing really wrong with a holiday to promote gifts and food, without messy religion, in a country that is eager to achieve prosperity. I said nothing.

As for Chinese religion, Buddhism was by far the strongest presence and my students, secular though they were, had it in their backgrounds. I discovered this outside of class, when Grant and I went with a group of students on a tour of sites in and around Beijing. An early stop on the tour was twenty or thirty miles outside the city and required a hike into the mountains to some Buddhas that had been carved into a cliff. The students explained about the various types of Bodhisattvas sitting in granite lotus positions, their explanations an interesting mixture of incomplete internet research and stories half remembered from childhood. One student showed me a Buddhist talisman that her mother had bought for her just before she was to go on a trip to a foreign country. Although neither she nor her mother is a Buddhist, they both liked the idea that the talisman might keep her safe.

"Do you have to believe in something for it to work?" she wanted to know. "No," I reassured her, "I don't think you do."

The same tour took us to the 云居寺 (Yún jū sì), or Cloud Home Temple, beautifully set in mountains that could be dimly glimpsed from Beijing on the rare clear day. We entered the temple through a building in which sat an enormous gold, fat, bald, laughing Buddha of a style I have only seen in China or in Chinese restaurants in America. Around him were four huge, fearsome carvings that were said to be of heavenly kings. Through the building was a courtyard where the first structure that caught the attention was a monumental gate with a plaque noting that it was called the Eternal gate. It had been destroyed by the Japanese in the Sino-Japanese War but rebuilt later.

The temple was quiet and beautiful. Soft music played and it was easy to feel it as holy. One of my students noticed this reaction on my part, was puzzled, and asked me what "places like this" meant to me. There followed a discussion about the way people respond to certain types of places, to certain kinds of beauty, and to religious ideas and stories. Those responses could be so strong that some people dedicated their lives to them and became monks and nuns. Several students were curious about monks and nuns in the West. Answering their questions, I remarked that I could imagine making the choice to come to a beautiful place like this and dedicate my life to something in which I believed.

The student who had asked the first question about places was unsympathetic. "I can't imagine it," she said. "I want a lover."

I mentioned that I had gotten the impression that in the East it was a well-known path for a person to become a monk or nun after a full life rather than dedicating oneself young, as was the ideal in the West. I happened to know of a Chinese actress who had done this, I said, one who had played a character in a TV version of the *Dream of the Red Chamber* that Grant and I had watched.

They knew the actress I meant. "Yes," said the same student who had been firmly against the nun's life, "I heard that she had breast cancer and if she had chosen to take treatment rather than retire to a temple she could have been cured."

A friend of a friend of ours was a Buddhist monk who went by the honorary title "*Fǎ shī*" (法师). The word 师 (*shī*) means "master" or "teacher." 法 (*fǎ*) is the Chinese character for "law" and is the ordinary translation of the Sanskrit "dharma," referring to both the order of the world and the teachings of the Buddha. We were privileged to visit *Fǎ shī* at his home at 法源寺 (*Fǎ yuán sì*) or Source of Dharma Temple, an ancient and especially revered Buddhist establishment in southwest Beijing with a history going back to the Tang dynasty, when Beijing was a small place on the outskirts of the empire. More recently, the temple suffered during the 1968 Cultural Revolution, as most religious sites had, being turned into a mortuary. In the late 1970s, when it had been returned to use as a temple, much cleansing had to be done, both literal and ritual. Today, it is attached to a Buddhist teaching center next door to the temple enclosure.

In the first courtyard of the temple there is, as in most Buddhist temples in China, a drum tower and a bell tower. Also like the other temples we had visited, this had a series of courtyards separated by buildings housing increasingly impressive statues, which were works both of art and of reverence. In the largest of the buildings, containing the largest of the statues, devotees intently paced counterclockwise around the inner perimeter, while outside a brazier sent up incense smoke.

Fǎ shī lived in a little dormitory space accessed by an alley off a main temple courtyard and was a casually dressed man in his early forties. He offered us some tea and told us how his mother had been a devout Buddhist and how he had come to the temple as a monk when he was young. He was seeing a re-emergence of Buddhism in China that he found encouraging; the atheism of the Communist Party had left a spiritual vacuum that people needed to fill. He was concerned about this lack and about the futile ways people tried to fill it. "They all want money, money, but they don't think any further," he said, sadly. He has taken people on trips to Sri Lanka where, he says, Chinese people are surprised that people with so little money are capable of being happy. He was interested, too, in the way that Buddhism was perceived by others, especially in the West. "All they know of us is Shaolin Temple. That is not the way most Buddhists really are," he remarked.

Shaolin Temple is famous as the home of a martial arts discipline. Jackie Chan made a movie about it, and *Fǎ shī* was probably right that this movie was many Westerners' only experience of Buddhism, and also right to dislike the impression it would leave. My efforts to study Christianity with my students might have shipwrecked, but I did not think they would be better served by reading *The Da Vinci Code*.

Later, at another Buddhist temple, I had an experience that made me think again about how hard it is to discuss religion. The 法海寺 (*Fǎ hǎi sì*), or Sea of Dharma temple, is famous for its murals, which many say are the most beautiful paintings in China.

The paintings are so fragile that the temple is kept locked and in darkness to protect them. When we had paid a sizable entry fee by Chinese standards (100 rmb, about $17), a tour guide gave us flashlights and carefully unlocked the central building that held the murals, cracking the door as little as possible against the sunlight.

It was pretty exciting to be in the dark and see beautiful colors on far away walls, visible only in small pools of light. The room echoed like a large cave, giving an impression of endlessness. The murals were on three walls of the room and one side of a freestanding wall. The other side of the freestanding wall was the backdrop for three giant sculptured Buddhas that, whenever the flashlights caught them, loomed with pearl-white eyes. These were later sculptures, the tour guide said dismissively, which had been brought in to replace the originals that had been destroyed during the Cultural Revolution. Much had been destroyed then, she explained, adding that it was a miracle that the murals had survived. Taking a breath, she asserted that the destruction meant that we could get a feeling for the freshness of the original colors of the murals because the statues that had once covered the bottom edges of them had been torn away. It was a determinedly cheerful view of a sad history. On one of the walls on which the murals were painted, I saw what looked like bullet holes.

We lit up the murals one at a time, leaving the rest in mystery and darkness while the stories unfolded. The two side walls were covered with landscapes in mostly muted greens and pinks, defined by sharp edges of Prussian blue or black, with sometimes a burst of concentrated delicacy in a flower or a person. You might run your flashlight down a river, with bamboo bridges over it, then follow some trees or grasses upward, suddenly to be surprised by a lotus, a peony or, even higher, a placid Buddha in the heavens, surrounded by rich robes and loving, wise attendants. These paintings were roughly contemporaneous with the Western Renaissance, and the tour guide pointed out that they showed an understanding of perspective.

When we came to the back wall, she emphasized a vital difference between these paintings and those of the Western Renaissance in that these murals attended more to symbol and meaning than to realism. On the back wall was painted a huge vision of twenty gods, each telling his or her own story by postures, expressions, or accompanying figures of animals, flowers, or children. In the tradition celebrated here, the Buddha did not replace old gods, but entered into their stories and taught them the value of compassion, making them part of the Buddhist understanding. Brahma spread the seeds of creation, while Kali held eight weapons in her eight hands, although in demure Chinese robes rather than dancing.

Our tour guide invited admiration for the thick gold dust used to paint the brocades of the divine robes, as well as the intricate veins in the ear of a fox. The goddess with the fox had a lion in front of her and a leopard behind. I listened with interest to the explanation that, through word play on the animal's names, the painting was showing how future lives were ahead and past lives behind.

The guide and I were alone just then, and she suddenly turned her flashlight downward, making the shapes and colors we had been examining recede into darkness. Only our two faces could be seen in a cone of intimate light. In this hidden, quiet moment, she asked, "Do you believe that?"

I was silent.

Then she stated, resolutely, "I believe that."

I remembered this as I thought about the impasse in my class-room regarding stories about conversion to religious belief. If silence was all I could offer in response to the tour guide's heart-felt witness, I should not be surprised at my students' silence in response to St. Paul, St. Augustine, and the Emperor Constantine. Not only that, but during one of the silences around St. Augustine, a student had asked me:

"Do you believe in God?"

"It doesn't matter what I believe," I had replied sharply, surpris-ing myself by how quickly I shut the question down. Apparently I also didn't want to talk about religion. Conversation, however, requires willingness on all sides to offer real opinions. I didn't know exactly what was behind my students' silence on the subject of religion, but if I wasn't willing to talk honestly about it myself conversation would not happen.

And yet something needed to be said. As a teacher of humanities my hope was to help my students to discern their own deepest beliefs in order to bring them into the light of day to be examined. I didn't want a wariness about religion to cause them to conclude that deep beliefs could not or should not be put into words. If we respect each other's beliefs to the point of being unwilling to discuss them, then they divide us. I discovered in myself a passionate aversion to that result as an enemy of conversation. Conversation was one of the hopes I had brought to China, and my dream for the world. Words and artistic expression are the best ways we have to broaden understanding of human experience, to bring about creative empathy among people, and to push our culture-bound stories a little closer to truth.

I believe that.

So I had to discover how to get my students to find words for what was going on inside them. Although they might be distrustful of religion, they certainly had their own deep beliefs—we all do. I decided to take advantage of the indirectness of stories as a way to allow my students' ideas of what is true to emerge. I asked them to write a story to contribute to the world's store. To those who wanted more guidance, I suggested they write a story about someone who had a radical change of mind.

The results were fantastic. The stories they wrote, with wonderful creativity, further developed the ideas we had raised in our study of Rome, pushing them into places that I had not expected. One student, for example, wrote from the future about his experiences in America, describing through the lens of his excitement about adventuring his desire to protect his Chinese identity and his feelings for home. I liked his complaint, in the voice of his future self, that he was constantly celebrating holidays, as the American ones were added to the ones he wanted to honor from his Chinese origins. "Too many holidays" was not a problem of cultural encounter that I had anticipated.

Some wrote about past changes in their sense of identity. One student had been afraid of humiliation until he saw a friend fail spectacularly in public speaking but then shrug and try again. Seeing that his friend's identity was more durable than he had thought, he was persuaded that perhaps his own would bear some risk, or even failure, and come back stronger. He had been an Oedipus during Carp Week, and it was a pleasure to hear that his willingness to step out onto a stage was a chosen thing.

Each story was unique, but I could see a few common themes. A number of the stories reflected a sharp division between life as a good person and life as a bad person. "Goodness" was defined entirely as doing what society—often represented by parents—wanted the hero of the story to do, while "badness" was defined as doing what the hero wanted to do. In some stories, what the hero wanted to do was smoke, drink, or not do homework, but in other stories the hero wanted, against the pressures of society, to express an unusual opinion or give way to innocent feelings. One story-writer wistfully dreamed of choosing a few moments of childlike joy over a prudent, successful, long life. Another, imagining that she had only a few days to live, spent them eagerly pursuing beauty and meaning. These seemed to me to be interesting variations of Achilles' choice between a short, meaningful life and a long, less meaningful one—he was mentioned several times. Students were also mediating on the broader versions of this choice that arise in the contexts of state and empire, the tension between the order and uniformity offered by government and unruly personal characters who felt oppressed by order and uniformity. A safe passionless life might feel like a loss of the self, while a passionate life is dangerous and will likely be called selfish by society.

My favorite story was about a disease that caused people to explode if they told a lie. The consequences to society were exciting. Romance disappeared because lovers kept exploding. Business and government became impossible, too, as "BANGs" sounded repeatedly in the corridors of finance and power. Looking for someone to blame for these losses, people complained that the real problem was not lying but *believing* lies, because if lies didn't work, no one would tell them and no one would explode. So they began to stone gullible people. I took this student's story to be a wry commentary on our conversations about stories and truth.

I had assigned these stories just before the month off for the Lunar New Year. In a cover email to which her story was attached, one of my students offered a kind wish, made more meaningful by a small mistake in English. "Have a nice vocation!" she told me.

I do have. There's no vocation better than teaching.

Mathematics　数学

Chapter 8

Flatland, Mathematics and Society

Our unit on Rome caused me to change direction in the seminar. The original plan of marching through Western history would have called for readings from the European Middle Ages. There are wonderful texts from the Middle Ages, but I was now worried that the explicit religious language of those texts would distract from the focus of the class and hamper our conversations. I would have to find some other way to talk about the centuries in Western history when people rejected the cosmopolitan stories of Rome and lived under a single story they believed was true.

After much reflection, I decided to reach back to the Philosopher, the character that Ovid had used to voice the idea that constant change is the only truth of the world. The historical person behind Ovid's Philosopher, most literary scholars agree, was a Greek thinker named Pythagoras. Today, Pythagoras is most famous for his mathematical discoveries. My Chinese students had never heard of the Pythagorean theorem under that name, but they had encountered the concept in their mathematics classes and recognized the famous equation when I put it on the board: $a^2 + b^2 = c^2$, or, in the Greek geometrician Euclid's language, the square on the hypotenuse side of a right triangle is equal to the sum of the squares on the other two sides. At first the students were rather charmed to make a connection between a character from Ovid's *Metamorphoses*, this strange poem from the ancient West, and something they had encountered in what they thought of as their "real" studies. I made a mistake, though, by telling them the legend that immediately upon discovering this amazing the-orem Pythagoras had sacrificed a bull to the god Poseidon. I had thought of this as a humanizing story about how awed Pythagoras was to uncover so beautiful and elegant a geometric relationship, but they froze up when they heard he had reacted religiously (and with animal sacrifice, yuck), and Pythagoras receded into a primi-tive, incomprehensible past. Once again it was clear that any men-tion of religion was going to take the life out of the conversation.

Still, the moment that preceded the freezing—a moment of shared understanding with Pythagoras—set me on the path for-ward that would avoid religion and yet reflect accurately one strain of the development of Western tradition. Our topic was change, which inevitably invokes its opposite, the unchanging and perma-nent. Though in lots of Western thought the idea of the unchang-ing is expressed theologically in claims about God and the immor-tality of the soul, the unchanging had also been part of how the Western world thought about the meaning of mathematics. This was how Plato, influenced by Pythagoras, approached philosophy. Plato was deeply impressed that mathematical truths remain per-manent, even as everything else in our world suffers unceasing change. The world around us looks clumsy, inexact and subject to constant upheaval, but the relationships between numbers never alter, and neither do the relationships of geometry. The existence of mathematics and the human ability to understand it, therefore, seemed to Plato to mean that our minds have access to truths that never change. And if our minds can touch permanence and truth, then there must be something in us that is also permanent and true. Plato argued that this something in us that recognizes truth could connect us to the beautiful and the good and even be used to create a perfect city. Was he right that the unchanging nature of mathematical truth can help people navigate shifting, bewildering human society? In a seminar on the topic of change, the question was worth exploring.

There were obstacles down this path, too, ones that my Chinese students shared with their American counterparts. Students in both places seemed to believe that there were two kinds of people, those who were good at math and those who were not. By the time they had gotten to high school or college, they had put themselves inexorably into one or the other of the two categories. If they believed they were bad at math, they hated it. If they believed they were good at math they liked it, although mostly what they liked was how clever it made them feel to be skilled at its tricks. None had ever considered mathematics in terms of what it meant as a human experience: none had looked at it as a beautiful, unique aspect of the landscape of thought. And yet it is *amazing* that human beings can imagine perfect triangles and circles, even though we never meet perfect things in the physical world. Equally amazing is the whole concept of numbers, which are not in the physical world, either. Here is an apple, there is a tree, but where is "2?"

Those sorts of questions were so strange to my students at first that I don't know if they heard them at all. Mostly they laughed uncertainly. They were victims, as are most American students, of the world-wide educational separation between math and science on the one hand and humanities on the other. Outside of our little St. John's College, few students are trained to wonder about whether or how these human abilities can be thought of together as aspects of a full life, and even speak to the question of the best life.

I gave them Edward Abbot's *Flatland*, a fantasy novel about a rigidly hierarchical society of flat geometrical figures that is disrupted when a three-dimensional sphere intrudes into their world. My students, relieved to get back to a text that had a good story in it, mostly loved *Flatland*, although some aspects of the book were troubling.

"Why are women stupid and dangerous in this world? It's not fair!" Anne was indignant. It was the first day of our discussion of *Flatland*, and the students had read the first six chapters, which included a chapter called "Concerning Women."

"It's not our world," I offered. "Why should it bother you?"

"He means our world!" came several voices at once.

"Why do you think so?" I asked.

Anne was not to be distracted onto a conversation about allegory, even though I was already writing the word on the whiteboard. "If he thinks women are stupid and dangerous in the book, he thinks it outside the book," she declared.

The situation of women in the world of *Flatland* is certainly appalling. *Flatland* is written in the first person and the narrator is a Square, which makes him a respectable tradesman of the lower middle class. Social standing in Flatland is determined by how many angles a person has, with many-sided polygons who come close to being circles at the top of the societal hierarchy. Women, however, are straight lines and because Flatlanders believe that intelligence is related to the width of their angles, women are said to be brainless. Worse, women are dangerous because their sharp ends can puncture other figures and kill them easily. As a consequence, women in Flatland are tightly constrained, bound by onerous rules of behavior, never educated, and kept in the house as much as possible, although it is recognized that too much confinement might cause revolution. The polygons of Flatland are deeply worried about revolution and are aware that women would be potent weapons in any uprising.

Yet *Flatland* was not only an allegory about gender and social relations; it was an opportunity to see mathematics in a new light. I groped for a way to honor both themes.

"In this world, though, women really are different from men," I suggested. "They are straight lines, while the men are polygons. The difference is mathematical, which means there is a right answer. If people really are different, what's wrong with treating them differently?"

"Who decides who is different? Woman have different bodies here, too, but treating them differently is wrong," Anne insisted, still protesting.

The boys in the room had gone cautiously silent. Helena, trying to sort out two impulses—she agreed Anne that sexism is wrong, but she liked the book and wanted to be generous to it—said, doubtfully:

"Yes, but in this world, women have no angles, and no intelligence."

"How can they talk, then?" Janie burst in. "Anyone who can talk can think." This gave rise to several good-natured jokes at the expense of talkative friends, the boys joining in with relief, though still nervous about how to react to the discussion about the treatment of women in the book.

I thought I saw a way forward and asked, "So you think that the society of *Flatland* is wrong about how women should be treated. Do you think the author of the book, who made up the society, agrees with the *Flatland* society or with you?"

By way of making the question clear, I explained to the students that in a first-person novel it's not always easy to be sure whether the narrator's opinions are the same as the author's opinions. "Edward Abbott could be writing with his tongue in his cheek," I told them. That expression was so surprising to them that I had to spend a good five minutes on it, with my students solemnly taking notes while they experimented with making their cheeks bulge. English is crazy, really.

"Keep thinking about who to believe," I advised, as students began to pack up books toward the end of class. "There are different points of view. There's the main character, for example, the Square, who is describing the society of Flatland. Sometimes he seems to find it wisely arranged, but as the book goes on he comes into conflict with some of his society's most fundamental ideas. Then there is the author. The author has a whole different point of view, one that made him want to write a book. He has given us a story about a main character who receives a mathematical understanding, a claim of truth, that causes him to depart from the common understanding of the people around him. Why did he write such a story?"

The students disappeared out the door of the classroom, chattering in Chinese. I sat down heavily and let out an "ooph." The class had not gone as I expected. And yet, the more I thought about it, the more I liked it. Not only was I grateful to Anne for bringing up a reaction she really cared about, but I decided on reflection that she was perfectly right about what was important in the book. The seeming certainty of mathematical answers, applied in society, is what the book explores.

My Chinese students' views on women were interestingly uncertain. None of them suffered from any prejudice concerning equal academic ability. All recognized that bright academic stars were evenly distributed between genders, even in subjects often thought to be especially masculine, like mathematics. This was important because, up to that point in their lives, academic achievement was the standard that mattered most.

Their expectations for the future were almost as egalitarian, though not quite. They did not think that the girls were less likely than the boys to be professionals with their own income—the idea of being a housewife was not on anyone's radar. All of my students came from two-career families, as far as I could tell, and they expected that future for themselves. In the inverted-pyramid family structure created by the one child policy they were constantly and acutely aware that their parents and grandparents would depend on them for support.

And yet the students had some feeling that certain careers were more masculine than others, especially positions of political power. It was not that any professions were closed to women, but if a woman chose certain professions people would comment on the choice and would continue to comment on every promotion she received, particularly if she got to the top of such a profession. One

student did a research paper tracing out this sort of unacknowl-
edged influence on gender inequality in police forces in China.

Complicated feelings about Westernness were also part of the
mix. All my students, from an early age, had watched Disney movies over and over again to improve their English and I believe that
Chinese people often drank in the attitudes of Disney movies as
truths about Western life.[10] *Cinderella, The Little Mermaid, The
Lion King* and *Aladdin* were cultural references that my students
always found ready-to-hand.

Very few of my Chinese students felt they had the time to
experiment with dating, but Disney movies had firmly rooted in
all of the female students the conviction that someday their prince
would come. They held this unthinking belief even as they worked
hard to prepare themselves for their independent careers, and
I could not see that they had ever noticed any potential contradiction in those goals. I was glad, therefore, when Anne took her
tough stand against the misogyny reflected in the social arrange-
ments of *Flatland*.

I decided to roll with Anne's societal approach and converse
with the class about how the Flatland society compares with modern ideas about justice. Society—even the mathematical society of
Flatland—instructs us on what society believes to be true on many
things, including the proper status of women. Sometimes, however, one or another of us feels sure that society is wrong about
something it has taught us. How do we decide what, or whom, to
believe? Should we respect the customs of society and the wisdom

---

10   This possibility was a little disturbing when we found a copy of *Song of the South*,
made by Disney in 1946, for sale in our local DVD store. It is hard to get a copy
of this movie in the United States because it is set at a time and place in American
history that is painful to remember and offensive to many. The movie seems to be a
celebration of happy black folk contentedly living in poverty on the grounds of a rich
plantation, gladly sharing their quaint folk wisdom with the poor little rich white
child who is the hero of the story. My mother grew up in the American South and as a
child had loved the Uncle Remus books that were the basis for the movie. It was a hard
but important lesson for her and for me—who had loved to hear her read them—that
such stories could hurt people and that we must seek more inclusive ones.

of our ancestors? That seems noble and humble. Or should we trust our own inner knowledge, even if no one else can see it? We had met this question in the *Oresteia*, when individual heroes had to be folded into society. In *Flatland* it came wrapped up with the claim of truth in mathematics.

Wondering about societal conflicts in Edward Abbott's time, I sailed out on the Internet to do some historical research. *Flatland* was written in 1884, the year after Karl Marx' death. Societies were struggling with Marxism and anarchism. Labor unions were rising and suffragettes all over the British Empire and America were agitating for the vote. Elites who liked the status quo were worried about the possibility of revolution, as the lower classes, the non-elites, challenged the customs of society and shouted angrily that the wisdom of ancestors needed changing. Those times raised a question that perhaps our times do, too: how to decide between the traditions that society teaches—the society that has shaped us and preserves order—and the certainties that some people feel that society is wrong?

Plato and Pythagoras thought that the answer lay in mathematics. It's an entirely different strategy than the approach of the *Oresteia*. There, the answer was a political compromise, smoothed with respectful persuasion. By contrast, Plato and Pythagoras thought that mathematics, which seemed to deal with unchanging truths, would give a right answer, leaving no need to compromise. Plato dreamed that we could solve political disputes like mathematical problems, achieving a permanent peace, which would be better than the uneasy tension reflected in the *Oresteia*'s image of the Furies, the revenge goddesses, living underneath the city and always threatening to burst forth in anger.

Plato's dream is wonderfully attractive. If society could be based on unchanging truths of logic and mathematics it could be as perfect as the circles and triangles of geometry. The proper policies of the rulers would not be matters of personal interest or power but would be demonstrably right like Euclid's propositions.

Such well-founded, proven truths would persuade every rational person, even if the truths were as surprising as the unexpected geometrical relationships shown by the Pythagorean Theorem. Plato, for example—surprisingly for a man of his time—thought that logic demonstrated that woman were the equals of men and should have equal social status. This was true, he believed, regardless of the contrary wisdom of the ancestors.

Maybe a society based on mathematical truth could work, but in our classes on *Flatland* students continued to complain that the particular one described in the book, however mathematical, was not just. The girls remained indignant about the treatment of women, and the boys joined the objections to Flatland society when we talked about the history of Flatland's Color Revolt. There had been a time when Flatlanders had painted themselves different colors, which led to the discovery that colors could be used to deceive others about social standing, with anyone, even women, able to paint themselves to look like high level polygons. In the confusion of colors it was impossible to tell who was entitled by shape to be in charge, and all sorts of riffraff, even Irregular figures, disguised themselves as multi-sided polygons, put themselves at the heads of mobs and revolted, demanding power.

The Color Revolt had been crushed with great cruelty, and at the time when the Square was writing the secret of color was being hidden from the populace. In the years since the revolt, education had been focused on the central message that the most important thing in life is to be Regular—a perfect Triangle, a Square, a perfect Polygon—easily recognized and immune to the complicated sensualities of color. Any deviation from Regularity was shamed and harshly treated. Irregular figures, society pronounced, were dangerous, not least because they were often particularly talented and creative. Many of those born Irregular were sent or chose to go to hospitals to have their bodies re-shaped through risky surgery. Often they died there.

"Would you go to a hospital to be reshaped if you were Irregular?" I asked the students. They shuffled uncomfortably and did not reply, not wanting to imagine themselves in the role of society's outsiders.

"Yes, of course," someone finally said. I didn't see who, and it was said softly, as if the question I had asked was in bad taste.

"So all of you want to be as Regular as possible, to be just like everyone else in society?" I asked.

They balked at this, objecting that I had gone too far the other way. One of my best students, who was openly gay, argued that there was a wide range for Regularity, and it did not mean being exactly like everyone else.

"All Squares are exactly alike, aren't they?" I asked.

After a while, we agreed that all human beings wanted two contradictory things. We all want both to fit in society and to be special. They seemed surprised to expose this inconsistency in themselves, and I felt for them. My own long-ago experience was that the tension between those conflicting desires was at the heart of what was grueling about high school, a time in life when that tension is almost unbearably strong.

One episode in *Flatland* caused an intense conversation in our classroom, connected to this tension. The Square relates that because social standing is based on the number of sides a person has, many parents send their offspring, when still young enough to be pliable, to the same hospitals that correct Irregulars. There the high-class children undergo an operation to have their sides broken in two, doubling their status. Not only is the operation painful, it has a very low rate of success. "Scarcely one out of ten survives," the Square says. Yet Flatlander parents want social status for their children so much that they take those odds, subjecting their child to certain pain and likely death in the hope of seeing them climb upward in the social hierarchy. This story is an offhand aside in the book but it upset my students, who came back to it several times, making me wonder if it echoed too painfully the pressure weighing on them to succeed.

Once we had talked out our societal critiques, the mathematical aspects of the book began to come forward. Having explained his society, the Square then describes dreams and visions he had in one transformative night. First, in a dream he visits Lineland, where all of the inhabitants live along a line, unable to conceive of any other kind of life. The Square tries to explain to the king of Lineland that there is another dimension, but the king dismisses him as crazy. The Square laughs, smugly, at the foolishness of these limited creatures. It is a wonderful feature of the novel that, at the same time, the reader laughs at the Square's foolishness in just the same way. How ridiculous, readers think, smugly, that the Square should feel so superior to the Line, when both are so limited from the readers' *truly* superior point of view.

Then a visitor from the third dimension—a place inconceivable to the Square—comes to Flatland and intrudes upon the Square in his study. It is a Sphere but because a sphere cannot exist in two dimensions the Square can only see a circle that changes in size as the Sphere cuts through the plane of Flatland at different parts of his body. As readers understand, the Sphere is above or below the plane on which the Square lives and can enter the plane from anywhere, ignoring the barriers that seem solid to the Square from his limited perspective. At one point, the Sphere, from outside the plane, touches the inside of the Square. The Square reacts as we might if we felt a finger poking inside our stomachs.

The Sphere tries to explain the third dimension to the Square, just as the Square had tried to explain the second dimension to the Line. The Square reacts just the way the Line had, thinking the Sphere crazy. The Sphere makes all the same arguments that the Square had himself made, but the Square rejects them all, in the sacred name of Common Sense. Finally, the Sphere abandons logic and takes action, lifting the Square off of his plane and showing him his two-dimensional world from a three-dimensional perspective. After this experience, the Square is convinced at last of the existence of a dimension above his own.

We thought hard about that sequence of events in class, asking what exactly convinces people that something is true. Argument, mathematics, and logic are not convincing to the Square, even though it feels as if they ought to be the most convincing things. Few of the students wanted to think that experience was the only thing that convinces people; they preferred to believe that they were swayed by reason alone. Still, they could sympathize with the Square, who could follow the Sphere's mathematical arguments but could not take the final step of accepting their conclusions as true. Here at last we were getting to the ideas that I had wanted to explore through the lens of mathematics.

Once he has at last acknowledged the truth of what the Sphere is trying to show him, the Square begins to ask questions. Rather than worship the wisdom of the Sphere, as the Sphere clearly expects him to do, the Square astutely undercuts the smug sense of superiority that both the Sphere and readers had been feeling by taking the mathematics further. The Square asks about a fourth dimension, then a fifth, and forever onward. The Sphere is aghast, then contemptuous, but readers have to acknowledge that the Square is pointing, perfectly logically, in a new direction that we cannot define but that we know by mathematical analogy must exist. There were wonderful conversations in class about where the direction of these dimensions might be. The topic of time came up, which later flowered into a Carp Week theme. More than once there occurred in the discussion the incalculable moment when someone says something that she had never said aloud before, a welling up of wondering from a deep place that she had before thought too crazy to offer to others.

"How can logic show things we can't experience?" Cindy wanted to know. "Is logic real?" No one could agree on an answer.

Rather than ask the students to write a paper about mathematical ideas, which they clearly dreaded, I decided that our most important thoughts had been about different perspectives, reflected in *Flatland* by different dimensions. I asked the students to write stories from two different perspectives.

They responded magnificently. It is always wonderful, as a teacher, to receive evidence that students have heard the questions you hoped for them to hear. One of my female students wrote about two perspectives on love, contrasting the dream of a princess with a scientific view of mating behavior, concluding that humanity loves a puzzle. Another student looked at the world from two sides of the lens of a camera and mediated on the living stories created between the seeing and the seen. A third spoke with two voices about the chairman of a Marxist country. In one voice the chairman was brilliant, generous, wonderful, and inspiringly handsome, a leader taking the nation into the future. In a second voice the chairman was stupid, greedy, disastrous and ugly, needing to be resisted. Each perspective was passionately and persuasively offered.

Very few students wrote about two-dimensional versus three-dimensional perspectives. I decided not to worry about that, happy that they had fully explored two different ways of seeing. Such an exploration is the entryway to three-dimensionality because it adds depth. I was proud of all of them.

"How do you choose between perspectives?" I asked them at the next class, returning slyly to the question of belief. "How do you decide what to believe about the world?"

"I don't have strong beliefs. I'm open," said Mark, firmly.

To his surprise, this caused a general laugh. When he looked indignantly around the room, Janie explained, "You *always* argue. If anyone says yes, you say no."

"That's right," he answered, puzzled. "No beliefs. I'm always testing."

"So you believe that you should always test what people say?" I asked, smiling. "Isn't that a belief?"

"Not fair!" he said, mad at the gotcha.

"Why not? There must be some reason you believe that's a good thing to do. Shouldn't you test that belief? If I said to you that you should never believe anything until you have tested it for yourself, how would you argue against me?"

Feeling stubborn, Mark replied, "I would agree. No argument."

I appealed to the others: "Does anyone think that sometimes you need to accept things without testing them?"

After a pause, someone suggested that testing everything would take too long. "How do you choose what to test?" I wanted to know. This issue came up towards the end of class, so I couldn't tell if the silence that followed was running out the clock or resistance to the question. I wouldn't blame them for resisting, if that's what it was, as it is unpleasant work to face your own untested assumptions. Most of us are like Mark and believe we are objective—it is only other people, we like to think, who have careless assumptions and prejudices. Noticing that we have our own such things is no fun, while talking about them in front of classmates is even less fun.

I left the problem of what beliefs to doubt hanging in the air. It was enough to have explored the question of whether mathematical truth, with its seeming objectivity, could end all quarrels and form the basis for a just society. Even if Flatland was so limited in its vision that it was not that society, Plato's notion might still work, as our vision grows, I thought. Like so many humanities issues, that one is still open. Also like so many of these open humanities issues, it is still essential to talk about it and to notice our own deep beliefs, hidden as they are, especially when they sneakily present themselves as mathematically true even though they have not been tested. I hoped that *Flatland* had offered to my students the infinitely creative vision of being lifted off the plane of settled beliefs to see a perspective unimaginable from the ordinary dimensions of life. Books and ideas can do that.

Paradox 悖论

Chapter 9
Zeno, Galileo and Newton—The Mathematics of Change

In my quest to show my students that mathematics and science—their "real" studies, as they thought of them—should be seen as only one part of the wide human experience that humanities addresses, I decided that the class should confront the group of mathematical ideas that usually taught under the subject heading of calculus. Calculus was developed in the seventeenth century to analyze change; it was a radical change itself in how people thought of mathematics, as it applies mathematics not to the eternal perfections of geometrical objects, but to the physical movements of bodies on the Earth. Not only was this an appropriate subject for a seminar on change, it gave me a chance to re-create for my students a vision that had lifted me off the plane of my own settled ideas many years ago when I was an undergraduate at St. John's College. Like my Chinese students I had studied calculus in high school, memorized its tricks, and dutifully figured out answers to problems for tests. My teacher at St. John's, however, Mr. Swentzell, opened my eyes to a new direction when he taught me to study calculus philosophically, as a human understanding of change.

A philosophic approach to calculus meant that my seminar on change would have to go briefly back to the Greeks—specifically to the ideas of the pre-Socratic philosopher Zeno of Elea (about 490 to 430 BCE), who played with infinity. I thought my students would enjoy Zeno, who seems to have been an impudent person who liked to puzzle his friends. Twenty-five hundred years ago, he pointed out some paradoxes that, he argued, proved logically that all motion is impossible.

Zeno's most famous paradox was the "bisection." I described it to a skeptical class: "In order to move from point X to point Y, you have to get halfway there. To get halfway there, you must get a quarter of the way there. To get a quarter of the way there, you must get an eighth of the way, and so on forever. Because that process of dividing in half can go on infinitely, no one can move any distance at all without taking an infinite number of steps. But no one can take an infinite number of steps; it would take an infinite amount of time. Therefore, it is impossible to move." Obviously, I pointed out to my students, if motion is impossible, then there can be no change. I told them that if they were persuaded, we could end the class for the year.

Given that glittering promise, a few made a painful effort to believe Zeno's proof, squinting up their faces quizzically in the struggle. Especially in the light of all of our conversations about how people decide what to believe, it was a funny moment. Then they laughed and faced the fact that they could not bring themselves to take seriously such an obviously crazy conclusion. Yet, like so many philosophers and mathematicians over the last few millennia, they also could not immediately see how to prove Zeno wrong. "Just mocking him is not enough," I told them. "Show me a mistake in his reasoning."

Tyler stood up, walked around the room and said, "See, I move. It's possible."

"Well, you shouldn't be able to," I answered, drawing myself up to seem strict. "Logic says you can't, and in this classroom I will not allow anyone to defy logic." I gave him a stern order: "Sit down *right now*." Some of the kids laughed, while others looked at me uncertainly. Because many of my students still had to translate everything in their minds from English to Chinese, jokes that relied on pretend anger were a little dicey because they heard the tone of voice before they had translated the joke. I tried to be careful to make the straightforward meanings of my words match my affect, but sometimes I forgot. When that happened, students risked getting lost in a world where the meanings of words did not fit with what was actually happening—paradox.

No one could think how to refute Zeno's paradox. In order to move we must step through infinities, which must be impossible. Movement and change, therefore, must be impossible. Yet we do it anyway, happily ignoring the provable fact that we can't.

"Maybe mathematics and logic are not really very useful," I suggested. "In *Flatland* we saw that arguments based on mathematics and logic did not persuade anyone. Zeno goes even farther, showing that logic leads to things that *can't* be true. So what do we do with that?" There was silence, reflecting some frustration with being asked to take seriously something that was so clearly wrong. They were sure I was holding out on them and there was an easy answer to Zeno's paradox.

I pressed on: "Someone might draw the conclusion that logic and mathematics themselves are silly, only toys for elitist intellectuals. Be practical, such a person might say. Pay no attention to logic. Just do what feels right. You might call it the practical wisdom of experience rather than the mind." They continued silent, with a few shakes of the head, disliking this idea.

And yet the Chinese society I saw all around me seemed to be operating in this practical spirit, with limited interest in logical consistency. No one appeared to feel the need to make sense of the way both communism and capitalism were jumbled together in everything people did. In China, Communist Party oversight was everywhere—symbols of communism appeared constantly in flags, posters and public announcements—but also omnipresent were the marks of capitalism and the desire for personal wealth. Most of my students were unabashed about an ambition to get rich. Many were planning to get business degrees in college and were taking classes in entrepreneurship at BDFZ. Sometimes the whole campus seemed like a re-education camp for capitalism. The

Communist Party must have approved of all this or these classes would not have been taught; yet the Communist Party had issued a specific directive disapproving of teaching American-style principles of constitutional law, such as the separation of powers doctrine. The goal, I suppose, was to allow or encourage capitalism as a strategy for wealth, while cutting off any suggestion that there was a political ideology that accompanied it that might disrupt the Communist Party's hold on power. Maybe that will work. Still, perhaps because of my Americanness, I wondered if creativity, whether in technology or business, wouldn't ultimately lead to an ideology that insisted on freedom, subverting any ideology that tries to limit freedom.

In any case, the confusion was discordant. I noticed it first at a place called the Worker's Stadium, which I stumbled upon because my vanity demanded that I have my hair cut and colored. There were plenty of hair salons in the neighborhood around BDFZ, but to find one that worked on Western hair required going downtown to a neighborhood near the foreigners' district in which the Worker's Stadium stood.

Located inside a vast iron fence, attended by bored guards, the vast Worker's Stadium was built with clean, classical lines. In the large paved space around it were brilliantly white statues, about twice life-size, of healthy, happy, well-muscled, disciplined men, women and children engaged in various kinds of sporting activities. These statues were executed in the style known as "socialist realism" and were obviously meant to inspire. I'm sure, too, that when they were first conceived and built, they suited the spare, uncluttered lack of pretention in the stadium design, symbolizing the plain pleasures workers enjoyed during their well-earned leisure.

Since that time, however, capitalism had crept in like a swarm of small insects living off a larger host. Businesses, including my hair salon, had established themselves in the archways of the stadium and put up flashing signs that shouted for attention. Garish side buildings had sprung up containing bars and lounges and muscular security guards, before which limousines and Lexuses were parked. Simplicity was long gone.

While I was getting my hair done, three young women walked into the salon, bored and looking for something to do to get ready for an evening on the night scene in Beijing. They spoke English, although with a range of accents that made me think that English was the compromise language among them. They seemed to have no jobs and certainly showed no concern for money, as they examined the services offered, apparently in the hope of finding something to lift their evident ennui. I wondered if the lives that these people were leading was what my students were picturing when they said they wanted to be rich.

I resolved to impress on my students that, in the uncertain environment of this emerging China, where the idealism of communism was being colonized by the desire for money, it was important for young Chinese to think clearly about exactly why they wanted to be rich, what they would do with money, and what that implied about their deepest beliefs. Maybe the rising generation of Chinese to which my students belonged, with their unique experience of growing up in a country quietly shedding its ideology while trying to prevent another from forming, would find creative ways to deal with the conflicting tendencies around them. China is changing, even if some argue, like Zeno, that it cannot. Such a situation could be disastrous, or it could spur creativity in directions that would be helpful to the rest of us in an increasingly post-ideological world.

During the next class, I reminded my students: "Nobody seemed to like the idea that Zeno's paradoxes mean that mathematics and logic are silly and don't describe the world. Let's think about the opposite idea, then. Can anyone tell me who said this?" I wrote on the board:

"Mathematics is the language in which God has written the universe."

No one raised a hand, so I used the teacher's trick of offering the answer in the form of a question. "Does anyone know who Galileo was?"

"He was a great scientist," said Paul.

"He got the Church mad," added Janie, with some pleasure.

Alice spoke abstractedly: "He made the Earth move."

Sara agreed, seeing a chance to use an attractive word she knew, "heliocentrism."

"Good, yes," I affirmed, after asking Sara to explain to the class that heliocentrism was the idea that the Earth moves around the sun rather than the other way around. They wrote it down, on the chance that it might turn up on the SAT or on the TOEFL test.

"We are going to spend a long time with Galileo's ideas about the heavens when we talk about the scientific revolution," I told them, "but for now I want to talk about his notions of mathematics. He was the one who said that mathematics was the language in which God has written the universe. Why would anyone say such a thing?"

They waited for me to answer my own question. They had learned that I often did so, or at least gave them clues about the answer I wanted. Sometimes it seemed like the whole class was a challenge match where they tried to guess what I was fishing for, and I tried to trick them into saying what they actually thought. Neither of us wanted to move from these goals. It was easy to see why some teachers gave up on trying to get students to respond in meaningful ways and simply lectured—it might seem more honest to do so, and certainly less exhausting for everyone. But the reason lectures are less exhausting is that there does not have to be anything active going on during a lecture. Teachers can mindlessly enjoy talking while students mindlessly look attentive. Such a scene is a defeat. Nothing moves, nothing changes. In the labor of discussion classes, there is more action. Even when students were paying attention only to try to second-guess me, their concentration could, and frequently did, give rise to conversation. Then things might go anywhere. Most of the time the movements are small, but sometimes, once a real conversation arises, the whole universe can get redefined.

I tried a different tack, asking "How many of you have taken a class in physics?" Most of them had, as China is very serious about the hard sciences, especially physics.

"Did you have to do math?" I asked. Yes. With eloquent grumbles, they agreed that they had had to do math in physics class. There were all kinds of formulas they had to memorize in order to solve boring problems about bodies falling, sliding down inclined planes, and hitting each other.

"Does it seem strange to you that math describes physical bodies?"

No. Or, rather, they had never thought about it, as most people don't. After thinking it over, the students unanimously asserted that it was a pointless thing to wonder about. Experiment shows that physical bodies follow mathematical laws. It's as simple as that. Case closed.

It is not as simple as that. It was a drastic change when people began to believe Galileo's claim that mathematics governed physical bodies on the Earth. For most of Western history, people thought that the stars were divinely mathematical and regular, but that everything on the Earth was obviously chaotic. Galileo upended both opinions when he pointed a telescope at the moon and found flaws, and then dropped weights off a tower and found regularities. In our unit on the scientific revolution, I would have to make vivid for them how amazing these discoveries were.

In the meantime, we looked at how Galileo dealt with Zeno. The class read excerpts from Galileo's book *The Two New Sciences*, published in 1638, which discusses how uniformly accelerating bodies cover distances proportional to the squares of their times of travel. Galileo imagines that the speed of a falling body increases uniformly as time passes. He then constructs triangles whose heights represent passing time and the growing widths of which he conceives as an infinite number of lines stacked on their sides on top of each other, each standing for an infinitely small instant of time. The areas of these triangles, he argues, give the distance travelled, which increases as the squares of the times.

When called upon to go to the whiteboard and demonstrate to the class, the students presented this reasoning competently, but, despite my questions, they avoided thinking about its strangeness. It is strange to the point of outrageousness, though, to announce that a problem can be solved by stacking up parallel lines on their sides to make the area of a triangle. Lines don't have thickness! No matter how many of them are stacked up, even if it is an infinite number, they will never create an area. Galileo was flouting Zeno, making use of the concept of infinity in a way that defied Zeno's unrefuted paradoxes. Something was very odd in that strategy, but the students didn't want to think about it. Galileo's answers agreed with what they had learned in physics class and that was good enough.

We had time for only a brief look at Isaac Newton's even more shameless use of the infinite. The students had heard of Newton, an English physicist who lived in the seventeenth century, because of his discovery of the laws of force. He also invented calculus, which turned the infinitesimal methods pioneered by Galileo (and others) into a way to describe and analyze any quantitative change, anywhere. Projectiles and flowing fluids here on Earth, as well as orbiting planets in the heavens, could be understood by a single, integrated theory of forces. Enlightenment philosophers of the following century stood in awe of the power of reason in large part because Isaac Newton had shown how far reaching it could be. A poet wrote for Newton's epitaph:

> Nature and Nature's laws lay hid in Night.
> God said, "Let Newton be!" and all was light.

Yet Newton's views rested on uses of infinity that were completely outrageous. His invention of calculus involves velocities "at an instant." What sense does that make? How can a body have a rate of speed at a single, infinitely small point in time? Newton's answer to this question was to recommend thinking of these velocities as ratios between distances shrinking infinitely and times getting infinitely smaller—finite values for the velocities appeared just as all the quantities reached the end of infinity and evanesced. Really? Come again? How long does it take to reach the end of infinity? Newton's ideas are very strange indeed.

But his techniques work; that is, they give useful and consistent results, which silenced many contemporary critics of the new invention, despite the fact that it did not make logical, geometrical sense. Bishop George Berkeley, a contemporary critic of Newton who refused to bow to the vulgar effectiveness of calculus, described the entities manipulated by Newton's calculus as "the ghosts of departed quantities."

The students were bemused by the idea that someone might have doubts about a mathematical technique that worked. With so little time I settled for that bemusement, hoping it would grow in them as it had grown in the mathematicians of the nineteenth and early twentieth centuries. Those mathematicians tried and tried to make the useful infinities of calculus logically coherent but failed in all their efforts. In the end, these failures led to the mathematician Kurt Gödel's 1931 proof that mathematics could never be the solid, complete foundation for thought of which Plato had dreamed. The hope that mathematics could give us a proof for all true things was disappointed.

It was perfectly understandable that high school students might not want to confront questions at the foundations of mathematics. Students naturally resist the idea that the theories they are working so hard to master are and will always be works in progress. They prefer to believe that what they are learning is something unchanging and unshakeable, and any suggestion to the contrary seems like a betrayal of their hard work. Yet, looking bravely at the fact that nothing is unchanging and unshakeable, not even mathematics, is a doorway to creativity. Mathematical theories move—it's possible.

In a final effort to ask them to think about mathematics in a different way, I assigned excerpts from a 1949 essay *A Mathematician's Apology*, by the English mathematician G.H. Hardy, who wrote feelingly about the marvelous beauty of mathematics. Mathematics and beauty were two things that my students had not thought of together before—the combination challenged directly the habit of seeing mathematics as something entirely different from the appreciation for works of art that is associated with the humanities. I did see a little movement in this regard, I thought. At first, the students had seemed perfectly happy to have their lives divided up into separate boxes so long as they knew which one to refer to for which class. A few now had begun very tentatively to express thoughts about how such different perspectives might influence one another and to wonder whether, even outside of school, the idea of truth might require some single, unified perspective that embraces and accounts for the others. I fostered these thoughts as the precious pale green shoots of springtime.

My own thoughts about China were colored by my fascination with the strangeness of the mathematics of change. I saw an analogy between the impossibility of putting together communism and capitalism and the impossibilities of the infinite that Zeno had thought paralyzing but that Galileo and Newton showed how to manage. I had studied Newton at St. John's College, where his ideas are taught not from a textbook but from the original text of his book *Principia Mathematica*. We had talked a lot in that class about the outrageousness of "The Calculus," as our teacher Mr. Swentzell called it—somehow making the capital letters audible—and at the same time how, once that outrageousness was accepted, humanity gained what seems like an unlimited power to understand change. Accept The Calculus, even though it is not logically coherent, and humanity can predict the movements of the stars and planets, along with the fall of apples. Maybe China's embrace of the tensions between communism and capitalism will be fruitful like that.

Mr. Swentzell had given me another insight about the mathematics of change that had influenced my life throughout the years that followed our Newton class. In that class we had spent a long time with the Fundamental Theorem of the Calculus,[11] which Mr. Swentzell also spoke of in capital letters, his velvet Alan Rickman voice lingering over the words. Every student in his classroom, even the most math-phobic, was required to get up to the blackboard, draw the diagram, and demonstrate the steps of Newton's proof of this theorem. Mr. Swentzell said that he had a dream for us. He imagined us fifty years in the future scattered all over the globe. He hoped we would all prosper. But even if we never got wealthy by the standards of the world, even if we found ourselves in fifty years washed up in a seedy bar in Shanghai, dressed in a ratty ice cream suit or an evening gown that had seen better days, his dream was that we would still be able to prove the Fundamental Theorem of the Calculus on the back of a cocktail napkin. That kind of wealth, he told us, was permanent and unchanging.

When Grant and I visited Shanghai we stayed at a hotel that had been built in the 1930s, was a little run down and was located in an older part of town where the foreigners once lived. I thought it might have been exactly the kind of place that Mr. Swentzell had in mind. The rest of the city has changed a lot, though, from the days that had given rise to his fantasy. When we left the hotel to sight-see, we encountered a glittery, business-oriented Shanghai in which enormous amounts of money were sloshing around everywhere. The entire city was a madman's palette of garish colors. At

---

11   The Fundamental Theorem of the Calculus is the proof that differentiation and integration are inverse operations. For a fuller description, a textbook might be the place to look. Textbooks work well for some things. Even if something works, though, it might not be the whole story.

night, Shanghai has gone beyond mere neon and electric brightness and embraced the new possibilities of LED lighting. From the top of a tower called the Oriental Pearl, we admired the riot of color spread out before us, cut through by a dark expanse of river on which boats moved up and down glowing like fireflies on a Peter Max acid trip.

After visiting the tower we took a subway across the river to the business district to walk in the heart of all of those lights, making our way down a pedestrian shopping mall, a mile-long walkway lined with every imaginable icon of consumer excess flashing and calling for attention. While even one advertisement for something like a Rolex watch is an appeal to the avarice that values conspicuous consumption, a sixty-foot tall illuminated and animated advertisement for a Rolex watch is a commercial tidal wave. *Five hundred* such advertisements, for every imaginable luxury good, shouting from all directions, in the heart of communist China, is "an amped-up devil's interval of cognitive dissonance with the volume knob turned to eleven," as Grant described it.

Inside this bubble of the lure of money, looked down upon by fifty-foot mostly naked models displaying wealth, other sensibilities were valiantly struggling to persist. About halfway down the pedestrian mall, there was a crowd of shoppers and tourists standing in a circle a dozen or so yards in diameter, watching groups of middle-aged Chinese dancing in unison, a cross between tai chi and aerobic country line dancing. A few yards further along the walkway, in the center of the avenue, between fifty and a hundred people closely surrounded an elderly man with an easel that held hand-lettered sheets of paper. As he flipped the pages, the group sang in unison distinctly rhythm-heavy Chinese ballads. Q, our colleague from BDFZ who was traveling with us, identified the songs as ones "that were popular back in the forties." Communist revolutionary songs were being performed in the midst of the largest, glitziest consumer shopping frenzy in the largest, glitziest city of China.

The people singing did not seem old enough to remember the Long March or the Proclamation of the Republic in 1949, but most of them could certainly recall the days before the 邓小平 (*Dèng Xiǎopíng*) redirection and opening of the Chinese economy to Western influences. They reminded us of a communist version of Sarah Brown and the Salvation Army band playing revival hymns in the middle of Times Square, or Carrie Nation preaching a temperance sermon in Las Vegas. We watched and listened for quite a while, imagining the singers looking backward to a romantic ideal of simplicity and purity. Perhaps they hoped by this public singing to raise a question about the changes that new money and new power were bringing about in China. I imagined that these people were trying to say that change should be resisted with song and dance because it was impossible to reconcile the new economy—reflected in five hundred half-naked fifty-foot high Western models wearing watches and driving Lexuses—with what China had been. The paradox, they were singing, was too much. It was logically incoherent.

The rising tide of change in China, however, looked to be too strong for this objection. As Tyler had put it in our class on Zeno: "See, I move. It's possible."

Science 科学

Chapter 10

Brecht's *Life of Galileo* and the Coming of the Scientific Revolution

Since the early days of our time in China, I had known that the scientific revolution in the West was an important factor in China's internal conversations about education. In November 2012, in the fall of our first year in China, Grant and I attended The First Inaugural Conference for Liberal Arts Teaching in China, which took place at 西北 (Northwest) University, a highly regarded institution located in the city of 西安 (*Xǐ'ān*). Through our connections with the Association for Core Texts and Courses, which, like St. John's College, promotes the reading and discussion of classic books, Grant had been invited to give a presentation on the style of liberal arts education at St. John's. The only other American institution represented was Columbia University. To the extent that this constellation of colleges suggested that St. John's College and Columbia adequately represented American higher education in the liberal arts, the Chinese attendees got a ridiculously skewed picture that downplayed the tinyness and oddity of St. John's. It was as if the United Nations were to be represented by only two countries, China and Liechtenstein. There we were, though.

The conference brought together many people who, like us, wanted to get away from merely training students to do well on tests and instead move to a model of education that would promote creativity. It was a long-planned consequence of the experiments that had been going on in China since the 1990s, when the Communist Central Committee had mandated the inclusion of "general education" courses in high schools and colleges. The organizers of the conference were, I think, very conscious and hopeful that this conference might be a milestone in furthering conversation on how to do this. Certainly the conference had been beautifully and lavishly planned, even down to providing translation for the foreigners like Grant and me.

Our interpreter, N, was a student at Northwest University who was planning to make a career of translation between English and Chinese. She was nonplussed to get two of us to translate for but undertook the task with good grace. The three of us settled into chairs near the front of the large assembly room in which there would be welcoming addresses to the whole conference before it broke into panel discussions.

This was N's first time translating without a net—for people who did not know Chinese—and she found it harder than she had expected, I think, especially leaning this way and that as Grant and I asked questions from either side of her. Simultaneous translation is difficult in any situation and her task was further complicated because all three of us were embarrassed to be whispering to each other while high dignitaries were addressing us from the stage. The upshot was that, although I believe I got a general sketch of what was being said, my impressions of the speakers were informed as much by body language and imagination as by knowledge.

The speeches reflected a balance between doubts about the dangers of liberal education on the one hand and great excitement and hope on the other. When I look back over our two years teaching in China, such ambivalence is characteristic of the whole experience. Official China wanted the creativity promoted by the liberal arts in order to catch up technologically with the West, but from a political point of view, it feared the destabilizing effects of that same creativity.

A representative of the Communist Party opened the conference, as was the custom at all major occasions in China. The gist of this speech, I gleaned from N, was first praise for the Communist

Party, followed by the suggestion that the conference participants should be grateful to the Party for fostering the possibilities of liberal education. This message was met at first with a silence that seemed unsympathetic, as if the audience did not believe that the Party was unambiguously friendly to liberal education. It was painful to watch the speaker trying to make conciliating jokes at which no one laughed, although toward the end of his speech he succeeded in getting some friendly reactions. When, a few hours later, we encountered him on the elevator surrounded by his red-armbanded guards, I told him I had enjoyed his speech, which was true, at least in the sense of appreciating his efforts and being interested in the interaction with the audience. He shuffled, perhaps diffident, perhaps wanting no truck with pushy foreigners, perhaps unsure of his English.

The next speaker was the peppery, elderly, white-haired president of Northwest University, jovial-looking, and, it seemed, an amusing talker. His concern was with "university spirit," which is a matter for both anxiety and pride on a Chinese university campus because of the diverse roles it has played in twentieth-century Chinese history. "University spirit" in China refers not to pep rallies for sports teams but to the political uprisings that can boil out of college campuses anywhere in the world. In China, the government celebrates the student uprising that happened in 1919—the May 4th movement—in which Chinese students called for modernization in the period following the dissolution of the last imperial dynasty. University spirit also boiled up in 1989, however, ending in bloody conflict in Tiananmen Square, and the government doesn't want that occurrence remembered at all. Like creativity, university spirit is both precious and dangerous.

Against that background, this speaker was carefully cheerful about university spirit and liberal education. He argued that university spirit could be corralled to support liberal education, and he had some ideas about how to do that. His dream was that they would work together to the ends of the state. "Perhaps," I thought, doubtfully.

After the university president sat down, a tall, thin, distinguished-looking gentleman, also elderly, had to be helped on the stage to speak. He clearly enjoyed enormous respect. I was told later that he had a national reputation as a great teacher, which is a meaningful honor in China. He spoke of the possible contributions of technology to new kinds of teaching, citing online courses and a famous Harvard video about Justice, and mentioning with satisfaction that he might try something similar with Chinese subjects, having himself recorded for later generations. He believed that the West had succeeded in selling its culture to the world—and by Western culture I think he meant the concept of liberal arts education—because of the West's technological success. He wanted to use Western technology to sell Chinese culture, to fight fire with fire, although he was emphatic that the use of Western technology must not entail the surrender of Chinese identity. This reminded me of *Dèng Xiǎopíng*'s opening of China to capitalism in the 1980s when *Dèng* had pronounced that it was okay to become more capitalist but it had to be "capitalism with Chinese characteristics." Western-style liberal arts education was acceptable to this speaker only if it had "Chinese characteristics" and was used for Chinese purposes. I was doubtful about this recommendation, too, thinking that education is too unruly to be channeled like that.

The last speaker of the morning was the same generation as the previous two, somewhere in his eighties, stocky and vigorous, with a military-style haircut and one blind eye. He and the two previous speakers obviously knew each other well and were old conversational partners. It was his speech that made me aware of how important the scientific revolution was in those conversations.

The stocky man affirmed the points of the earlier speakers in emphasizing university spirit and the importance of liberal education with Chinese characteristics. He counteracted the cautious tone of the previous teacher, though, strongly defending the need for liberal education as a means to catch up with the West. He pointed out with a curious mixture of boasting and sorrow that China found the Pythagorean Theorem centuries before the West, and also understood astronomy, but that for some reason in the East these achievements had not led to astronauts. He felt this as a deep grief, it seemed. The suggestion, never quite said directly, was there must be some reason that the West and not China had been the stage for the scientific revolution, and that liberal education might be it. Because of that possibility it had to be tried, he believed, dangerous and Western as it was. Then he mentioned *Máo*, attributing to him the intention to appropriate Western ideas with the goal of surpassing the West and reasserting Chinese national pride. He claimed that *Máo* had a two-step program for China that was now being carried out. First, *Máo* intended to achieve material prosperity and then, second, he intended to turn to liberal education, which is the present task. The new movement in China toward liberal educational approaches was in fact, the speaker argued, following the far-seeing guidance of the Great Helmsman.

At this point, it seemed to me that the speech was mostly directed at the teacher who had spoken just before. The teacher had nodded through the first part of the stocky man's speech, but when the talk turned to claims of *Máo*'s wisdom and far-sightedness, he looked away and refused to meet the speaker's gaze, even though it was focused on him. China's truest scholars, I imagine, can never forgive *Máo* for the Cultural Revolution, the 1968 civil disturbance in which so many artifacts of Chinese culture were destroyed.

As we were leaving the morning session, I tried to get N to give her opinion of the concept of liberal education, seeking at least one data point on whether an actual student might feel university spirit on the issue. She resisted answering, being largely indifferent to the topics of the conference. She experienced general education requirements as just another burden added to the already overwhelming task of earning good scores on the various tests necessary to get her hoped-for good job. The extra requirements for general education credits were tiresome and irrelevant to that all-encompassing task. I asked her what she would do if she knew already that she would have a good job and so didn't have to worry so much about doing well in school. She instantly answered, "travel." "There you go," I said, "you have a dream of the life you want, a life that excites you. A liberal approach to education is to start with that, with what interests you, and follow it where it leads." She professed to like the idea but was wistfully certain that it was impractical, as was her dream of travel. She didn't think such things would ever be real for her. I hope she's wrong.

The question of why the scientific revolution happened in the West instead of the East is sometimes referred to as "the Needham Question." It was first asked in the 1940s by a British scholar of Chinese history, Joseph Needham, who made an exhaustive study of early Chinese technological achievements[12] and documented the stocky speaker's statement that China had invented all sorts of impressive things—gunpowder, the printing press—long before the West. It was devastating to Chinese national pride in these superior accomplishments when, in the nineteenth and twentieth centuries, the imperializing, mercantile, and technological power of the West seemed to marginalize China. Because of that psychological wound it is a burning question for some Chinese why the scientific revolution occurred first in the West and not in China. I did not know whether my students were interested in this question, but, even at the risk of exploring sore places, it seemed essential to ask them to look at something so vital to their society's internal conversations.

The topic of the scientific revolution is even more vital to the topic of change. Science and the technology it fosters have changed

---

12   Joseph Needham, *Science and Civilisation in China (Cambridge University Press 1954-).* This book is a compilation of Needham's notes and is still being published as those notes are edited. There are more than twenty volumes so far.

everything, perhaps the most radical change in human life since the awakening in the Axial Age. Most fundamentally from a philosophical point of view, the scientific revolution changed the kind of thoughts we value. In the ancient and medieval world, the desire for knowledge led to conversations about morality, beauty and divinity. In our modern scientific world the desire for knowledge leads to studying chemistry, physics and engineering, kinds of knowledge that seem to have nothing to do with morality, beauty, divinity or anything that feels personal. This new type of knowledge describes the natural world in a disinterested way that has made spectacular technology possible but is less helpful to human beings, including my Chinese high school students, trying to decide what is the best life. Focused on the new knowledge, none of us gets much training in how to understand what we feel, think, and believe. It is as if what counts as learning has been divorced from the actual experience of our lives.

"If you lived in a world without electric lights," I announced one morning in class, "you might spend a lot of time looking at the moon and the stars." The students nodded politely. Most of them had not seen stars very often, given the pollution and night brightness of Beijing.

Peter had seen them, having grown up in the country. He told the class about recognizing stars and constellations as they moved through the sky.

"Stars move?" wondered Cindy.

"Yes, stars move, I told them, "and almost all of them move in wonderfully regular ways—perfect circles in the sky. Imagine what they looked like to people during times in human history when there was no science and life was much more uncertain that it is now. They would have seemed to reflect grandeur and order and constancy, as in mathematics, entirely different from anything anyone encountered in daily life, with its confusion, meanness, greed, quarrels, wars, disease, back-breaking work, and all kinds of small, petty, ugly things. The stars are far above all that. If you lived in such times, you might say to yourself that heaven must be where the divine lives."

Janie shook her head, obviously unable to imagine saying such a thing, to herself or anyone else. The class began to go into its religion freeze. I tried to fend it off by grabbing for a Chinese insight. "Speaking as a Westerner," I said, off-handedly, "it looks to me as if the Temple of Heaven conveys the same idea."

I discovered at that point that some students who lived in Beijing had never seen the famous sights of their own city, including the Temple of Heaven. The students who had been there explained to the others that the Temple of Heaven is in downtown Beijing, within walking distance from the Forbidden City. Twice a year during imperial times, the emperor had processed there on a wide marble pathway from Tiananmen Square, accompanied by ceremonial fanfare. It must have been gorgeous, that parade, passing over the carved bridges and below the great gates of the city, then through a magnificent cypress garden that had been old even in imperial times.

When the emperor reached a certain great courtyard, he offered sacrifices for a good harvest. The place where he stood at the height of the celebration was a dais, raised above the immediate surroundings and feeling like the focal point of the bowl of mountains that circled the city. There, at the center of the capital city of the Middle Kingdom, the emperor, it was believed, communed with the divine at the meeting point between Earth and heaven.

Nowadays anyone can stand there for 20 rmb (about $3.00). As at many of the old imperial tourist attractions, there is nearby a booth where people can rent robes and hats like those that the emperor would have worn in the special imperial color of bright yellow, a color forbidden to anyone else in the empire. When Grant and I visited, I enjoyed watching people putting on these robes, stroking the yellow cloth and imagining themselves as the emperor of China. I did not try on the yellow robes myself, but I did pay my 20 rmb to stand on the dais where the emperor had stood, feeling the universe swirl around me as if I were the unmoving pivot of all that was. Perhaps the tourist attraction was popular not only because it is fun to imagine being the emperor, but because it gives rise to nostalgia, in our cold, scientific times, to dream of being at the center of the universe, touching heaven.

The reason that I brought it up in class was that the Temple of Heaven was unique in being round. The Forbidden City, the structures at the Summer Palace and all the other ancient imperial buildings are square or rectangular. Only the Temple of Heaven is a circle.

"Yes." my students informed me, when I asked about this, "Heaven is round, Earth is square." It was a principle of ancient Chinese cosmology.

"Why is heaven round?" I wanted to know, and when there was no answer, I speculated that the roundness of heaven might have to do with the perfect circles of the stars. It did not persuade them, but I counted it as a win anyway because it kept them talking.

Someone pointed out that the full moon was the most perfectly round thing that a person would have seen in a pre-scientific age, as it sailed beautifully in the sky. Mention of the moon led the conversation immediately into poetry. Every Chinese child memorizes poetry from the *Táng* dynasty (about 620—900 CE), and some of the most famous of those poems are about the moon. There was one in particular that moved me:

Looking at the Moon and Thinking of One Far Away

The moon, grown full now over the sea,
Brightening the whole of heaven,
Brings to separated hearts
The long thoughtfulness of night....
It is no darker though I blow out my candle.
It is no warmer though I put on my coat.
So I leave my message with the moon
And turn to my bed, hoping for dreams.
—*Zhāng Jiǔlíng* (张九龄)

During the Autumn Festival, which takes place on the full moon of October, there are special cookies to eat called moon-cakes. The custom in the evening of the festival is to look at the full moon, like the poet, and think of those you love who are far away but who are also looking at the same moon. Grant and I ate quite a few mooncakes in our first homesick autumn in China, thousands of miles from our family. Even though the time difference meant that we couldn't actually see the moon at the same time as our children, we took comfort from *Zhāng Jiǔlíng's* sentiment. The pre-scientific world, East or West, attended better than our modern world does to the yearnings of the human heart.

Just before class ended I handed out copies of Bertolt Brecht's play *Life of Galileo* and asked the students to read the first five pages, promising that we would do more reading in class. The play was an abrupt change of subject from the day's conversation, and the students may have wondered why we had spent class time on the Temple of Heaven and the poetry of the moon. I was content, though. I hoped that the attractive picture of the Chinese emperor standing at the central point connecting heaven and Earth would help them feel how shocking and upsetting it was when a similar pre-modern vision in the West was rejected by Copernicus and Galileo, who insisted that the sun and the moon and the stars do not revolve around the Earth, the emperor, the Catholic Church, or any of us. Despite how important we feel to ourselves, the heroes of the scientific revolution showed us that the Earth and the authorities on the Earth are not the center of anything. We are tiny chunks of matter in a universe full of such chunks, common as dirt. Also, ever since Galileo focused his telescope on the moon and saw flaws there, it is harder to see the moon either as *Zhāng Jiǔlíng's* embodiment of human longing floating above the sad separations of earthly life, or, in a Western medival way, as created by God to give light at night in the firmament of the heavens. Through a telescope, the moon is as blemished and defective as any squalid daily scene. Galileo's telescope debased heaven to the level of Earth. It was a radical change.

I was surprised by the students' reactions to the Brecht play we read together in the next few classes. I had assumed that his Marxist analysis would seem right to them and that they might expect their Western teacher to challenge it. They had a more complex reaction, though, coming from a society in which Marxism is the entrenched establishment rather than, as it was for Brecht, the revolutionary future. This came out first when we read aloud, taking parts, one of the most dramatic scenes in the play. Just after he has announced his world-shattering findings about the moon, Galileo is visited by Catholic Church dignitaries, followers of Aristotle who consider Aristotle the final authority on the heavens. These scholars despise Galileo's new picture of the sky and wish to argue with him, ready to demonstrate to him logically, with syllogisms, that Aristotle's reasoning about the heavens is both sound and beautiful. They sneer at Galileo's silly mechanical contraption, through which he claimed to see flaws on the moon.

Galileo responds to these Aristotelian sneers by pointing to the telescope. He refuses to answer or even hear their arguments, implying that arguments were useless. What mattered was to look through the glass and see for themselves that there are shadows and mountains on the moon. It was a rock like any other rock, not a divine heavenly creature. The scholars refuse, with scorn.

When in my classroom I asked why an Aristotelian scholar would refuse to look through the telescope, David spoke up urgently, "He believes what he has learned. He is resolute." I must have looked puzzled because Sam undertook to explain, struggling a little more than he usually did with his English. "The scholars are resolute that culture holds high social harmony. Good spirit."

The other students became restive, reacting strongly in ways I could not quite figure out. I gathered that Sam was translating phrases—"high social harmony;" "good spirit"— that were a part of their childhood in Communist China.

Time ran out just then, before I could decide how to respond, and the class disbanded quietly. What a strange moment! I appreciated the connection that David had made, although it was hard to sort out. Brecht had no sympathy with his scholar-characters, as David seemed to. I imagined that Brecht had created the scholars to represent, in the *Máo*-speak that some Chinese still use among themselves, "metaphysicists" or "idealists," insulting terms for foolish intelligentsia who turn away from the practical world in which the workers live. David, however, instead of admiring Galileo's defiance of authority, empathized with the Catholic Church officials obeying the teachings of their "Party," so to speak, and rejecting dissent. Dissent is bad for the people. By that measure, Galileo was bad for the people. David's position, if he had carried it out fully, would have had him arguing that it is more important to adhere to high social harmony and create a good spirit than it is to find out the scientific truth about the heavens. I didn't know if David would have gone that far, but I was sure that Brecht would have been horrified.

In the next class there were sharp differences of opinion. Some students enjoyed Galileo's defiance of religion, while others, like David, felt for the members of an institutional authority trying to maintain uniformity of thought. We talked about Brecht's interpretation of the behavior of the newly elected Pope Urban VIII, who earlier, as Cardinal Barberini, had shown friendliness toward Galileo and his theories. One scene portrays Barberini being dressed elaborately in multiple layers of papal regalia while the Cardinal Inquisitor presses him to take action against Galileo. As the man is buried in clothing, so the private opinions of the individual Barberini are smothered by his institutional obligations. Finally, he tells the Inquisitor that he may "show [Galileo] the instruments," meaning the machines of torture. When I asked the students' opinions about this, one said, "He was right. He has to do what is necessary to save the people from distress."

Other students argued that science was a more trustworthy authority than religion, so that Galileo was a hero to defy religion. They mentioned Achilles, which made me do a quiet, celebratory fist pump. The argument was that Achilles, like Galileo, refused to go along with what everyone wanted him to do, even though that choice put the army in danger, because he sought his own truth and his own idea of the best life. In response to this appeal to the heroic nature of the dissident, David persisted in defending the importance of social harmony, saying that social harmony leads to the best life for everyone. There was some scoffing at this, but even the scoffers were shaken a little by David's contention, which was based on a sentiment that they had heard all their lives.

The class' conversation reminded me of the concerns I had heard the speakers express at the liberal arts conference. Galileo, though a hero of scientific creativity, was a dissenter from social harmony, which meant that the official authorities had to worry that students would learn the wrong lesson from him. If students were taught to admire Galileo for his scientific creativity they might admire him also for his struggle against authority. Is there any way to get one without the other? "Probably not," I thought.

I had no idea what would win out in a contest between the society's desire for uniformity and the students' unselfconscious, creative personalities, and I saw that contest often. At the beginning of our second year at BDFZ, for example, when we arrived at the school about a week before classes were to start, we found the students in the midst of mandatory military training. At first, it bothered me to see students I knew dressed in camouflage, marching crisply and calling out militant songs and chants. They were troublingly impressive, all in unison like that. I was witnessing a Chinese army, united and strong, the vivid personalities I had known in class buried in the service of military force.

But as we stood and watched, someone in the formation saw us and flashed us a "V" sign, which our students loved to do. Another gave a wave and an eye roll. They were, we found out later, mostly bored with military training, and it was reassuring to watch them dive for their cell phones the instant they were dismissed. Marching within that army, each of them had remained irrepressibly him or herself.

In Brecht's reading of Galileo, he is not just being an irrepressible personality or a curious scientist who is caught up accidentally in the questions of authority. Brecht writes as if, when Galileo looked at the moon through a telescope and saw that the moon was made of the same material as the Earth, it was an intentional, revolutionary act, designed to challenge the political meaning of the idea that the heavens are made of divine material. For Brecht, therefore, the most important thing about Galileo's work was not the science but that the de-centering of the Earth led to the idea that, despite appearances, there is no natural basis for political authoritarianism. True authority, Brecht argued, does not come from on high, but comes from the practical experience of scientists and of workers who engage directly with the material of the world. This, in turn, means that political power should be given to workers, who by hard work have gained practical knowledge resulting in the production of goods. I had thought this political reading of Galileo as a hero of the workers might spark an interesting conversation with students raised in a country run by the Communist party, but though the play gave rise to good conversation on various issues, that particular set of ideas did not seem to attract much student interest.

Maybe Brecht's political argument failed to gain traction with the students because it was not what I myself found most interesting about Galileo. I cared more about the duality of Galileo's insight. The fact that the heavens and Earth are made of the same stuff can lead to either of two conclusions. Although the Church chose to be insulted by the idea that the heavens are not special and divine, it is possible to look at the same idea and chose to be excited by a nearly opposite conclusion, that the Earth might not be inherently corrupt and chaotic, but also ordered, like the heavens. If the heavens with their mathematical perfections were made of the same stuff as the Earth, then mathematical rules might govern both. It is this way of looking at what Galileo did that brought about a far-reaching change in scientific investigation; scientists began to explore a mathematical structure not only in the heavens, but in what was in front of our eyes on Earth. That shift might be the second greatest change in human history, after the Axial Age awakening to consciousness.

When I assigned the students a one-page paper on the subject of science it was, to my happy surprise, evident that they had been thinking hard about science in a great many ways. One, for example, spoke to the theme of conversation:

> Science makes communication a lot easier and our lives more efficient and convenient. Our lives are more publicized but with probably more of shielded hearts because of the common public exposure caused by advanced technologies. It is both harder and easier for people to be self-conscious and faithful considering that people are less willing to public their emotions with invisible platforms (for example, text messages and online chatting systems), but it is the convenience of technologies that brings the mass knowledge and viewpoints which accelerate the process that people need to gradually attain self-consciousness.

What a strong and lovely idea, the "shielded heart" that we must develop in our much-connected world.

Another group of students compared science to the humanities. I was glad to see them thinking about the strange—in my mind unnecessary, even pernicious—separation of the two types of human experience. Interestingly, their attempts to unify them went in both directions. One student was impatient with the humanities:

> Comparing with the humanity, science is a subject that make more sense. In the world of science we can discuss some things real or somethings near our life. Electrons, gravity and bacterium those

are the things that really exist. In humanity, we discuss more like justice which is a kind of things that is not real and do not have a perfect definition.

Then, being unable to reject completely the personalness of the humanities despite their lack of perfect definition, she added:

> However the process of proving science is the most beautiful part of it. Someday you will discover a things that you are the first one who knows it in the world, I believe the feeling must be wonderful.

I hoped that she would one day get that feeling.

Another student's similar thoughts about the contrast between science and the "critical thinking" of our humanities class took a different turn:

> I think the best part of science is that there will always be an answer. Sometimes I really admired those scientists because they have hope. Whatever how tough their research is they believe that there will be an answer, and that feeling is really great. For me I am now really confusing about everything. After I got into high school many opinions that I have believed for several years was not trusted anymore, and now I am lost. I do enjoy the feeling of talking about humanity problems. That is, I know I probably will not find a correct answer forever, but the pain and enjoyment appears at the same time. However, I start to feel like I need something to believe. Like science, even it is not true, but I can convince myself. Critical thinking kind of makes me to doubt about everything and that hurt a lot. I now really envy those people who can be really determined about their view of the world (even thought it is wrong). I think at this time I need to learn some science. I want to have a faith.

I felt a little guilty about offering something that hurt so much, but many of the best things do. Furthermore, it might not work for this student to retreat to the supposed certainties of science, as there are painful uncertainties there, too.

Someone else pointed that out, agreeing that in her early years science was essentially comforting in the way it ensured that the world was basically logical, and logic was safe. I loved the first line of her piece: "When I was young, science makes me feel fearless." Her English verb tense was wrong, but her thought was bold. When she got older, she wrote, she discovered that science led to all kinds of strangeness, strangeness that challenged her understanding, shattering the feeling of comfort that logic had once given her. For example, she learned that we are not solid matter as we feel, but mostly emptiness through which electrons fly—it is scary to know that so much of the world is nothing.

One student directly took on the observation that science can simultaneously seem amazingly clear, puncturing superstition, but then also plunge us into its own kind of mystery:

> Before the revolution of technology, people all live under the consciousness of religion, which means that everything can be explained by God. However, scientists just easily offer a powerful chance to crack these beliefs and then lead human into a brand new age. In addition, the result of the revolution of science essentially brings people into a much more mysterious dimension. One perfect explanation from Albert Einstein, "The most incomprehensible thing about the universe is that it is comprehensible." The world formed by science is totally without border. There is always something unknown for scientist to explore. In contrast, there would be nothing unknown when people live under their beliefs of God. Common people would always satisfy under the name of God. Finally, science straightly offers this chance to get rid of the religion and also to let this world be much more unknown.

Great use of the Einstein quote.

Three or four different students independently suggested the interesting idea that the logical approach of science and mathematics was a means of perception like vision. One wrote: "In my opinion, math is a kind of sense just like sight and smell." With regard to science versus the humanities another of these students suggested that, because science was a different means of perception we should pin down the proper objects of this specialized sense so that there would be no confusion about what it should be used for. You don't use eyes to hear music, and you don't use science to feel your humanity.

The imaginative thinking in these paragraphs was exciting. More than once in China I heard Chinese people say, resignedly, that the Chinese were not creative. I suppose this opinion might have been part of the wounded feeling that came about because the West had gotten ahead of China in technology. Nothing in my experience with Chinese students, however, supported such a belief. Their writings on science and the humanities broadened my own perspective and made me feel optimistic about the future that these students would help bring about.

No doubt there are many possible answers to the Needham question of why the scientific revolution happened in the West rather than the East, but my small classroom experiment suggested that liberal education unleashes creativity in just the way that people attending the First Inaugural Conference for Liberal Arts Teaching in China had hoped. That creativity will necessarily show us new landscapes. I can understand why there are fears about exploring these new landscapes—judging from what has happened since the beginning of the scientific revolution, they will bring about changes that will threaten to overwhelm the institutions and traditions of the past. They may be unstoppable.

Tradition　传统

Chapter 11

Bacon, Darwin, and Confucius—the Scientific Revolution and Old Wisdom

I t is a big question whether science will overwhelm the institutions and traditions that have shaped how we understand our humanity. As our seminar on change proceeded through the scientific revolution, we read one scientist who was wary of tradition, Francis Bacon, another who was treated as an enemy by the institutions of his day, Charles Darwin, and came at last to the philosopher of science Thomas Kuhn, who offers an explanation of science's lurches away from traditional understandings. The class was a little shell-shocked by so many ideas being raised so quickly and reached no conclusions. Outside of class, pursuing my conversations with China, I meditated on the question through the wisdom of the ancient Chinese philosopher Confucius, whose love of tradition and humaneness promised some steadiness in the ferment of a quickly changing world.

My students had mixed feelings about the way that the sixteenth century pioneer of science Francis Bacon seems to despise tradition, at least on a first reading. Bacon was the person who, in the midst of the literal and figurative explorations expanding sixteenth century England, saw vast possibilities for science to make improvements in the practical circumstances of human life. For him, the goal of science was not political or philosophical insights, but hands-on change in our physical lives. The ontological status of the moon was all very well, but what excited Bacon was inventing things that might make our time on the earth longer and easier. He set about doing this by creating a systematic and skeptical approach to scientific research that did not rely on great geniuses making brilliant intellectual breakthroughs but could be done by anyone following his plan for accumulating useful knowledge. Bacon gave us the scientific method.

Though Bacon's prose is elegant—some have argued that he ghostwrote Shakespeare's plays—it is not easy and my Chinese students struggled to understand it. Once they did, they were both appalled and attracted by his argument that it was wrong to have a blind respect for the thinkers of the past or to revere them as elders. The first step in the scientific method, according to Bacon, is to get rid of false idols, by which he meant traditional approaches to the world. Bacon was particularly scornful of Aristotle as he argued that old thinkers should be thought of as children, since we are *their* elders, from the point of view of the development of human knowledge. Besides, he claimed, their best work has been suppressed as too controversial. In the river of time, Bacon announced, the weighty matters sink, and what comes down to us from the past—Aristotle's understanding of the natural world, for example—is the light, useless material. Bacon knew these ideas were scandalous to his contemporaries; he wanted to push people out of their constraining, traditional understandings so that they would do the work needed to march into a new, modern world, a paradise of scientific knowledge. The students enjoyed that, although they grinned furtively at each other over it, wondering, I imagined, if their parents and grandparents would approve of these disrespectful ideas.

"So," I said, "shall we toss aside all of these old books we have been reading?"

A few joking students said "对! (*duì*, Yes!)," but most of the class did not like the idea. They had gotten things from these books, and it did not seem right to despise their wisdom.

Then another argument was raised; in a low, cautious voice someone said: "I don't want to get rid of tradition. I want to preserve it."

When I asked why, it turned out that this person had made a disturbing connection between the impudence of Bacon toward the ancient Greek thinkers and the losses suffered to the artifacts of Chinese history when *Máo* had ordered the obliteration of the past during the Cultural Revolution. In the Cultural Revolution there were harsh, sad losses. I had even heard a rumor that a teacher at BDFZ had been killed, thrown off one of the buildings we all walked by every day.

Silence followed the mention of the Cultural Revolution, and then Lily said, firmly: "In a new world, we still need wisdom."

"What do you mean by wisdom?" I asked.

She didn't answer, and Tyler stepped in. He had established in the class that he was a science-minded person, good at math and unafraid of the modern world, so he felt he could be gentle to the past. "We can change, make a better future, and keep the ancient things," he said. "They show us time."

At the end of class, I posed an unanswerable question that I think about often as a teacher of classic texts: "Those wise people in the ancient world, in the Axial Age, their lives were very different from ours. Does their wisdom apply to us now?" People looked puzzled, so I made the question more specific, asking, "What would Confucius say about the scientific revolution?" The students shook their heads, laughed at the strangeness of the question and filed out of the classroom.

Confucius would probably be extremely dubious of all these new technological conveniences, I thought, as I settled into my office to write down the notes of the day. And yet he himself offered new ways of seeing things that he must have hoped would make life better. I imagined, daydreaming, that I was sitting among Confucius' disciples in the Axial Age when the Master said: "To study and at due times practice what one has studied, is this not a pleasure?" This is the first line of Confucius' *Analects*, a book that has had a huge influence on Chinese society for more than two thousand years. Was it an original idea in Confucius' time that study was a pleasure? In his politically fractured world, mostly dominated by war, perhaps it was.

Confucius' disciples must have recognized truth in this saying of the Master or they would not have written it down and given it pride of place in their collection of the Master's wisdom. They must themselves have felt pleasure as they explored with each other the exciting possibilities of thought and knowledge. The desire for knowledge is a different kind of desire than the ordinary desires for plenty and power that govern so much of what people do with their lives; in the Axial Age it must have seemed rare, new and precious. The disciples of Confucius, however, did not hold it entirely separate from the political world. At due times Confucians would practice what they had studied, using the new knowledge they had gained to advise the warrior lords in how to remake their world into an ordered, harmonious place of proper ceremony, ruled by the Confucian concept of *rén* (仁); that is, humaneness.

I liked the notion that in trying to get my students to take pleasure in learning I was doing something in keeping with one of the greatest traditions of Chinese culture. My daydreams about Confucius, though, were not because I wished to admire tradition, but because it was a pleasure to imagine Confucius' ideas when they were new, just created. Confucius valued tradition and venerated the ceremonies and customs of the 周 (*Zhōu*) dynasty that had flourished many years before him. In addition, filial piety (孝, *xiào*)—respect for parents, rulers, and elders—was for him among the highest of virtues. And yet there was a contradiction between Confucius' admiration for tradition on the one hand, and the innovative nature of those ideas on the other and the way that those ideas changed the world. Confucius might have seen people living in the *Zhōu* dynasty as his elders, but Francis Bacon would have said that they were children compared to him.

Maybe, despite their seemingly different judgments about the proper attitude towards tradition, Bacon and Confucius could have conversed together. There is a contradiction in Bacon, too, which appears in his opinions on studying and reading books—on liberal education, in effect. At the beginning of each of our classes in China, Grant and I distributed a memo about the skills of reading, talking, and writing that we wanted our students to learn. It began with a passage from Bacon's essay *"On Studies,"* written in 1625. We only quoted the last line of the excerpt, but the whole passage gives a sense for how Bacon understood study and books:

> Crafty men contemn studies, simple men admire them, and wise men use them; for they teach not their own use; but that is a wisdom without them, and above them, won by observation. Read not to contradict and confute; nor to believe and take for granted; nor to find talk and discourse; but to weigh and consider... Reading maketh a full [person]; conference (talking) a ready [person]; and writing an exact [person].

The wise read books to use them, weighing, considering, and interpreting them through the lenses of their own observations. Thus, despite the zest with which he attacked Aristotle, Bacon did not intend that old ways of understanding be ignored, but that classic texts be weighed and considered as materials for the observations of our lives, making them part of the present conversation. "That describes my job!" I thought, with pleasure. In *Analects* 2:11, Confucius expressed this same idea as he showed me my ideal as a teacher: "A person who can bring new warmth to the old while understanding the new is worthy to take as a teacher." For the rest of my teaching time in China, that saying served me as a North Star.

Reassured that what I was doing was not in conflict with Chinese educational tradition, I skipped lightly over a lot of scientific history and then assigned the class some Darwin, hoping that they would see how Darwin's work on the theories of evolution and natural selection created a whole new picture of the power and strategy of change. Before Darwin, it had seemed to many that animal species were permanent and unchanging. Darwin showed instead that the animals we see today, including ourselves, have come about through small explosions of change followed by competitive selection. He showed that nothing remains the same, not even our own bodily shape and our understanding of how that shape came about. No wonder he caused a firestorm! If animal and human nature has no permanence, then we cannot be sure that it makes sense to look to past traditions for guidance, since it could be that we have evolved away from the old wisdoms and they should be destroyed. That reasoning would mean that the Cultural Revolution was the right move. Were this the case, then the scientific revolution really is simply a disaster for the humanities, as many critics of the modern world argue.

The students did not take up these ideas, instead seeing the whole Darwin episode as a repetition of the Galileo story, where religion persecuted science. It seemed to be easier for them to condemn the bigotry and intolerance of Western religions than to look squarely at the problem that the East and the West share: what is the right relationship between ancient wisdom reflected in tradition and the modern, explosive new discoveries of science?

I spent a little class time on relativity and quantum physics through some short stories by the physicist George Gamov about a man named Mr. Tomkins, a mild-mannered bank clerk with an interest in physics and a wonderful ability for imaginative dreams. He dreams that he is in a town where the speed of light is twenty miles an hour and relativistic effects are visible. He also dreams of being so small that he can witness the astonishing, counterintuitive world of quantum physics. I hoped these stories would make modern physics feel unthreatening and accessible. Judging from the diffidence, fear, and grousing in class, however, most of the students were unable to get past the idea that relativity and quantum theory could only be understood by impossibly smart people. I was sorry to see this kind of self-denigration in students so young. I wanted them to believe that they could grasp all knowledge and that all knowledge was desirable.

Perhaps this was how people long ago reacted to the new understandings of the Axial Age. Confucius, the Buddha, Homer, Isaiah, and Zoroaster were all pointing to worlds that made little sense from the point of view of everyday life. Maybe when the sages first began to teach a lot of people thought that what they were saying could only be understood by impossibly smart people. I think the sages would be sorry to have their teachings be put out of reach in that way, ossified into elitist tradition that does not engage the new.

Our final direct look at science was through Thomas Kuhn's *The Structure of Scientific Revolutions.*[13] Kuhn's writings brought more comfort and fire to the classroom, especially when he offered this picture to illustrate how the same information can be interpreted in starkly different ways:

Is it a duck or a rabbit?

Kuhn argues that science does not proceed by smoothly gradual accumulation of data, as Bacon imagined, but goes in lurches, what he calls "paradigm shifts." The scientific community might for centuries look at something and see an obvious rabbit (the

13   (3rd ed. Chicago, IL: University of Chicago Press, 1996)

Earth at the center of the universe, for example). Then somebody points out that it is possible to look at exactly the same thing and see a duck (the Earth orbits the sun). The students had fun pretending to argue that the picture was objectively one or the other, pointing to evidence and insulting each other's perceptions. Duck and rabbit factions formed and held together with mock loyalty. We also spent a day on other optical illusions, just to roll with the liveliness.

Once the idea of paradigm shifts had become part of our shared vocabulary, a question arose that perplexed all of us: can a paradigm shift ever be a mistake? This was not really a question tethered to science. It was clear that the whole class, including me, were wondering about whether revolutions in knowledge—like the revolution that was occurring for both myself and my students as we worked to see the world from the perspective of a different hemisphere's traditions—were always a good thing. In the end we settled cautiously on the answer that more perspectives are always good, so that seeing both the duck and the rabbit was always better than only seeing one of the two.

"Do you think that science has made the world better?" I asked.

"Of course!" said many, pointing to medicine and iPhones.

"No," said others, pointing to weapons and iPhones.

There was no agreement.

A few days later, Grant and I took advantage of a break in the teaching schedule to travel to 曲阜 (Qū Fù), the home of 孔子 (Kǒng zǐ), Master Kong, latinized in the West as Confucius. Qū Fù, the place where Confucius had taught, had been the scene of my daydreams as our class considered the role of tradition and how radical new ideas take hold. Ever since our early classroom conversations about the Axial Age I had tried to bring alive in my mind's eye what it might have been like to have the new idea of self-consciousness opened up for the first time. If the scientific revolution was a change in thinking every bit as radical as the Axial Age, then my students and I and the whole modern, newly scientific world had an experience in common with the people in the Axial Age—all of us are trying to make sense of the changes in human life brought about by new kinds of knowledge.

Because of these reflections I was excited about seeing *Qū Fù*, now a center for tourism around Confucius. Most improbably, we had a friend near *Qū Fù*, a former student of Grant's from St. John's College, D, who was in China visiting her family and had kindly offered to lead us around some of the sights. The second line of Confucius' *Analects* is "To have friends arrive from afar, is this not a joy?" I hoped D would feel it so.

The ride to *Qū Fù* on the fast train from Beijing took a little over two hours. In another of the ambiguities we met often in China, the magazine provided in the seat pocket was called "Fellow Traveler." In America when we were growing up the phrase "fellow traveler" was used to accuse someone of being sympathetic to Communism and had the same insulting tone as "pinko." Was the magazine title a coincidence or was somebody joking about the American expression? No way to tell.

Grant sat next to an old gentleman who struck up a conversation in English. He looked Chinese but was in fact a tourist visiting from Australia, his family having moved there from China in 1948, when he was quite young. It took Grant a moment to put the date in context: 1948 was the final year of the Nationalist - Communist war on the mainland before the People's Republic of China was declared in 1949. The man's family had evidently left China to escape the communists, and now he was coming back as a tourist to the province where he could trace his family's history for eleven generations. He had brought with him his daughter, his son-in-law and his two granddaughters hoping, I supposed, to connect them with the Chinese traditions that he remembered and valued. At one point, he reached into a bag and pulled out some packets of a Chinese dried fruit snack, something that he had perhaps enjoyed as a child. He turned back to the seat behind us where his granddaughters were sitting, playing on their iPads. "Do you want some?" he asked. They shook their heads. His wife, beside him, observed dryly, "Nobody likes those things." His grandchildren were Westerners, for better or for worse.

D met us at the train station. She flagged down a taxi, which dropped us off inside the old city walls, next to the great stone Gate of Respecting the Saint near the entrance to the Confucius family compound. Confucius' descendants were still the most prominent people in *Qū Fù* right up to 1949 when they relocated to Taiwan, and they still come back to attend to family rituals, also, I again supposed, to reconnect to Confucian Chinese tradition. D got us tickets for the Temple of Confucius, the family mansion and the cemetery where Confucius is buried.

Our visit was in January, at the opposite end of the calendar from peak tourist season in *Qū Fù*. It was very cold, the gardens around the mansion were barren, and there were not many visitors, although there was nevertheless an enormous number of people trying to sell tourist tcotchkes. A long street was lined with vendors offering trinkets: brass Buddhas, figures of Confucius, glass ashtrays, prayer beads, child-sized imperial-era scholar's caps with pigtail attached, models of fighter planes made out of used rifle shells welded together, and paper, porcelain, cloth, plastic, glass, and metal depictions of Chairman *Máo*. There were more hawkers-per-tourist capita in *Qū Fù* in January than at any other time of year, and D continually ran interference for us, shooing away hopeful guides, carriage and rickshaw drivers and salespeople. Some got upset at her protection of us, complaining to her in Chinese that it was her duty to her fellow Chinese to help them get the foreigners' business. It had been a tough winter.

Like other temples we have visited, the Temple of Confucius is not a single building but a complex of structures built along a single axis. These are not quite so impressive as the Temple of Heaven in Beijing, but they have a balanced beauty. In the center is the Apricot pavilion where Confucius lectured to his disciples, and I was glad to be able to gather an image of the place that would be useful in my daydreams. I also loved the idea of having a temple devoted to a teacher—that is not an idea that has caught on in the West.

The Confucius family mansion was an old-style Chinese compound, with courtyards and widely separated buildings that were mostly empty and unrestored. Such places raise in architectural form questions like the questions that come up with classic texts—how should we converse with the past? We explained to D how Thomas Jefferson's home at Monticello in Virginia had been restored almost to perfection for the tourist trade, so that visiting there was like walking through a series of quaint period piece dioramas. James Madison's home a few miles away, however, was less well-funded and showed its age, requiring a good deal more imagination. Which of the two was the right way to treat history, the one that tried to display it as if time had stopped or the one that, as Tyler put it, showed time? The second strategy, even when it comes about by lack of funding, seems to me to allow better for the Master's advice to "bring new warmth to the old while understanding the new." Applied to books, that means to me that we should not read classic texts because of a wish to live in the past. We should read them first because we wish to take pleasure in their beauty and brilliance and second because we wish, in due time, to put them to use in our own lives.

Once we saw the major sights, D took us to 济宁 (Jǐníng), an hour's drive from Qū Fù, to have dinner with her family. In a gesture of extraordinary generosity, her uncle drove us from Qū Fù to Jǐníng and her father did the cooking. Dinner was a banquet of tofu rolls, broccoli, sautéed tofu, steamed dumplings, chicken, a delicate soup, all surrounding a broiled fish that we attacked with chopsticks. Neither D's parents nor her uncle spoke English, and Grant and I were unable to dredge up much of the Chinese we had learned, so there was really no conversation. D was very accommodating about translating compliments on the food, but she refused to translate Grant's praise of her as a student, insisting she was a "humble Chinese girl." Traditions of hospitality and of filial piety lived on in Confucius' home region.

The next day D met us in the hotel lobby and escorted us to the bus station, sending us back to *Qū Fù* for some more sight-seeing and the train home. Having seen the main tourist sights the day before, we now walked away from the tourist center of the town and down a street lined with shops that seemed to cater to the local market, selling everything from food and clothing to cell phones, tobacco, jewelry and eyeglasses. There were so many optician shops that for a while it seemed that the only way we would be able to stand someplace warm for a few minutes would be to have new glasses made.

A few yards further on we came across a storefront advertising what we had actually been looking for: "Coffee" (咖啡, *kā fēi*, a rare borrowed word). It wasn't Starbucks, but it was a good faith local effort in that direction. We were welcomed and shown upstairs to a dim, cold, empty room. On one side were shelves with decorative fans and other Chinese aesthetic touches, in this case, a row of porcelain puppies with big eyes. On the other side were couches along the wall. We chose the seats nearest to the heating unit, which had been turned on when we arrived, and were given menus written entirely in Chinese. The only things I understood were the prices, so we ordered two of a deluxe item (35 rmb, about $5.00), which turned out to be mocha drinks topped with whipped cream; pistachios came on the side.

A few moments later we heard a familiar voice from the stereo behind the counter downstairs: "Take me hooooome ... country roooads! To the plaaaace ... I be-loooong! West Virginia, mountain mama, take me hooooome ... country roooads!" I wondered if the shop staff had picked this song out of respect for the Americans upstairs, or whether it was popular in China. Here we were, huddled alone in an elongated, chilly, shadowy second floor room in Confucius' hometown of *Qū Fù*, China, listening to John Denver's

1970 hit song about the Appalachian back country—a vivid experience of cultural mixing.

At the train station, we enjoyed another Chinese delicacy: Kentucky Fried Chicken. The Colonel can be found in most cities in the Middle Kingdom and D had told us that KFC in China is better than KFC in America. Indeed, the mushroom and seaweed soup that I ordered was better than the mushroom and seaweed soup that I have eaten at any American KFC. The wasabi chicken was also good. The cultural patterns of the world are in chaotic turmoil.

Our trip to *Qū Fù* was wonderful, but I was as confused as ever about the proper place of old wisdom amidst the new. Everything around us in China, right down to the mutations in the menus of American fast food restaurants, seemed to present the question of how tradition can or should be honored in the modern world.

There is another dimension to this uncertainty. Confucius' thought was banished from China during the early Communist years, treated as one of the traditions that had to be eradicated to prepare for the Marxist utopia to come. Yet it is making a comeback, at least according to some. More than one person we talked to argued persuasively that a restored Confucianism would, in the end, be the story that replaced Marxism as the heart of Chinese self-understanding. However, because Confucianism was lost to China for half a century, its return has come by way of Singapore and other surrounding countries where it had been preserved in expatriate Chinese communities and in Western universities. Consequently, the Chinese are learning their own traditional story from foreigners, confusing issues of identity yet again. I did not know what to make of it all.

The third line of Confucius' *Analects* is "To be patient even when others do not understand, is this not the mark of the gentleman?" I imagined the Master's patience with my questions and was comforted.

Humanity 人性

Chapter 12

Frankenstein—Considering the Dangers of Science and Technology

The next book our class read, Mary Shelley's *Frankenstein; or, the Modern Prometheus,* spoke directly to the doubts and confusions about science expressed in our conversations. *Frankenstein* pushes the question to the farthest point by making us wonder whether our scientific creations are changing what it is to be human.

So far in our seminar on change we had mostly talked as if the changes we looked at were all for the better. Even when we sometimes questioned it, our discussions had assumed a triumphalist story in which history progressed from the philosophical awakening of the Axial Age through the civilizing compromises of cities, which led to the unification of empire resulting in a community of shared belief and learning, until finally science provided the objective truths that enabled technology. The past had steadily improved until it culminated in us, right now, in this classroom!

It was time to look seriously at an alternative story, a critique of technology and of the modern world it had made. We are still at the early stages of technological humanity, after all. Even assuming we avoid destroying ourselves with advanced weaponry or by poisoning of the earth—a big assumption—it is easy to see dangers ahead. Some serious scientists think that "The Singularity," the awakening of artificial intelligence, may be near. Artificial Intelligence (AI) scientists working towards this goal seem excited, but they may create a monster when they succeed in bringing forth a new form of intelligent life.

There are many surprising things about the original story of Frankenstein's monster, especially for those who associate it mostly with Boris Karloff in heavy green make-up looking creepily out of horror movie posters. The book does not present an ordinary narrative with a third person teller of the tale, but instead is a series of documents, offered like evidence in a law case for the reader to decide. Once again, as when we discussed the *Oresteia*, our class was undertaking the role of jury considering a world historical question. This time the question was not about justice, but about science and humanity.

There is also in the book an unexpected focus on the North Pole, which acts as a magnetic attraction to an assortment of characters. In 1815, when the book was written, no one had yet reached the North Pole, although apparently people had been trying. The writer of the letters that comprise the book is a ship's captain on an expedition to find the North Pole who meets two travelers, one chasing the other. The rest of the book recounts what the first of these travelers, Dr. Victor Frankenstein, tells the ship's captain about why he is engaged in this chase and the origins of the creature he is chasing. The ship's captain hears how Dr. Frankenstein made a creature through a combination of science and alchemy, as well as how he deserted his own creation in horror and disgust. The monster, bereft, tries to fend for himself but is everywhere rejected for his ugliness. He seeks revenge on his creator and kills Dr. Frankenstein's brother and wife. As the tale is being told, the ship's captain sails closer and closer to the North Pole, a place fixed, icy and inhospitable to human life. Dr. Frankenstein warns the captain against scientific ambition, which, he seems to imply, leads to such cold, deadly places. When Dr. Frankenstein dies after telling his story the creature returns to mourn him, then drifts away on the ice, forever lost (maybe he's forever lost or maybe not—like her Hollywood imitators, Mary Shelley left room for a sequel). The

ship's captain, horrified by the testimony of these terrible consequences of chasing scientific ambition, obeys Dr. Frankenstein's
warning and abandons his search for the North Pole, turning
again towards the warmth of human community.

During our classes on *Frankenstein,* I changed my teaching
approach a little and asked the students, two by two, to lead the
class and be responsible for creating conversation. I wanted them
to gain the experience of noticing how a conversation was going,
although I worried that the experiment would result in panicked
lectures. To my glad surprise, it didn't. Whether because they sympathized with their fellow students who found themselves on the
spot, or because they anticipated the day when they would have
to lead the class themselves, everyone spoke up more for student
leaders than they did for me, trying to help their temporary teachers have a successful class. In addition, many of the teaching teams
produced PowerPoint presentations on their part of the book.
PowerPoint is immensely popular in China. When Grant tried to
give his talk at the liberal arts conference without PowerPoint he
was met with such horrified incredulity that he ran back to our
hotel room and created a deck of PowerPoint slides in twenty minutes flat. For our seminar on change I had been reluctant to allow
PowerPoint, thinking that it might distract people from the more
austere pleasures of reading. In the end, though, I had to admit it
worked well to keep the class alive.

"Technology helps the humanities!" Sam pointed out, triumph-
ing over my doubts.

On the first or second of these types of classes, when the two
student leaders had gotten through their assignment and run out
of things to say, I stepped in to fill out the time, asking, "Does anyone know who Prometheus was?"

No, but, at a nod of encouragement, the students took out
iPads and phones to consult Wikipedia, and were impressed that
Frankenstein showed up in the article. Several voices interrupted
each other to tell the story of the Greek titan who gave humanity

the gift of fire and who was horribly punished for it by Zeus. I asked why it made Zeus angry for humanity to have fire.

"Fire," someone summed up the discussion that followed, "gives light but also burns; it cooks food but also makes metal for swords; it begins science, which can be used for both bad and good."

"And what does the name "Prometheus" mean?" I continued, knowing they would be glad to get another question that could be answered by looking at their computers. "Forethought!" the student with the quickest fingers and the fastest download time called out, naming the curious ability that humans have to make plans for the future. Human forethought was why we began to invent things to make us feel safe from our enemies and to protect us from dangers that we saw coming—disease, food shortages, weather and natural disasters. The improvements to our lives that forethought allows was what Francis Bacon hoped for from science.

Forethought, however, is only as useful as our predictions of the future are accurate; that is, maybe not very useful at all. Forethought has had some spectacular failures. For example, although Francis Bacon predicted rightly that science would provide ideas for products to improve our lives and protect us from our enemies, he failed to foresee all the ways that science could be threatening as well as promising. The threats coming from our technology have taken various forms at different times. For my students and me, climate change seemed the most urgent threat, while for my parents' generation it was the atomic bomb. In the nineteenth and early twentieth centuries, when Marx wrote and *Máo* was studying at *Běi Dà* university, the threats created by science came from the cruelties of the industrial age, reflected in the horrors of World War I.

Perhaps a Maoist would see an analogy between *Máo* and Prometheus, claiming that *Máo* had brought Karl Marx' Western scientific/economic analysis of capitalism and communism to China the way Prometheus had brought fire to humanity. It was easy to see how the analogy might seem plausible and to empathize also with the hopes that there might have been for *Máo*'s gift of economic fire. If Marx' foresight was accurate—and Westerners were scientifically clever, after all, so why shouldn't it be?—then adopting Marxism would mean that China could push ahead to Marx' predicted worker's utopia before the West got there. True, Marx' analysis seemed to expect that the workers' revolution would be a response to the abuses of an industrial age of development that China had not yet gone through, but that didn't matter. The beauty of foresight is that, because the inevitable future is known, there is no reason to endure the dreary, predictable middle of the journey—just fast-forward to the good part. In the early decades of the twentieth century the Soviet Union was one of the least industrialized nations of Europe, but it was trying the same dodge, leaping forward to the communist utopia. *Máo* might have thought that China should do that, too, and beat the West to the future, healing the wounded national pride that surrounds the Needham question of why the scientific revolution had not happened in civilized China instead of in the unrefined, crude West. Such a strategy would use the West's own science in the form of the economics and historical analysis of Marxism to humiliate the West as the West had humiliated China, leaving the West to choke on its outdated, contemptible, capitalist greed. I could see the appeal of this ambition for China. It would be an ambition to re-make humanity as great or greater than that of Dr. Frankenstein. The question raised by *Frankenstein*, however, is whether our forethought will be good enough to judge whether we have changed humans so much that we are no longer human.

"Maybe computers will usurp us," suggested Sara. "They will establish algorithms to predict the future."

After a moment or two on the definitions of "usurp" and "algorithm," I asked: "Do you think that's possible? No one has succeeded in predicting the weather yet; do you think that humanity's future would be easier to predict?"

"Yes!" declared some students emphatically, confident that AI was on the way, and that it would be able to do pretty much anything, including predicting the weather and the future, surpassing human intelligence. Others didn't believe that computers could be so independent of their makers, and Mark asked, cynically, "Who programs the computers?"

Another student wondered whether predicting the future was even a good idea. Wouldn't it destroy creativity? Tyler, so often the lover of science in our classroom, spoke up strongly for that argument, saying, "I don't want to know it. I want to make it."

After class, I decided to take a break from literature and walked to a fruit and vegetable store just outside the gates to our school, where we went every two or three days to pick up a few things. It was a good place for a little Chinese practice, too. The storeowners were sporting about our terrible accents, and helpful about kinds of produce that we did not recognize. That day I succeeded in asking for apples (苹果—*píng guǒ*). I was rewarded with a big smile and a bilingual response: "Okay-了."

I sat down on a bench outside the shop, across the street from a retirement home. Men and women who looked to be in their eighties and nineties, dressed with classic black severity, sat on a low wall in the sun, watching the bustle around them, sometimes conversing.

I wondered how the twenty-first century looked to them and how their life's experiences compared to what they had foreseen when they were the age of my students. People who were now in their mid-eighties likely had grandparents born during the imperial period and had been told stories of what China had been like in that time. Their parents would have lived through an interval of struggling warlords in the 1920s and 1930s, and their own memories might extend to those bewildering years. They would have heard of the Long March in 1934 and seen relatives and friends choose allegiances between *Máo Zédōng's* communism and Chinese Nationalism under another leader. Many of them would have come of age around the time of the Japanese occupation of China and World War II. They would have been young adults in

1949, and maybe some had been among the cheering crowd at Tiananmen Square when *Máo* had faced south on the balcony of the Forbidden City and declared that the new People's Republic of China would march into the Marxist utopia.

Then they saw the long years of *Máo's* rule: the partitioning of land as socialism was established in the 1950s; the invitation to let a thousand flowers bloom, when dissent at first seemed welcome and then was punished; and the Great Leap Forward, the effort to increase production that had ended in failed harvests, misery and starvation for millions. They would have been about fifty during the Cultural Revolution, when gangs of teenagers and twenty-something Red Guards had attacked all forms of counter-revolution, whether Westernism, religion, or ancient Chinese tradition. I wondered if they had felt threatened, if they approved, or if some of them had been present at the public humiliations. Now, after these long, eventful decades, these witnesses to the development of modern China sat in the sun surrounded by smoggy air, the noise of traffic, flashing neon signs of businesses—including Western chain stores—and half completed construction projects, all signs of the capitalist turn that China has taken under *Máo's* successors. The times they had seen!

As I returned to the school, I passed the enormous rock with *Máo's* calligraphy on it. I traced the engraving with my finger and my mind returned to our class discussions, considering the role of forethought and Western science in *Máo's* history and the development of his ideas. China, like the ship's captain in *Frankenstein*, now seemed to be turning away from his ambition.

I was unsure what the students thought about *Máo*. His name came up from time to time in various classes, and I believe they accepted the idea that he had been great—at the very least because he was on much of the currency—but I never heard anyone express either admiration or critique. I did not know if they were being cautiously reticent, or if they said little because he felt to them like ancient history.

There was censorship of material related to *Máo*, which might have contributed to a reluctance to speak about him. Once, as a result of an entirely unpolitical conversation, Grant tried to look up the Beatles' song "You Say You Want a Revolution" on the internet, not remembering that Chairman *Máo* was in the lyrics. As far as we could tell, the lyrics to every other Beatles song could be found, but that particular one was censored on every site. It was odd and gave us a shiver.

It was also not obvious how the students felt about communism generally, or about the Communist Party. We were astonished to find in the political philosophy class we taught that the students had never read the *Communist Manifesto*. We assigned it, but in our class discussion, the students seemed curiously distant from it. They had to ask what "*bourgeoisie*" meant. None seemed to see any connection between what Marx was talking about—the dictatorship of the proletariat, the withering of the state and the classless society—and what was happening in China today. It was left to us foreigners to argue that Marx was proposing a radically interesting idea: that alteration of material circumstances would alter the nature of humanity to such an extent that old ideas of greed and corruption would fade away. The students were unconvinced. These qualities haven't faded away in China. Nor has the family shown any signs of disappearing, despite Marx's confident assertion that it is a bourgeois institution. Q, our faculty colleague who joined the class, was perhaps the strongest voice speaking up for Marx. She expressed an affection for the image of the workers' paradise that Marx paints in the *Manifesto*, where "the free development of each is the condition of the free development of all,"[14] even though she understood it as a dream, like the Christian idea of heaven. The nature of humanity has not been altered by communism, at least not yet.

14　Karl Marx, *Manifesto*, section 2, last sentence.

The experiment with making a new type of human was equally equivocal in our class discussions on *Frankenstein*. "Is the monster human?" Alice asked. The question seemed to be the product of arguments outside the classroom.

David looked at her in surprise and said, forgetting his English, "不是人 (Not human)."

"Why not?" challenged Anne, prepared for David's reaction and ready to take it on.

This was the beginning of a passionate exchange. People felt strongly on both sides of the issue, each amazed that anyone could disagree with what was so clear to them. For some it was obvious that the creature was human; he could speak, think, and he wanted love; his feelings had seemed to them what any human person might feel and they could imagine themselves in his place. He was responsible for so much death, though, that others could not empathize with him and did not want to try, being offended at the idea that he was human. Particularly contemptuous, Paul wanted to know whether, if his classmates sympathized with the creature, they would sympathize with all murderers. He asked whether his classmates would be willing to listen compassionately when murderers told of being unloved and deserted in early life or explained how necessary a murder was for some good end, or any of the excuses people give for doing horrible things. Pleased at the baffled silence that these questions produced, Paul then made a common debater's mistake of putting a winning argument in the form of a general principle. He claimed confidently that people who killed others put themselves in the wrong and outside of society, ceasing to be human.

Jack, always competitive, pounced on that. "Soldiers?" he said. "Revolution?" A storm came down on Paul's head, as students spoke over each other in their eagerness to point to the heroes of wars and revolutions as proof that great human beings could do very ugly things. I don't know if any of the students who piled on Paul were thinking about *Máo* as an example of a great human being who did some ugly things. I was proud, though, that some-one brought up Achilles.

Class ended on yet another undecided question.

There is a celebration of *Máo* at the National Art Museum, an immense edifice in Tiananmen Square. It often seemed to me that the Chinese have in their minds a different sense than I do for the size of things, the ordinary relationship between human beings and the spaces in which they live. Private homes are much smaller than I am used to, while public squares and buildings are mind-blow-ingly big. I see this contrast in Chinese landscape painting, too, where tiny human beings and human doings are barely discernible under brooding, looming mountains so enormous that their crests float above clouds. Human beings are small in this vision, which may be related to a comment that I heard several times in China. It happened once at a train station, for example. We were standing in line for a ticket, and had been for a while, so we struck up a con-versation with the English-speaking Chinese woman behind us. We chatted about a lot of things, but, not surprisingly, the conver-sation kept returning to how long the line was. She finally shook her head, lamenting that everywhere was always so crowded and said: "there are too many of us." I was taken aback, and then sad for her. I don't like the idea that people feel as if they are one among too many, faceless extras in the world's drama. It must be hard to feel valuable, or to take up much space in the landscape, if you tell yourself that story.

Máo looms in Chinese society like one of the mountains in a landscape painting. The central space of the enormous National Art Museum was devoted to sculptures of the Great Helmsman in a variety of sizes and artistic styles, all reverential. A more enclosed, but equally large space nearby housed the "Art of the Revolution," paintings portraying the Chinese Revolution and the commu-nist victory over the Nationalists in 1949. Within this room was a multitude of cheerful communist faces, each more dedicated than the last to socially responsible goals such as boosting China's steel production. I was especially attracted to one painting that was, unmistakably, "*Máo* crossing the Delaware." It was presumably a scene from the Long March, but *Máo*'s pose was just the same as George Washington's in Edward Leutze's famous painting of an heroic moment in the American Revolution. The Chinese version reproduced perfectly a sense that the hero, imprudently standing up in a small boat, knew he was making history. There may be a different sense of space between China and the America, but the story of revolution has some things in common.

In our next class discussion on *Frankenstein* we returned to the topic of stories that had been such a big part of our earlier conversations about Rome. Now we examined the topic of stories in the light of the question of what makes humanity. Frankenstein's creature, having learned to read, discovers a discarded backpack with three books in it: Johann Wolfgang von Goethe's *Sorrows of Young Werther*, Plutarch's *Lives of the Noble Greeks and Romans*, and John Milton's *Paradise Lost*. These three books provided the only stories available to the monster to understand the people around him and humanity in general. Of course he was confused! The sentimentalized romanticism of Goethe's novel contrasts sharply with Plutarch's austere exhortation to duty and virtue, which is shot through with harsh, cynical and gossipy politics. Add to that Milton's condemning story of original sin—with its perhaps unintentional celebration of Satan's rebelliousness—and anyone would be perplexed about who human beings are, exactly. Frankenstein's creature's own story is cruel perhaps because none of the stories he found allowed him to make sense of how to be human.

When we reached this conclusion in class, someone asked whether that made the creature any different from any of us? There are contradictory stories everywhere, we agreed, and it is hard to decide which of them to choose as the story that, in trying to foresee the future to make our life's decisions, we will accept as truth and take as our model. Reading *Frankenstein* made us want more than bare truth in a model story. An acceptable model story had to be one that teaches humanity and compassion, as well as feeling true.

A number of writers have observed that China is a country in need of a new story, as the Communist narrative is in trouble. The triumphalist story of the inexorable march of the proletarian revolution, like the triumphalist story of science, has led to uncertainty about whether its goal is too cold and inhuman, like the North Pole in *Frankenstein*.

One story I often heard in China was about the pride taken in the accomplishments of China through its long history, a pride that my students had shown in the classroom when we talked about the identity of China or compared China with the West. I saw it too when we went to see the Great Wall.

It was November of our first year in China when, guided and accompanied by Q, we took a bus to 八达岭 (*Bādálǐng*), a rebuilt portion of the Great Wall only 50 miles northwest of Beijing. The bus climbed through the increasingly dense fog of a gray day up steep mountains. As we went higher I was amazed to recognize in the natural scene before me some of the landscapes I had admired in Chinese paintings. I had thought those landscapes must be exaggerated, but there they were—narrow, rocky mountains with patches of trees clinging to their impossibly steep slopes, shooting up so high that clouds and fog were below them, their summits seemingly detached and resting on haze. We humans felt tiny, making our insignificant way among these vast, dominating masses.

The wall at *Bādálǐng* is a reconstruction of how the Great Wall had been in the mid-*Ming* dynasty, although with added iron hand-rails for elderly pedestrians, and periodic restroom facilities for tour groups. The top surface had been designed to be wide enough for eight soldiers to march shoulder to shoulder. If the *Ming* had been thinking of modern crowds, they would have made it even wider, as far more than eight tourists, mostly Chinese, were clambering along it in both directions simultaneously. Every half mile or so were guardhouses from which the imperial troops had observed the frontier but which were now bottlenecks as the crowds surged back and forth.

The wall clings to the mountain ridge. Where the ridge was flat, so was the wall, and where the ridge leapt upward the wall leapt right along with it, at vertical grades steeper than the streets of San Francisco. In a modest concession to people who had to navigate these leaps, the *Ming* engineers had inserted shallow stairs when the vertical grade went above 20 percent.

I saw an elderly Chinese couple struggling slowly up one of these vertical grades, jostled on every side by sightseers in more of a hurry. They looked to be in their mid-eighties, like the people in the retirement home near our school. The man was eating an apple, and from time to time would stop and take a bite as the two of them labored up the stairs to reach the next guardhouse. An over-excited child skipping down the incline collided with him, and the half-eaten apple went flying over the edge of the wall, no doubt to join debris that had been thrown there for centuries. I braced and held out my arms to catch the man in case he fell, but his wife had already steadied him, so the best I could do was to mime sympathy over the lost apple. He refused to be dismayed, seemingly unshakably proud and happy to be there celebrating one of the great achievements of China. Smiling at me, he reached into his pocket and triumphantly pulled out another apple.

It was a pleasure to see his pleasure in being at the Great Wall. Yet the wall as an occasion for admiring pride is not the story that China has always told. Cruelty and disregard for human life went into the Great Wall's construction. A poet wrote in the twelfth century that the Great Wall was composed of the bones of the peasants who died building it. Even worse, the wall eventually failed in its purpose of keeping out invaders, and China was conquered and ruled by the northern tribes whom it had been built to exclude. This bleak history meant that, for centuries, the Great Wall was remembered as a symbol of the brutality and ineffectiveness of imperial rule, an interpretation to which the communists were especially attracted. Somehow, however, perhaps around the time Richard Nixon saw the wall and suggested that it had been built by a "great people," a new story began to take hold: although the builders of the wall were oppressors, they were still part of Chinese history and thus, the new regime thought, it made as much sense to identify with the oppressors as with the oppressed in telling the story of the Great Wall. All is China. Ticket booths went up, tour buses began arriving and Great Wall T-shirts, hats and snow-globes appeared in Great Wall gift shops. A fresh apple had been pulled out of a pocket.

After our trip to the Great Wall, whenever we went to buy apples and walked by the people from the retirement home near our school I thought of the old man and his triumphant smile. Perhaps he gave an answer to the question of what story people of his generation can tell of the events they had seen in their long lives. Those astounding events mark Chinese history as incalculably impressive. Like the Chinese emperors who built the Great Wall, *Máo* constructed something on a colossal scale. Even if it turned out unexpectedly, rebuking the Promethean, scientific effort to foresee history and careless of the small lives of ordinary humanity, a jury cannot render a verdict. The magnitude of the undertaking is larger than judgment can reach.

经典　Classics

Chapter 13

Conversing with the Great Books of China

All the time I was offering Western classic texts to my Chinese students I was myself soaking up the Chinese books that I had decided to read when the question of Chinese identity came up in the classroom during our unit on Rome. I was not trying to become a scholar of Chinese classics by reading these books; I wanted to approach them as we approach all classic texts at St. John's College—"take up and read,"[15] beginning my conversation with them from where I was, in all my ignorance and interest. I had been encouraging my students to do that with the great books of the West, and by reading the great books of China I hoped to empathize with their experience.

In the pause between our change seminar's conversations about the scientific revolution and the next topic of political change, I got a chance to take stock of my project of reading these Chinese classic books and to think about how my world was being enlarged, sometimes uncomfortably. New personalities carrying new perspectives had come to come to take up space in my mind, as I hoped they had for my students. They had met Achilles from the *Iliad*; I had met the Monkey King from the Chinese classic novel *The Journey to the West*. Both characters are fascinating and confusing at once, rich and puzzling. Now that they both lived inside us they could converse about the stories and understandings that

---

15　These are the words of a voice that St. Augustine heard in a garden in Milan. St. Augustine's life changed when he did as the voice said, took up a book and read it. St. Augustine, *Confessions,* Book 7.

had separately shaped China and the West, perhaps creating something new for a globalizing world.

Some modern books are already in a conversation between China and the West, at least at the level of politics. Henry Kissinger's *On China*[16] was popular while we were living in Beijing and I read it, although with some distaste. I was a rebellious hippie during the early 1970s so that for me Nixon and Kissinger were such equivocal political figures that I could not judge dispassionately the story that Kissinger told. Still, the experience of reading a history book written by someone I distrusted was valuable because it shed light on an ambivalence my students might feel. Reading outside the tradition of one's culture, because it can trigger a similar distrust, makes the reader hesitate between two ways to approach the book. On the one hand, a text from a distrusted source or a foreign culture could be read in the spirit of semi-hostile anthropological inquiry, in which the point is to gain insight into alien thinking. My hippie past tempted me to take that attitude toward Kissinger: "Look! Here's how a war criminal thinks! How strange and interesting!" On the other hand, such a book could be approached as a bridge, a way to empathize across our different experiences and seek a common humanity through understanding the wellsprings of each other's traditional stories. That latter was my naïve idea, and the basis of my grand dream of conversation.

Though I suppose we all inevitably take both approaches—I grudgingly found Kissinger persuasive in some ways—the situation is especially opaque in China because so many stories are already mixed. Having once adopted the Western ideas of Karl Marx, now roaring ahead with Western-style capitalism and playing catch up with the scientific revolution, all while seeking a unique nationalistic vision which honors its millennia of civilization, China's attitudes toward mixing stories were open. When Grant's Plato class read the *Phaedo*, the dialogue in which Socrates

---

16   Henry Kissinger, *On China* (London: Penguin Books 2012)

talks about the afterlife and cheerfully anticipates conversing with great figures of the past before drinking hemlock and dying himself, a student came up to Grant after class and asked earnestly: "Will Karl Marx be there in the afterlife?"

"Yes, he will," Grant assured her.

I set aside Kissenger's modern conversations with relief and picked up the *Records of the Grand Historian*, by *Sīmă Qiān*, the near contemporary of Plutarch who, like Plutarch, told his history through biography. I loved it. *Sīmă Qiān*, with brilliant humaneness, tells the mythical stories of China from the earliest days of the legendary Yellow Emperor, makes us admire with wonder the self-sacrificing filial piety of the fabled early emperors, and then leaves mythical stories behind to describe with unsparing realism the fractured time of the Warring states that lasted until China was at last united under the First Emperor Qin. The First Emperor Qin, who desperately sought immortality and who caused the terra cotta warrior army at *Xī'ān* to be built to accompany him in death, came to live in my imagination along with other vivid characters from *Sīmă Qiān's* life histories. What moved me to tears, though, was a letter by *Sīmă Qiān* to a friend of his, in which he writes of his falling out of favor with the Emperor, who condemned him to be castrated. His contemporaries expected *Sīmă Qiān* to commit suicide rather than submit to such humiliation but *Sīmă Qiān*, like Oedipus, declined to abandon the world, telling his friend: "I have things in my heart that I have been unable to express fully …"[17] While the disgraced Oedipus turned from suicide in order to follow a light of inner knowledge, *Sīmă Qiān* chose to live, despite dishonor and shame, because he was an artist who could not bear to leave his creations unfinished. I don't know if my students knew this story, but I hoped so.

---

17   Sima Qian, *Records of the Grand Historian, Qin Dynasty*, Burton Watson, trans. (New York: Columbia University Press 1961), appendix two, 235.

Next came the four great classical novels of China: *The Romance of the Three Kingdoms*, a fourteenth century work attributed to *Luō Guànzhōng* (罗贯中); *A Dream of Red Mansions (or The Story of the Stone)*, by *Cáo Xuěqín* (曹雪芹), dating from the eighteenth century; *Outlaws of the Marsh*, attributed to *Shī Nàiān* (施耐菴) and of uncertain date, though probably between the fourteenth and sixteenth centuries; and *The Journey to the West*, attributed to *Wú Chéngēn* (吴承恩) in the sixteenth century. Although it seemed unlikely that many of my high school students had read these massive books, I had noticed in the bookstore that all four of them had been turned into a great variety of video productions, children's books, and abridgments, so they were in the air and had likely influenced the way my students thought and felt.

Romance of the Three Kingdoms is the story of the disintegration of the Han dynasty in the second and third centuries of the Common Era. Its first lines are famous in China: "The Empire, long divided, must unite; long united, must divide. Thus it has ever been."[18] This seemed to reflect a sense I thought I saw in many people around us in Beijing that China, however it is defined, somehow abides, enduring all political changes and remaining itself. The book is about wars and the struggle for power, loyalty and disloyalty, martial trickiness and political stratagem. It was probably the lens through which my students interpreted the warrior culture of the *Iliad*. I tried to imagine seeing through those lenses, finding that the books were both like and not like. There were no gods anywhere in the *Romance of the Three Kingdoms*, for example, which was perhaps why my students were so perplexed by, and contemptuous of, the gods of Homer.

In *Romance of the Three Kingdoms*, life is often matter-of-factly cruel, but also marked by nobility. At the beginning of the epic,

---

18   Luō Guànzhōng, attributed to, translated from the Chinese with afterword and notes by Moss Roberts *Three Kingdoms* (Berkeley; Beijing: University of California Press; Foreign Languages Press 1995), vol. 1, 1.

three warriors, gathered in a peach garden, swear their loyalty to each other and to the diminishing Han dynasty. Over many decades, the three remain brothers amid military disasters and equivocal successes. They are plagued by personal failures and the painful difficulty of accomplishing what they set out to do. Thus it has ever been.

Outlaws of the Marsh is a story of bandits outfoxing the powerful. The characters in the book encountered more tigers than Robin Hood did in Sherwood Forest, but, as with Robin Hood, *Outlaws of the Marsh* rests on the premise that if only the true king could see what the evil ministers are doing in his name he would correct it. The idea of kingship itself is never questioned. This story in their backgrounds was no doubt part of why my students resisted Livy's claim that there was nobility in Rome's founding principle of "no kings!" The story about the true king has power in the West, too, as the legend of Robin Hood shows, but in China, there was no countervailing tradition. There was no Livy to be astringent about King Richard the Lion-Hearted's many flaws, and to show that Robin Hood's trust in him was undeserved.

A Dream of Red Mansions, also called *The Story of the Stone*, was reportedly *Máo*'s favorite book. That seems odd at first because on its face it is a sentimental and sympathetic description of the household affairs of a great Chinese family of the eighteenth century, a kind of "lifestyles of the rich and famous." The fortunes of the family fall, however, and perhaps *Máo* saw in this a picture of the inevitable changes of class that would lead to a different type of society. Or perhaps he simply loved what anyone who reads this book must love—the enchanting beauty of the world that the author creates.

A Dream of Red Mansions has been turned into a soap opera many times, most successfully in a 1980s version that continues to be popular. The set for that version still exists, and it is possible to go there as a tourist and dress up as characters in the story. The soap opera versions almost entirely skip the parts of the story that

I found most extraordinary, the different ways that China and the West have treated divinity. In the book, some of the characters have a backstory in heaven. The main character is a stone, for example, a piece of the sky that was left over when a goddess repaired the heavens. Two wanderers, a Taoist and a Buddhist, encounter the stone and take it with them to enter the human world. The Taoist and the Buddhist are a striking pair from the point of view of the West, where there has been so much bloodshed over religious disagreements. The two travel together amicably, never discussing which of them is right about their beliefs. In the West, if a Christian and a pagan travelled together, the pagan might be sophisticatedly tolerant, but the Christian would never stop trying to convert the pagan. In some ages of the West, the pagan might end up burned at the stake. With the Taoist and the Buddhist monks wandering in a friendly way through her mental landscape, no wonder my student Janie distrusted Western religion.

When the stone is born as a human, he is 宝玉 (*Bǎoyù*), the scion of a wealthy Chinese family. The importance of his status as a heavenly stone is never wholly clear so it is not surprising that the TV version concentrates on what happens within the family compound, especially on his relationships with the women around him. That aspect of the story is wonderfully human, sensitive and beautiful; all the characters, especially the women, are vividly sympathetic, living lives soaked through with poetry. They spend their time in a garden that is also soaked in poetry and that has affected Chinese gardens ever since the book was written. The names of places in the Beijing Summer Palace that sound strange to a Western ear—The Palace of Benevolent Longevity, the Hall of Pleasing Rue, the Tower of Fine Sunsets—all sound like relatively down to earth versions of the names given to places and perspectives in the garden from A *Dream of Red Mansions*—Seeping Fragrance Pavilion, Where the Phoenix Alights, and Approach to Apricot Tavern.

On a trip to the south of China we saw what might have been the historical inspiration for the garden in the *A Dream of Red Mansions*, the Humble Administrator's Garden, the largest garden of 苏州 (*Sūzhōu*), a city in which garden architecture is an ancient and revered art form. The Humble Administrator's Garden answered a question that a cousin of mine had asked, wanting to know what we saw in China that was heart-rendingly beautiful. This garden was it. When I read *A Dream of Red Mansions*, I was inclined to find the novel's descriptions of subtle perceptions of beauty and shades of feeling a little beyond belief, or at least beyond my coarse Western sensibilities. In the Humble Administrator's Garden, even crowded and a little run down as it was, I could see the beauty that the book described. Streams, stones, and hillocks were as carefully placed as trees, plants, and structures, so that every step taken entered a different, contained and cultivated world with different joys presented. Here too were evocative names: the Pavilion of the Snow Fragrance and Colorful Clouds, the Whom-to-Sit-With Pavilion, the Small Room for Listening to Rain.

Cáo Xuěqín, the author of *A Dream of Red Mansions* had, like his character *Bǎoyù*, been born into a great Chinese family, and may have spent time in childhood in the Humble Administrator's Garden. In his adult life he was poor, so poor that he died of starvation before the book was finished, a sad passing for the creator of a work so celebrated in China that academic specialists—called "Redologists"—are hoping to make the site of the author's birth a tourist attraction. A British friend of ours, who helped develop Shakespeare's birthplace at Stratford-on-Avon for the tourist trade, was invited to China to consult toward that end. When we heard P was coming to Beijing we arranged to meet—I wanted any advice I could get from him about how to interest my Chinese students in the classics of the West.

Over a drink at a Beijing hotel, P and Grant and I talked about the ways in which books take shape from a society, then shape it in turn, an exchange like the way a skillful gardener works to bring natural beauty alive by art. I believe that *Cáo Xuěqín* was thinking like this when, in the first chapter of *A Dream of Red Mansions*, a character in a dream passes through a great archway that is said to be an archway of illusion, on which is written:

> When the fiction's true, truth becomes fiction;
> Real becomes not-real where the unreal's real.

In an appropriately confusing way, that couplet captures the exchange between books and reality. When fiction is true to life, it affects the way people see so completely that there is no distinguishing the book from the world any more than art can be separated from nature in a garden. After P and Grant and I had reached this elevated insight, we then had fun inventing Chinese names for the world literature garden: Homer: The Hall of High-Hearted Heroes; Shakespeare: The Pavilion for Exploring Humanity; *Cáo Xuěqín:* The Grove of the Memory of Delicate Beauty.

I saw some conversations between literature and reality going on under my nose in China but I could not tell if they were careful cultivations or wild growth. This confronted me almost every time I turned on the TV in China because the show that was playing was nearly always a popular TV live action version of the most ubiquitous of the four great novels of China, *The Journey to the West*.

The main character in *The Journey to the West* is 孙悟空(*Sūn Wùkōng*), the Handsome Monkey King, who is an icon of Chinese life. He has no family, being born from a stone, and was taught by a Patriarch from a distant land who makes him promise never to reveal who taught him. Then, with the power thus gained from outside the mainstream of ordinary hierarchy, the Handsome Monkey King upsets the heavenly order of the divine Jade Emperor, wreaking havoc in heaven, eating the peaches of immortality, and stealing the longevity elixir of *Lǎozi* (老子), the father of Daoism. No one can stop him until the Jade Emperor sends for the Buddha, who tricks him and traps him under a mountain for five hundred years, after which, to gain his freedom, he converts to Buddhism and accompanies the Buddhist monk 玄奘 (*Xuánzàng*) on a journey to fetch Buddhist scriptures from the West—that is, India, the home of the Buddha. Throughout many adventures on the journey between China and India, the Monkey King is always impudently clever, amusing, and amazingly powerful, controlled only with great difficulty. He is ultimately controlled only by himself.

The Journey to the West seemed to be about liberal education! The book identifies *Sūn Wùkōng* as the Monkey of the Mind, the embodiment of the irrepressible sassiness of reason, which exists outside hierarchy, and which mocks and angers established traditions unless it can be tamed and made to support and accompany them. The ritualistic, traditionalist court of the Jade Emperor is unnerved by, and cannot defeat, *Sūn Wùkōng's* extraordinary ability to transform into any shape or creature he chooses. In this way, the book suggests that Mind Monkeys who think for themselves can be a threat to governments concerned with order and resistant to change. And yet Mind Monkeys are indispensable to the journey towards wisdom. I began to think of the students in our liberal arts experiment as Mind Monkeys. With that vision, even small disciplinary issues that I sometimes had in my classes could seem charming, like signs of life, and useful on the way to bringing alive the classic texts we were reading.

In the book, the unruly Mind Monkey is essential to the mission of the Buddhist monk *Xuánzàng*, who has been sent by the Emperor 唐太宗 (*Táng Tàizōng*) (r. 626-649 CE) to the West to bring back Buddhist scriptures. Emperor *Tàizōng*, who is considered one of the greatest emperors that China has ever known, the model for all later emperors, promoted religious and philosophical tolerance, celebrating new ideas as beneficial for his empire. *The Journey to the West* contains an account of Emperor *Tàizōng* considering an objection raised to Buddhism by one of his advisors, who argued that, as a foreign doctrine, Buddhism should be kept out of China. After hearing discussion of the matter, the Emperor *Tàizōng* overruled the objection.[19] He was apparently persuaded by arguments that virtuous Buddhist practices would be good for the nation and concluded that all of the Three Teachings—Confucianism, Daoism and Buddhism—were worthy of honor. At his command, the expedition that included the Mind Monkey made the grueling, adventurous journey to bring back the Buddhist scriptures and contribute to the civilized, inclusive greatness of China.

Though not an obvious part of the live action version of the story that we saw so often on our Chinese television station, Emperor *Tàizōng's* tolerance and curiosity, as well as the idea that it is a good, heroic thing to travel West to gain wisdom, must make an impression on the Chinese children who read all the cartoon books and watch the videos of the story. *The Journey to the West* was so pervasive that I was moved to wonder why it suited the purposes of the Communist Party, which controls all public television in China, to make this story so much a part of their children's formation. Probably the reason was simply that the book is an immensely attractive tale, as well as a Chinese cultural accomplishment, but I wondered if *The Journey to the West* was in the thoughts of the Chinese authorities who opened the door to the Western concept of liberal education in their quest to spur a creativity that would catalyze Chinese technological achievements.

This last conjecture is particularly attractive, as it suggests that the tolerant inclusiveness of Emperor *Tàizōng*, who believed that new ideas would benefit his empire, still lives among Chinese rulers. Growing up in America during the Cold War meant that I tended to see communist nations as sources of repression, secrecy, and censorship, a tendency that had been supported by our experience of censorship in China. For that very reason, I love it that China also has *Sūn Wùkōng* and *The Journey to the West*, which

---

19   *Wú Chéngěn, The Journey to the West*, trans. W.J.F. Jenner (Beijing: Foreign Languages Press 2011), vol. 1, ch. 12, 271-72.

offers openness and inclusivity as ideals, as well as the training of the mind as a means for making a society great. The Mind Monkey's irrepressible impudence can be trusted to insist that this history returns and returns until it is accepted.

Sūn Wùkōng

Reading Chinese classics helped me feel more in conversation with China, and better connected to my students' backgrounds. It also fit with an experience I had several times in smaller cities in China, less used to foreigners than Beijing, where sometimes complete strangers would come up and ask to take their pictures with us. I was not sure how to understand this, although I always said yes. It could be that they saw us as curiosities, so that their interest in us was merely anthropological or even hostile, given some of the history between China and the Western "red-haired devils" ("Look! That's what a war criminal looks like! How strange and interesting!"). The pictures we took together, though, showed people on vacation smiling together, like friends, which must mean empathy. In the context of *The Journey to the West*, I choose to see these exchanges as expressing a wish to make connections with different ways of understanding. I believe that one way to strengthen those connections is to read each other's classic books. I also believe that this is part of the best life, to read with care, sympathy and openness the most excellent productions of human culture.

Emperor *Tàizōng* says to us:

> Consider the cinnamon flourishing high on the mountain, its flowers nourished by cloud and mist, or the lotus growing atop the green waves, its leaves unsoiled by dust. This is not because the lotus is by nature clean or because the cinnamon is itself chaste, but because what the cinnamon depends on for its existence is lofty, and thus it will not be weighted down by trivia; and because what the lotus relies on is pure, and thus impurity cannot stain it. Since even the vegetable kingdom, which is itself without intelligence, knows that excellence comes from an environment of excellence, how can humans who understand the great relations not search for well-being followed by well-being?[20]

---

20   *Wú Chéngěn, Monkey and the Monk: A Revised Abridgement*, trans. and ed. Anthony C. Yu (Chicago: Chicago University Press 2006), 490.

Law　法律

Chapter 14

The U.S. Constitution and Discussion of Political Change

My change seminar had reached the point when it was time to talk about political change. I resolved to face squarely the kind of change that, in China and in other places in the world, had brought people shouting into the streets, the kind of change that was the darkest fear of the Chinese authorities cautiously experimenting with liberal education: *revolutionary* change!

I thought long and hard about how to approach this topic. For one thing, living in a communist country that asserted considerable control over what was taught in its schools I wondered whether teaching about political change was quite wise. I had no idea exactly what the Communist Party line was with respect to the various revolutions of the world and, in my ignorance, I would undoubtedly depart from it. I couldn't decide whether by doing so I would risk a re-education camp, or whether the opinions of foreigners were too absurd to be a source of interest to the government.

I decided to place my bets on the latter. When Grant and I were growing up in America there were no bogeypeople more frightening than communists, who seemed faceless and uniform. Referring to the victory of communism in China, pundits in newspapers and later historians asked American politicians accusingly, "Who lost China?" as if the Chinese Revolution was something for which American politicians should be blamed. The reality of our experience with China did not match up very well with these childhood impressions. China had never been lost—it was right here all along! Not only that, but every Chinese person we met was entirely human with understandable feelings and purposes, and no one we met in China believed that American politicians had been responsible for China's Revolution. With this history of American overblown importance in mind, I tamped down my own self-important notion that my classroom would be of interest to anyone outside it.

Generally, it seemed to us that China was much too involved with the enormous difficulties it faced in its internal affairs to care much about anything we might say. Modern American pundits, the intellectual heirs of the "Who lost China?" faction, often warn their readers that China seeks to surpass the United States as a world power. If that happens it will be because America has stumbled, not because China is bending its might toward global domination. Rather, it seemed to us that China was like a giant finding its balance; sure it has great strength, but it is preoccupied with the challenge of standing upright.

In planning for how to talk about political change, I drew on our earlier experiences in China, including the political philosophy class that Grant and I taught in our first year at BDFZ. That year, 2012, Grant and I had sent away for absentee ballots so we could vote in the American presidential election between Mitt Romney and Barack Obama, who was seeking a second term. When our ballots arrived, and before we filled them out, we brought them in to show our students.

Anne took my ballot in both hands, put it down, smoothed it out, and touched one of the little ellipses next to the names of candidates. She took a pen and held it over the paper, making me think that she might vote: perhaps she was imagining how it might feel to color in that space. Then she asserted, challengingly: "The American president is important to the whole world. Everybody in the world should vote in the American election."

That idea had never occurred to me. I was taken aback and even offended at the notion that people from other nations should get a voice in my government. Some students around the table were nodding, though. Unwillingly, I thought about people all over the world following an election that might have a huge effect on their lives but in which they were not allowed to participate. It must be frustrating. And yet, wait a minute—I'm the one who pays taxes in America! Nonsense, I wanted to say, back off!

When the ballot came around to David, he pushed it away with irritation, perhaps reacting to Anne's comment by finding a reason to believe that voting was stupid, so it didn't matter that he couldn't vote. He said: "Governing requires skill. There is no voting on what doctors and scientists skillfully do, why should there be voting for government officials?"

One or two other voices rose to support this assertion, arguing that governing well requires expertise and should only be open to people who have been trained in how to do it, as doctors and scientists are trained in their professions. Without such training, elections would put the wrong people in power.

At almost the same time as the American election, China was also choosing a leader. Beijing was hosting the Eighteenth National Congress of the Communist Party of China. The contrast in politics between the American election and the Chinese choice of a new leader was stark. There were no political TV ads, yard signs, or billboards in China. On the contrary, censorship was fierce; it was forbidden to roll down the windows of cars because the Communist Party didn't want anyone handing out leaflets. The internet slowed to a crawl and an ominous yellow page with a picture of binoculars and a vaguely threatening message popped up for even seemingly harmless searches. We were told that of the approximately twenty million people who lived in Beijing, two million were employed as censors, spending their days in enormous warehouses full of computer stations and making dangerous opinions and information disappear from the web.

Nevertheless, dissident opinions managed to get themselves expressed in subtle ways. The Chinese language has an enormous number of homophones, differentiated only by characters. So, for example, the phrase "Eighteenth Party Congress," when spoken aloud, sounds like the phrase "This is Sparta!" from the movie *300*, though different Chinese characters would be used to write the two phrases. In speaking, people differentiate between homophones from context but the Chinese language offers immense opportunities for people who wish to speak equivocally in order to get around censorship. While the Eighteenth Party Congress was going on, "This is Sparta" became a code phrase for complaining about everything that felt wrong. "The pollution is terrible today," someone might say, to which another would respond, "This is Sparta."

From the public's point of view there was no suspense and no participation in the Chinese choice of a leader—the street vendors had been selling DVD biopics of 习近平 (*Xi Jinping*)'s life for months. People wondered what the choice might mean for them and speculated on what effect *Xi*'s early life experience might have on his policies, but they did not express the view that they should have a say in choosing the new leader. I gathered that, despite the grumblings we heard about Sparta, many people looked upon government in a way consistent with David's argument. It seemed right to them that choosing a new leader was done by experts, not by them.

Ideas about political authority in China interested me as a lawyer. From my point of view, the Chinese had a curious idea of what constituted a law or a rule. Draconian obstacles and prohibitions existed everywhere, but people routinely found their way around them. A rule, therefore, was not what the authorities *said*, but what they chose to *enforce*. The only way to find out what would be enforced was to break the rule and see what happened. Thus, a good deal of rule-testing took place all the time, an understandable human reaction the result of which was that the strict laws and regulations did not command much respect. I saw this dynamic even in small ways around our school. For example, all doors in the large granite and concrete complex of the Dalton Academy had electronic locks, and most of them were locked all the time, including the classrooms. But everyone in the school knew of certain windows and doors that could be propped open or otherwise jimmied, so the locks never seriously impeded anyone, including me. Every morning I limbo'd my way into the room with the treadmills through the loose third window from the right. There was a peaceful co-existence between rules and ways around them.

Getting around silly obstacles is unobjectionable, but sometimes this attitude toward rules was more troubling. Once, walking with H., we passed an enormous building with a wraparound LED display. H pointed it out as the headquarters of one of the Dalton Academy's competitors, at least in the sense of being an institution that was helping students be accepted into American colleges. The strategy of that place, however, was to figure out how to game the system. The business provided pre-written college entry essays, resumes with false claims, and also allowed it to be believed that it could show students how to beat the SAT and TOEFL. H remarked, "There's no stigma to this kind of cheating in China. People argue that if you can get away with it you must be clever and thus deserve to get into a good school."

In the class I taught on American law, I made the issue of authority a theme. On the first day, after a brief description of the circumstances that brought about the American Revolution, I wrote on the classroom whiteboard the word "Authority" and asked the students where authority came from. The customary initial silence followed, but finally a few answers trickled uncertainly in: parents? the government? teachers? (some friendly giggling). Ideas started coming faster: friends? tradition? logic? books? The students scanned my reactions to try to see which answers were right. I wrote them all on the board and asked, "If someone wanted to start a revolution, which of these sources of authority would he or she look to?" Hesitantly, they concluded that a revolutionary could not look to the government, and probably not to parents, nor tradition, observing that loyalty to government was one tradition, but if the government was itself violating tradition there might be a loophole. Friends, logic, and books could be authorities, they thought. "What about nature?" someone blurted out excitedly, "Is that authority?" It went up on the board, and I handed out copies of the Declaration of Independence to read for the next class.

The class on the Declaration was lively. I was unprepared for the crowd of questions about Thomas Jefferson's famous evasion of the question of where the authority for revolution comes from: "We hold these truths to be *self-evident*, that all men are created equal ..." Passions ran high on this claim among my students. Apparently there had been arguments over it in the dormitory the night before. I did my best to pour gasoline on the fire.

Some students thought that the Declaration of Independence was right and that equality among people was self-evident. "Look at tiny babies—all of them are the same," they argued, giving rise to a give-and-take in which people spoke eagerly over each other—"no, it was self-evident that people were *not* equal. Some are tall, some short, some smart, some artistic, some musical—everybody is different! If America was founded on the claim that everyone was the same, it was founded on a lie. Is there a difference between being the same and being equal? Even if there were, how can you say that anything was self-evident about it? Maybe the smarter people really were better. Certainly it was the smarter people you want running the government. But people who thought themselves smart could be the stupidest of all."

When we got to the U.S. Constitution, these arguments resurfaced. The U.S. Constitution, I argued, does not try to find the smartest, best, and most virtuous people to be president or members of Congress, or judges. Instead, it sets up legal structures and procedures whereby these three branches of government will police each other. This is the heart of the doctrine of the separation of powers. The great insight is that human beings must stop looking, fruitlessly, for a good king or a trustworthy central organizing authority; human history teaches that no one can be trusted with power. In that predicament, the writers of the United States Constitution believed that the only thing to do was to invent procedures that would contain the inevitable quarrels among people seeking power and make those quarrels productive. Such a system should work whether the people in charge were good people or not.

My students hated the notion that no one could be trusted with power. They were sure that there were smart and virtuous people who could easily be found and put in charge of the government. I tested this belief with as many questions as I could think of, fending off a haunting sense of how much the Chinese government would disapprove of what I was asking my students to wonder about. "Do virtuous people want power?" I asked. "What kind of people *do* want power?" And "What happens to virtuous people when they gain power?" They were taken aback by these challenging questions. Every day for a week or two, I wrote on the whiteboard a saying by Lord Acton that is famous in Western political thinking: "Power tends to corrupt, and absolute power corrupts absolutely."[21] Every day one of my students would object, having thought of a new argument to try to prove that saying false.

Many of those arguments revolved around education, which was an especially fun conversation because, although we teachers had spent enormous amounts of time thinking about the students' education, the students themselves had never questioned it much. Tasks had been set them, information presented to them, and examinations administered as hoops to be jumped through, but it had not occurred to them to wonder why they were studying the particular things they did—this was new territory.

---

21   "Power tends to corrupt, and absolute power corrupts absolutely. Great men are almost always bad men." John Dalberg-Acton, First Baron Acton, *Letter to Bishop Mandell Creighton,* April 5, 1887 published in *Historical Essays and Studies,* edited by J. N. Figgis and R. V. Laurence (London: Macmillan, 1907).

"If a person has a good education they will do right," a student would argue, hoping to refute Lord Acton. "They will not be corrupted by power."

"So," I responded, "you are saying that education teaches virtue? Can virtue be taught?" They laughed, recognizing the question from their study of Plato's *Meno* in Grant's class. I was glad to have them see, in the context of our class on law, why people care so much about that question. If virtue could be taught, societies would not need doctrines like the separation of powers or need to worry about power corrupting people. They could just teach virtue to everyone so that everyone in government would be incorruptible.

Someone remembered that, as children, they had all taken classes on virtue and how to be good. That caused more laughter, as they mockingly quoted from multiple choice tests they had taken on how to behave well:

If you have a disagreement with a classmate, you should
1. beat him up
2. steal his backpack
3. throw a rock at him as he walks home; or
4. meet and discuss your differences with him in an open and honest exchange of views.

The students were not inclined to think that such tests had taught them to be virtuous.

Still, they did not want to concede that virtue could not be taught and that power would always tend to corrupt. So I asked, "If virtue classes are not the way to make people good, is there a kind of education that will? What kind of education would cause people to become the good people you need to have good government and a good society?"

"People should study history," one student offered. "They should learn examples to follow and not follow." This seemed like a wise approach, so we began to explore historical examples of good and bad people. Unless we went very far back in history, there was disagreement over whether a particular person was to be admired or not (no one brought up *Máo*, certainly not me). Finally, I asked them who they actually admired—who did they themselves use as examples of people they most wanted to be like? Many of the names that came up were celebrities, both Eastern and Western. They were famous, wealthy, and talented but not primarily known for virtue.

One class was taken over by a faculty applicant doing a demonstration lesson. She led the class for forty-five minutes talking about the elements of political theory, beginning with problems of cooperative behavior. At one point, she asked the students to devise rules for a hunter-group who wanted to deal with possible cheating among its members. Part of the class came up with a sort of democracy, another part with a primitive monarchy, but the winning suggestion, acclaimed by support from the entire class, was a system in which everyone was called upon to share the game they had successfully hunted while a single person was given authority as supervisor to make sure that everyone followed the rules. Who would supervise the person in authority? They didn't get that far.

For the first paper in the American Law class, I asked the students to write on the United States Constitution, particularly about how they would analyze the doctrine of the separation of powers, as well as the related doctrine of the rule of law, the gift of the Roman Empire to Western political thought. The rule of law as it was developed in America is the principle, deeply embedded in American ideas, that the law is the highest authority in the society, higher than any person. The most famous statement of this principle was made by John Adams, the second president, who proudly avowed that the United States is "a government of laws, not of men."[22]

Several students compared the U. S. Constitution with the Chinese Constitution. One laid both the similarities and the differences at the feet of Confucius, pointing out that the Chinese Constitution has clauses guaranteeing freedom of speech and freedom of the press, but somehow those guarantees do not play the prominent public role in mainland China that they do in America. This student argued that this has come about because the rule of law does not seem admirable when approached from the point of view of Confucian tradition, according to which laws should not control human beings because the truly humane person is above and better than law. For Confucius, the ideal was for people to be good enough that they did not need laws.

This comparison implied a critique of America's doctrines, of which we are so proud, suggesting that people who feel the need to establish a rule of law must be conscious of not being very good people. I learned later that in raising these issues I had inadvertently stepped into a discussion that had been going on elsewhere in the school. In their class on Chinese heritage, one of the teachers was teaching the Communist Party's position on the strategies of the U. S. Constitution. "Chinese do not need a separation of powers doctrine," he claimed, "because we are not weak and greedy like Westerners!" That, at least, is how my students characterized what was said; this particular teacher didn't interact much with the foreign faculty and the students may have attributed to him an argument that they did not want to express to me as their own opinion. Hating the claim that power tends to corrupt—which leads to doctrines like the separation of powers and the rule of law—they suggested as the view of this other teacher that these

---

22　John Adams, "Novanglus Papers," no. 7, *The Works of John Adams*, edited by Charles Francis Adams, (Boston: Little, Brown 1851), vol. 4, 106.

doctrines might be needed in the West because Westerners were simply not as culturally humane as Chinese.

Resisting this idea, I dutifully undertook to use my legal training to advocate for it. I had to admit that it was Westerners who had come up with the theological notion of "original sin," according to which human beings were so deeply, ineradicably flawed that only the sacrifice of God's Son Jesus could rescue them.[23] Obviously—I argued for my client the Chinese heritage teacher—Westerners recognized their own capacity for deep evil, an evil that the innocent Chinese had suffered from so horribly when oppressed by Westerners during colonial times. The Chinese, by contrast, had never sailed around the world to exploit other peoples but had been content to enjoy their own highly civilized society. China does not need the doctrines of the separation of powers or the rule of law, I concluded the argument, because China does not have a tradition of the uncompromising condemnation of human nature. Therefore, China can rely on its rulers to be fair and just.

Discussion of such issues exposed a running comparison between East and West that was a big part of my students' lives. They liked and spent time with all things Western—movies and music, Grant and me and the other American/European faculty at the Dalton Academy, and especially Western technology (Steve Jobs was enjoying a vogue in China when we were there)—but sometimes they felt bad about doing so, as if they were deserting their own traditions. The Dalton Academy students in particular may have felt torn in this way because they had decided to go to America for their college education, a decision that could perhaps cause an internal tension, the effect of which was unresolved. Maybe this tension, which I felt too, as I learned to appreciate wonderful things about China, would drive us all back defensively to our respective nationalisms (Westerners are not worse people than Chinese!). Or maybe there will be the opposite effect,

---

23   See St. Augustine, *Confessions*, Book 2.

as people experience through conversation the humanity of those who might otherwise have been enemies. The political change that is coming to the globe may depend on how we have this unpredictable conversation.

Some of the most important events of political change in China are tied to Peking University, *Běi Dà*, which was near BDFZ. We spent some time at *Běi Dà* because a group of BDFZ students was exploring the formation of a tour-guide company and wanted to try out a business plan. As foreigners, we were called upon to play the targeted customers in this experiment. The organizational skills of the student group were not yet well developed, however, and the tour quickly devolved into uncertain, shy whispering into index cards the order of which did not reflect the layout of the campus. We got as far as the library where, the tour guide told us—in halting English after some shuffling of cards—*Máo* had studied when he was a student at *Běi Dà*. After that, we faculty members wandered off by ourselves to enjoy a walk around the campus under the informal guidance of Y, the BDFZ biology teacher, who was an alumna.

Běi Dà has always been a center of the "university spirit" that I had first learned about at the liberal arts conference we had attended in *Xī'ān*. The most famous episode of university spirit, the May 4th (1919) movement that inspired *Máo* during his student years, started from the campus of *Běi Dà*. So had the student uprising that culminated in bloody conflict at Tiananmen Square in 1989, which the government does not want discussed, but which came up often in quiet ways.

We walked to the meeting spot from which the 1919 uprising launched, and perhaps the 1989 one, too, although that was not commemorated. Nearby, unexpectedly, was a statue of Miguel de Cervantes, the author of *Don Quixote*. Cervantes presents Don Quixote as someone who went crazy from reading too many books, which made him, I thought, a strange character to celebrate on a university campus. When I looked it up later, I discovered that the statue was a gift of the Spanish government in 1986 in recognition that Don Quixote was a popular figure among early twentieth-century Chinese intellectuals, the instigators of the May 4th movement. It seemed that both Spain and China believed that Don Quixote's special brand of book-driven craziness was linked to the idealism of university spirit. Don Quixote and the twentieth-century Chinese political activists were all idealists, seeing around them what their stories would have them see, and imposing their longed-for, admirable stories on everyday life, banal and often ugly as it is.

Honoring Don Quixote's creator in this place of university spirit seemed to imply, however, that the quest for a perfect society was a crazy delusion or at best an impossible dream, as the musical version of *Don Quixote, Man of La Mancha,* calls it. And yet, having in my childhood been overwhelmed when the impressive actor Richard Kiley sang that song, I decided that maybe the further message that many people have read in *Don Quixote* is also there, that chasing an impossible dream is worth doing, is admirable, is a better life than one without dreams. Political change, which can be hard-nosed and cynical, is also full of dreams. It is a kiln in which dreams are fired. Sometimes they crack, but sometimes they harden into something beautiful.

As we turned back towards the central campus, I stopped to study a nearby bust of a dignified and courageous-looking man. Y told me he was *Cai Yuanpei*, the president of the university in the early twentieth-century who had attracted to the campus the kind of free thinking that undoubtedly contributed to the May 4th movement. I wasn't sure why I liked the look of him so much—I did find out later that he was a strong advocate for women's education—but I lingered admiringly. I'm told that the students at *Běi Dà* tend to this statue on Tomb-sweeping day, the holiday on which Chinese families visit and keep in good repair the graves of their ancestors. As a fighter for liberal education for everyone I adopt him as my ancestor, too, and will try to keep his memory clear.

Y then led us to the lake at the center of campus, a lovely expanse of water with a pagoda presiding gracefully over it. There, university students walked, jogged, studied, and hung out talking in the afternoon sun, an idyllic academic scene. On a hillside overlooking the lake there is a monument to Edgar Snow, an American journalist, who is described on the stone as: 中 国 人 民 的 美 国 朋 友 (*Zhōng guó rén mín dè měi guó péng yǒu*): "The Chinese People's American Friend." This was the longest phrase—eight characters in a row!—that Grant and I had by that time been able actually to read. It was hard to convey to our Chinese friends how giddily proud we were of ourselves at this achievement, which any Chinese six-year-old could exceed.

In 1937 Edgar Snow wrote a book called *Red Star over China*, which lionized *Máo* and his army, presenting *Máo* as an inspiring, effective leader with progressive ideas and hopes for China. To Western readers who found *Máo*'s political rivals difficult to deal with, this view was immensely attractive. The West responded to the hope that such a personality might rise to power, and *Máo*'s struggle against Nationalist China became a popular cause, especially in America. It's hard to remember this history, given the demonization of communists that Grant and I grew up with in the 1950s. Political change, including changes in political orthodoxy, can happen bewilderingly quickly, and catch people off-guard.

Y told us that when the Cultural Revolution came many of *Běi Dà*'s most beautiful and valuable artifacts were sunk into the lake in the hope that they would escape destruction. The strategy had been mostly successful, but rumors persisted that some things were still under water. Looking around at the peaceful scene, I tried to imagine the competing bands of Red Guards who had fought each other at *Běi Dà* during that awful time, each claiming to be the purest revolutionaries. One man, 邓朴方 (*Dèng Pǔfāng*), had been tortured and thrown out of a third-story window from one of the buildings around us. He was paralyzed as a result. Just ten years later his father, *Dèng Xiǎopíng*, who had also been tortured by the

Red Guards at *Máo*'s specific direction, became the most powerful leader in China, stepping into the lineage of *Máo* and showing no resentment over his sufferings or those of his son. Political change may be the most volatile of changes.

This wide range of impressions about politics in China were in my mind as I set about to address the topic of political change in my change seminar. I was too ignorant to talk about China's history or its revolution, nor did I want to push the ideals—equivocal in China—of the American Revolution. Finally, I remembered the famous story of an earlier conversation about political change between people from America and people from China. Preparing for his visit to China in 1973, President discovered that 周恩来 (*Zhōu ʻĒnlái*), *Máo*'s trusted and scholarly second-in-command, took an interest in French history, having spent time in France. Subsequently, when he and *Zhōu* were alone during the visit, Nixon undertook to make polite conversation and asked *Zhōu* his opinion of the French Revolution. *Zhōu* thought about it for a while and responded, "It's too soon to tell."

Many people doubt the story, or explain that the two men misunderstood each other, but it is still a wonderful answer. The French Revolution exploded over Europe in 1789 and neither then nor now can people agree on what it meant, or how to feel about it. It had been in the background of our *Frankenstein* conversations, too, so there would be connections with our previous work. The French Revolution, I decided, would be a diplomatic way to talk about political change without coming too close to home for either China or America.

En avant, then—to the barricades!

Time　时间

Chapter 15

Burke and Paine—History, Carp Week II and Time

Time was on our minds at this point in our China stay, both in and out of the classroom. Inside the classroom, I thought about the nature of time because my decision to discuss the French Revolution meant that I would have to teach some history. At St. John's College there are no history classes any more than there are textbooks. Students read only original texts and expect those texts to fend for themselves, relying on a general knowledge to supply any needed context. I didn't think I could do that with Chinese high school students, who might not have any generalized sense of Western history, let alone the details of French history. Respectful of the rule of law as I am, even I know that sometimes rules need to be bent, including the St. John's rule against mere facts in the classroom. I asked the class for brief historical reports on the events and people of the French Revolution.

As with our earlier mathematics classes the students were startled that their humanities course was stepping outside of philosophy and literature, but they were sporting about it. I gave each student a revolutionary figure or episode—the *Ancien Régime*, Robespierre, the trial of the king—and asked for a two minute presentation. I did not tell them the chronology of their subjects in advance but called for the reports in chronological order. They either had to figure out themselves when they needed to be ready, which was valuable, or they had to be on constant alert. That was less good but still valuable. There was considerable scrambling as history was disentangled and put in order like a word jumble.

I supplemented the students' presentations with a PowerPoint (China had convinced me of PowerPoint's usefulness) showing some images from the French Revolution. I also, reluctantly, lectured between their reports.

The lectures did what lectures do: the students relaxed and their attention slipped away as I mentioned dates and names that meant little to them. It was a struggle for me, too, as I encountered the difficulty of trying to tell the story of the French Revolution as neutrally and colorlessly as possible so as not to prejudice the students for the conversations on philosophy and literature to come. No wonder such lectures are boring and no wonder St. John's avoids them.

With relief at getting back to original texts, I gave them excerpts from Edmund Burke's *Reflections on the Revolution in France*, an English conservative's meditations on the dangers of political change, and from Thomas Paine's *The Rights of Man*, a radical revolutionary's counterattack against Burke's views. Together, these texts interpret the French Revolution in contrasting ways, revealing a fundamental philosophical quarrel between Burke's defense of the cohesive power of tradition and Paine's rallying cry for the compelling justice of reason. In historical terms, it was the Romantics against the Enlightenment. I asked the students to choose up sides.

"Old ways must go if they hurt people. Reason and justice are better than tradition," argued Mark and Anne, in the voice of Tom Paine.

"Our identities, our stories, come from tradition," answered Jack, siding with Burke and recalling themes from our earlier classes.

"We can honor tradition and still be reasonable," claimed others, seeking harmony.

Once we got into Burke and Paine's original writings, I stumbled upon a better resource for teaching history than my earlier efforts at neutrality. Even-handedness is boring, but Paine's casual descriptions of his friends George Washington and the Marquis de Lafayette brought history to life as a drama played out by real people who do not know the ending of the story they are creating. The challenge of teaching history, I was beginning to see, is to try to get students to enter sympathetically into another time. Three centuries of time have turned the tense ferment of uncertainty that surrounded the French Revolution into a story that, looking at it from a contemporary classroom, seems dully inevitable. I needed to work against that, to get my students out of their place in time so that they could envision the passionate clashes of the French Revolution as if they were in it.

The subject of time was coming at us from other directions, too. Grant turned sixty, which caused us, reluctantly, to face the fact that the events of our early lives, still important and vivid to us, were as unimaginably distant and faded to our students as the French Revolution. In addition, the end of our time in China was in sight. Our feelings about that were mixed. Or, rather, we acknowledged that they *should* be mixed even though they weren't really. We knew perfectly well that our adventure in China [had been/ still was/would be in memory] absolutely wonderful, fascinating, marvelous. This knowledge sat sullenly in our heads alongside an active, energetic, nearly frantic desire to go home. On the refrigerator in our little apartment we taped three calendar sheets—April, May and June of 2014—and crossed off the days. Each particular day went roaring by too quickly for all we had to do in it but together they moved with glacial slowness.

Time was the theme of our last Carp Week in China. I did a workshop on Kurt Vonnegut's *Slaughterhouse Five*, in which the protagonist Billy Pilgrim comes "unstuck in time." This meant that the events of his life are no longer ordered chronologically. He jumps about among the things that [happened/happen/will happen] to him in the course of his whole lifetime, as if all of the beads of [memory/experience/anticipation] had come unstrung. Among the events of Billy's life is a visit to the world of trans-temporal aliens from Tralfamadore, who perceive all of time at once and can admire a lifetime as if it were a painting or a mountain range.

They are as passionless about the events they see as if they were listening to a neutral lecture about the French Revolution. Students reading the book found it confusing, amusing and strange. I found it completely believable.

In the workshop, students recalled past events from their own lives and imagined events from their futures. Each event, real or imagined, was written on a slip of paper, mixed up in what we called "life boxes"—origami cubes—and then drawn out at random to make "Tralfamadorian narratives." First you go to school. Then you die. (So it goes.) Then you celebrate Tomb-sweeping day. Then you are born. Then you get married. Then you go to a restaurant to meet some friends. Then you have a great time teaching a Carp Week workshop in which you are simultaneously desperately dreaming of the past and future at home in America. Time was as confused as a word jumble.

Grant's workshop read the first sections of Einstein's 1905 paper "On the Electrodynamics of Moving Bodies," which argues that fundamental problems of electric and magnetic fields can be sorted out if we are careful about what we mean by the word "now." The insight has a Tralfamadorean flavor to it, and Einstein's result, showing that space and time are far more intimately linked than had ever been thought before, leads to a picture of time spread out alongside space as a fourth dimension, as if we had been lifted off our *Flatland* plane. The students wanted to use this vision to learn to time-travel, but Grant insisted that they start with simpler stuff such as electromagnetism and the weirdness in the Maxwell Equations that led Einstein to reconceive the relation of time and space. It was an opportunity to play with some iron filings and magnets that Grant had found, neglected, in a laboratory storeroom downstairs. Nothing is more effective than a bar magnet and iron filings to show that there is more going on in seemingly empty space than meets the eye. Place the magnet under a piece of paper, sprinkle the filings on top and lines magically appear, a phenomenon that fascinated Michael Faraday in the nineteenth century and fascinated Grant's students just as much, which was a little odd. Judging from their science textbooks, these students had already encountered some rather advanced ideas, and yet magnets and iron filings seemed like a novelty to them. Perhaps science teaching in China, like humanities teaching, is too much a matter of relaxing to lectures. No wonder they had trouble traveling in time and making history real to themselves.

In an even more undignified mortification of the passive model of teaching, Grant's class used skateboards to illustrate uniformly moving frames of reference. Einstein's thought-experiment of synchronizing clocks in different locations with light-beams and mirrors was recreated with steadily walking students representing light bouncing back and forth between mirrors (other students) posted at opposite ends of the hallway. It was not as persuasive as a subway train running at three quarters of the speed of light, but it was a lot cheaper and fun, too, watching students zip about impersonating photons.

There were two afternoon seminars with faculty members and class participants from all grades mixed together. For the first we read Ray Bradbury's 1952 short story "A Sound of Thunder," the story that originated the phrase "butterfly effect." Bradbury imagines a time-traveling dinosaur-hunting safari to the Jurassic age on which one of the participants accidentally steps on a butterfly. The chrono-tourists return to their own time and discover it has become a fascistic nightmare.

The week before, trying to learn from the last Carp Week, we had had a practice seminar for faculty members on this story, and some teachers could not resist fantasizing about what events in history they wanted most to change (shooting Hitler was a popular choice). For others, it was an opportunity to reflect on the difference between the contingency of the future and the fixity of the past. We trample on butterflies all the time in our present; it's no crime to alter the future, and if time travel could make our past as malleable as our future, why not change it? We would then always inhabit the conditional tense, unstuck not just in time but with respect to reality. Our quasi-Tralfamadorean lifeboxes would contain not only things that have happened/are happening/will happen, but everything that *might* happen, as well. Maybe there are an infinite number of parallel universes in which an infinite number of Grants and Marthas did or did not go to China, and maybe the French Revolution has occurred or not occurred in an infinite number of ways on infinite timelines.

Our second schoolwide seminar reading was philosophy straight up: selections from St. Augustine's *Confessions,* Book 11, on Time. It was a bold, possibly reckless, maybe even lunatic choice. Separating St. Augustine's religion from his philosophy with selective edits is no more possible than using a pair of tweezers to separate the gin from the vermouth in a martini, but Grant nevertheless came up with two thousand words that posed Augustine's classic paradoxes of time and included his famous response to the question, "What was God doing before he created the world?" Answer: "Making Hell for people who ask impertinent questions!"

According to Augustine, time is a deep mystery. "If no one asks me," he wryly observes, "I know what it is. If I wish to explain it to him who asks me, I do not know." With this much the students agreed heartily, but his next steps lost them. Our idea of time, Augustine argues, is divided into three: past, present, and future. But that division presents a paradox, for the future does not exist yet and the past is already gone. As for the present, it is an infinitesimal instant that is always disappearing. Thus the entire world and everything in it is vanishingly small, a quivering flirtation of transitory passing-away poised between two gulfs of nonbeing. In my seminar, the Chinese students worked their way through Augustine's argument, but they didn't buy the way he mapped time onto the points of an imaginary "time line," with the past to the left and the future to the right. Their understanding of time was not geometrical, but emotional. Sure, they agreed, there are three kinds of time: the future is what you fear, the present is what pressures you and the past is what you regret—all three are terribly real. They feel the past bearing down on them always, even when they are not perfectly clear where it comes from or what it means. The hand of the past can take the form of parental authority, appearing as the responsibilities of good socialist citizens, or the glaring ancestral attentions of five thousand years of emperors, sages, poets and warriors. The present is no better; always full of impossible demands, books to read, projects to finish, tests to take. As for the future, it occupies their attention more than the past and the present combined. If the future weren't real, then for what have they suffered through a decade or more of school so far, with a prospect of four, five, six or more years to go? Sorry, Augustine. It just won't fly. These Chinese students could not believe in the infinitesimal, inconsequential present.

I saw during Carp Week just how hard it was for one of our Chinese students to break out of her structures of time, and how she felt when she did. Grant and I were returning to the classroom building, earnestly discussing how Carp Week was going. Approaching the entry to the school, we were startled when one of our best students suddenly leapt through the door out into the day, shouting and jumping as high in the air as she could. Every line of her expressed delight, joy, wide-openness, and energy. At the very height of her spring she saw us standing near, smiling. Immediately mortified, she collapsed all the way into a ball on the ground. Her friends gathered round, half comforting her and half laughing with us at how ridiculous it was that being surprised by teachers while being happy should feel so humiliating. There was no room in her life for an unguarded present, no matter how infinitesimal.

Another Carp Week workshop showed off the smear of time in a different way. In the presentation at the end of Carp Week, the students in a workshop on English verb tenses enjoyed taking out their hatred of English grammar in a clever play showing the strangeness of English when it comes to time. This production worked just as the Carp Week faculty planners had hoped by making Grant and me look carefully in our Shakespeare class at how Shakespeare, who is unequalled for clever plays, treated time in *Henry V*. We had been teaching the *Henry* plays and, when we came back from Carp Week, had eased into classroom work by screening Kenneth Branagh's version of *Henry V*. One of Shakespeare's most famous speeches—the St. Crispin's Day speech ("we happy few; we band of brothers …")—is from that play. This speech is only slightly less familiar than Hamlet's "To be or not to be" and there is a reason it is so well known. It is a magnificent display of King Henry's ability to shape the world around him with words, including the way words treat time. On the eve of the battle of Agincourt, he and his army face a desperate situation. The French enemy outnumbers them massively and French soldiers are fresh, with the best ground, the best horses, and every other military advantage. King Henry has only words with which to put heart into his troops. In a stirring, rallying speech, he conjures the image of a common soldier who "outlives this day and comes safe home." This man, years in the future, will gather his friends to a feast annually on the anniversary of the battle, St. Crispin's Day, and will bring that day's events back to mind.

> Old men forget; yet all shall be forgot: But he'll remember, with advantages, what feats he did that day.

There on the battlefield, King Harry recasts the desperate present in which the army finds itself, turning it into the nostalgic past of a hoped-for future. His words almost defy the capacity of the tense-system of English grammar but they express a simple truth. We don't live only in a point-like present. We are entangled in a network of memories and anticipations whose form and meaning are partly given but also partly made, and remade, continually.

This insight from Carp Week's far-reaching blend of fantasy, relativity theory, science fiction and philosophy helped me in my change seminar, shedding light on *Zhōu 'Ēnlái's* statement to Nixon that it was "too soon to tell" the meaning of the French Revolution. I hear in this that for *Zhōu 'Ēnlái* the French Revolution was still unfolding; its meaning would change as its consequences played out and as people conversed about it from different circumstances and at different removals of time. My difficulties with teaching history made more sense in this light. History is fluid, needing to be shaped by words but then subject to being shaped again.

These new ideas of time also made Grant and me feel better about the seeming tension between loving our years in China and longing for home. Like King Henry's soldiers, or perhaps like Tralfamadorans, the spreading out of time gave us courage to see the adventure from many places on the timeline. We thought: If we out-live this time in China and come safe home then each year we'll gather and feast our friends and family on the Lunar New Year. We'll wear the silk jackets that we got here and point to souvenirs of our trip.

> Old people forget, yet all shall be forgot,
> But we'll remember, with advantages,
> Our time here. Then shall these places and events—the Dalton Academy, our conversations with students, the Forbidden City, the gardens of *Sūzhōu*, Carp Week – Be in our flowing cups freshly remembered.

The memories unstick me in time.

Change 改变

Chapter 16

A *Tale of Two Cities* and Views of the French Revolution

With minds full of a sense of time happening all at once, our seminar on change turned to Charles Dickens' *A Tale of Two Cities*. The book offers a novelist's look at the quarrel between tradition and reason that the political philosophers Burke and Paine had joined, translating the quarrel from philosophical abstractions to the intense experiences of private, sympathetic lives and making the reader feel what is at stake. Dickens shows us ugliness and injustice in the tradition-bound pre-revolutionary society of France. He also shows us ugliness and injustice in the tradition-destroying French Revolution. He makes vivid the irrepressible struggle between the beauty and security of tradition on the one hand, and the need that people and societies feel, seeking justice and reason, to defy tradition and create something new on the other hand.

A Tale of Two Cities was at first hard for my Chinese students. The English was much more difficult than that of Vonnegut, as bad or worse than that of Burke or Paine. Dickens is so elliptical that sometimes it is hard to figure out exactly what has happened to the characters, or what they have done. One whole section of the three I was teaching entirely missed a central plot point—the murder of a wicked Marquis, the uncle of the main character Charles Darnay, who inherits and renounces the title. Reading the murder scene aloud in class helped a little. It was fun, too. I went broad, giving readings as emotional and energetic as I could. With Dickens a reader can go a long way in the direction of exaggerated pathos, and the students enjoyed it. Even so, I had to stop several times and explain what was going on.

I wondered whether assigning the book was a mistake. Hard as it was, however, they needed to be able to handle Dickens and other books as hard or harder in an American college classroom, so we soldiered on, with lots of explanations and theatrical readings. Gradually the students became familiar with the way Dickens slides around between real historical events and the metaphors he uses to give meaning to those events, swapping historical particularities and timeless truths back and forth, watching them speak to each other.

On the day our class talked about the storming of the Bastille, I asked, "Would you have joined the crowds in the streets of Paris?"

Two or three of the guys, wanting to display a willingness for action, cried out "对! (dui) Yes!" They were in a rollicking mood, maybe because it was spring and the end of the year was coming. "Throw over the old cruel regime, try something new, better."

Alice and Cindy looked worried. Sara shook her head. "Warm-hearted impulse has cruelty, too."

"Seven prisoners, seven heads," remarked Tyler, agreeing with Sara's observation that sometimes people who are acting with the highest motives can be just as cruel and destructive as any criminal. Tyler was pointing to the fact that, as Dickens dramatically presents, only seven prisoners were released from the Bastille, while seven people were killed in doing it.

The unruly guys had gotten to punching each other in a joking way, not in the mood for a conversation. I went over and stood next to them. They suppressed themselves, looked angelic and muffled laughter.

Alice said, as if testing herself in her imagination, "I would be there, but I would not join in the action." Then she added, wistfully, "I would want to. It was the right thing to break the power of oppressors." Others shrank back. It was clear that many of us would have stayed away, even hid if we had to.

Janie, as always, had a strong opinion: "Any change is good when life is bad. Fight to make things better!" Mark applauded this, probably because he always liked it that Janie's fierceness was so energizing. Another little tussle broke out in his corner of the classroom.

I turned to Tyler and asked, "When Dickens shows us the seven prisoners next to the seven heads, what do you think he is saying?" I had a few prompting suggestions in reserve in case Tyler had no answer, but he came back readily.

"It was equally good and bad," he claimed. "Balance."

I liked the wide range of reactions, the make-up of a crowd. Some people want to disrupt because they are restless and bored; some people are idealistic; some go shrinkingly with the flow; some hide and some are excited by strength. All of them were there in a high school classroom, and maybe they are there in political movements, too, each with their individual approaches, perhaps adding up to action together, perhaps not.

A stack of books slammed loudly to the floor. Tom had been shoving Paul and had knocked them over. Fortunately, time had run out for the class so I did not have to be the disciplinarian. Of all my duties as a teacher, I disliked that most. They were young, the weather was great and they were almost done with school—of course they felt bursting, even rebellious. I announced the next reading over loud chatter as they poured out the door toward the sunlight, making raucous footsteps.

Dickens sets individual lives within the great movements of history, putting the past and the future in conversation. The first story in A Tale of Two Cities is about the beautiful, young Lucie Darnay meeting her father after he had spent many horrible years in the Bastille prison, before the Revolution. Then, in a chapter called "Echoing Footsteps," Dickens takes a seven-year leap in time and describes the events of those years as the echoing footsteps of things that had happened in the Darnay household. I thought of Shakespeare's *Henry V*—Dickens was using the the same time-bending strategy as the St. Crispin's Day speech. It's a strange way to tell a story and confused my Chinese students.

Then the chapter lifts its eyes to a public stage on which more famous footsteps can be heard. France was in crisis: the French Revolution had come! A monarchy that had lasted for a thousand years disappears with bewildering speed, which must have felt to many like a bolt of lightning, sudden and inexplicable. Dickens' work, though, lets us hear the years of echoing footsteps that lead up to it, growing louder and louder until they are the tramp of marching feet. As they march through the streets of Paris, the metaphor changes. The waves of sound become the breakers and whitecaps of an ocean in a storm.

The public storm is composed of private lives, though. While the surging roar of marching feet rushes towards and floods the Bastille, Dickens shows individual people acting for their own purposes, pursuing the small intentions and histories of private characters. One such character enters the cell where Lucie's father spent many dreadful years and removes certain hidden documents, to be brought out later as damning evidence in the trial of Charles Darnay. As Dickens presents it, all the seemingly abstract ideas and gory or noble deeds that were played out in Paris on the day of the storming of the Bastille had private and personal feelings pushing behind them like tides. Dickens hears history as a welter of echoing footsteps in many directions, all impelled by individual emotions. Some resonate with others and rise to a shout or a storm; others conflict with and cancel each other. This idea matched the many contrasting personalities and opinions in my classroom, making up our conversation.

Trying out this auditory notion of history, I looked up from the French Revolution and cocked an ear at China. I wondered if the echoing footsteps of the past were gathering into a swell. One or two of our colleagues expressed the view that China was about to be torn apart by dissent. "Perhaps," I thought, though it didn't feel that way to me, on the peaceful campus of BDFZ. On the other hand, most French people probably woke up the morning of July 14, 1789 expecting an ordinary day in an ordinary summer like any other.

Sometimes I caught hints of how little I had seen of China, moreover, and how little qualified I was to guess at the future. Now that the weather was warmer, I had given up the treadmills in the gym in favor of jogging around the school's track, about a half-mile oval surrounded on three sides by a wall that marked the boundary of the BDFZ campus. On the school side of the wall were murals that celebrated the 2008 Beijing Olympics, showing stylized athletes doing spectacular feats. The other side of the wall was more mysterious. Every time I ran by I smelled the unmistakable odor of hashish. There might be, just over that wall, something entirely different going on than I had met in China. The crowd that would make up the future was broader than my experience.

I also tried to imagine how individual lives might have come together in the past in China to make the tidal waves of great events. On one of our visits to Tiananmen Square, I spent time meditating on two of the political flood events that place had seen. I craned my neck looking at the forty-foot high portrait of *Máo* that hung over the balcony on which he stood on October 1, 1949 to proclaim the birth of the People's Republic of China, then I turned around and envisioned the cheering crowds responding to him. Dickens would say of that crowd, waving and surging like a single sea, that it was made up of all sorts of people pursuing individual lives. I tried to think who they might be, each of them. There were veterans and survivors of the many long years of battle that had finally led to that moment, but there must too have been some who, perhaps genuinely and perhaps cynically, were more recent converts to Communism. Some, I suppose, were just swept up in excitement while others were busily calculating what the new government would mean for their ambitions, or for their families. *Máo* had shown a strong hand, which was no doubt attractive to many, and practically everyone, I'm sure, was glad of a resolution to what had been nearly two decades of war. What a day it must have been! At least some of the people in that crowd must have believed that a new dawn for the human race was at hand. I envied them.

Skipping ahead forty years in my imagination to a time when the proclamation of the People's Republic made echoing footsteps in the memory, I thought about what happened in that same Tiananmen Square on June 4, 1989, as members of a pro-democracy movement that had been stirring and gathering force for a long time became a wave of students arriving at the city square from *Běi Dà*. Perhaps that crowd also believed that it would carry all before it and establish a better future. Possibly a few of the same people were there, forty years older but again hopeful. The end was different, though. Soldiers opened fire on the protestors, killing or wounding hundreds. I imagined the shots ringing out and the crowd screaming and running through blood, the wave dissolving into terrified persons.

After that terrible clash, the 1989 protests persisted for a little while. The next day one lone protestor stopped a line of tanks by standing in front of them, daring them to run him over, trying to make the tide rise again with his lonely effort. Despite the killing on the day before, the driver of the tank stopped for him. Harshness had reached a limit. It seemed that China was struggling, unsure what to do, trying to find a balance. In that uncertainty, the sounds of the echoing footsteps fell away. The pro-democracy movement appeared to dissipate, or perhaps to flow underground.

And yet I also saw evidence that the echoing footsteps and currents of June 4, 1989 continue in the private lives of people I met in China, although still in a divided way. One day I found myself in conversation about June 4, 1989 with someone I will not identify, although I will assign her a gender, just for convenience. She had not been at the protest herself but she knew people who had been. She had been planning to go, but her father, a Communist

Party man, had warned her off. He had seemed to know that the government would meet the marching protestors with deadly violence. Her friends had gone, though, and some had been injured and some killed.

Something about the way she told the story, looking into the distance, made me think that she had told it many times before. I had the impression that, among people her age, it was treated as the great event about which everyone had a story, in the same way that Americans of a certain age tell each other where they were on September 11, 2001, when the World Trade Center towers came down. The footsteps of the 1989 Tiananmen Square marchers were still echoing in her life and the lives of people telling such stories.

She ended her story and then, after a little pause and for no apparent reason, she turned to face me directly and told me a completely different story. This one was about a meeting at her workplace where a dispute about the direction of the organization had gotten heated. Just when things seemed to be falling apart, a Communist Party official stepped forward and offered conciliatory guidance, pointing out to both sides which of the two alternative paths was more public-spirited. This had calmed things down and brought consensus, in accordance with the Party's wishes. She seemed to want me to appreciate the role played by that Party member at that scene. Then, after describing this happy result, she turned away again and smoothed her hair back with both hands, lacing her fingers behind her neck and standing silent for a while, looking at the ground. She was a portrait of mixed feelings. The currents and footsteps in her head were roiling.

Back in revolutionary Paris, Dickens changed the metaphor once again. In the years after the liberation of the Bastille in storm and flood, a fire burned in Paris, a chaos of undirected, blazing passion, all with unclear motives. Some people said they wanted to invent a new kind of government and to do that, they shouted, the old foundations had to be mercilessly destroyed, including the aristocratic class that had profited from those foundations.

The guillotine took up a place in the center of the city. No one could really tell whether a new type of government was possible, though, or whether that was even what the so-called Republican heroes handing out death sentences were trying to do. It was easy to believe that their real goal was to destroy their personal enemies and secure their own power. People in London, the second of the two cities of Dickens' book, were immensely frightened that the flames might spread from Paris to England. It reminded me of how people talked about communism when I was growing up, as if it were a forest fire raging that must be controlled to prevent it from engulfing the world.

The lives of Dickens' fictional characters were caught up in the Reign of Terror as it burned. Lucie Darnay's husband Charles Darnay—the heir to the wicked Marquis murdered by a revolutionary cabal earlier in the book—was captured by the new Republic and condemned to die for being an aristocrat.

In the classroom, I had been experimenting with a new teaching technique to get the quieter students to talk. At the end of every class, I asked them to reach into a hat and draw out a slip of paper on which was written a question about the upcoming assignment. Next class, each person was required to read the question and answer it, inviting and leading discussion.

One day Anne read her slip of paper: "From the point of view of the revolutionaries, was Charles Darnay guilty?"

The book presents Charles Darnay's as obviously innocent of all wrong-doing and flawless in every way. He was one of those pasteboard heroes full of virtues that Dickens sometimes creates, rather boringly. The alcoholic, cynical Sydney Carton, a rowdy lookalike to Charles Darnay who has attached himself to the family, is a much more interesting character. Sydney Carton doesn't care at all about politics, while Charles Darnay, although accused by the Revolutionary Council of being subversive because of his aristocratic heritage, is sympathetic to the Republic, hating the injustices his uncle the wicked Marquis has committed.

I suspected, rightly as it turned out, that Anne's contrarianism would not let her be railroaded into defending so tiresomely virtuous a person as Charles Darnay, no matter what Dickens was trying to do. I had not forgotten her spirited defense of Agamemnon's murder of his daughter, way back in our discussions of the *Oresteia*. "Yes, Revolutionaries are right to condemn Charles Darnay. Society must destroy the old class system," she argued. "It's bad for one man, but good for the new country."

There was a small chorus of disagreement. One of the students from my American Law class claimed that the whole point of society was to protect individuals, not the other way around. "Society can't protect anyone if society is destroyed," said Anne, vigorously. "Protecting society from threats is the most important thing."

"Charles Darnay is not a threat!" someone called out. "He believes in justice!"

"He is a symbol of aristocracy and old, bad tradition," said Anne, who seemed to have thought her position through, no doubt knowing she would be standing against the class and Dickens, too.

Tracey, who had only spoken once or twice this semester, said suddenly: "No should make war on tradition. Too much is lost."

After a short silence Sara turned to her. "Glancingly you reference the Cultural Revolution." The Cultural Revolution had been an express war on tradition, seeking to have the "four olds"—old customs, old culture, old habits and old ideas—completely eradicated. It was remarkable how often it had come up in our class discussions. Tracey nodded and replied, "So many people killed. So much beautiful history is gone." The silence that often came with memories of the Cultural Revolution descended again.

I didn't break it because I was reflecting on a conversation I had had with someone I had met outside the school who remembered the end of the Cultural Revolution. "In our village," he had said, "there were reports on the radio that those four had been arrested," referring to the so-called "Gang of Four" who were arrested on October 6, 1976. "Everybody knew that things would be different from then on. There was dancing in the streets and much confusion. So much that, when I fell down and skinned my knees, no one noticed." Big events can swamp small lives.

Anne had meanwhile been working on a comeback to this powerful equation of the French Reign of Terror with the Chinese Cultural Revolution and now took a clever tack. "Tradition is not always beautiful," she announced. "Especially women are hurt by tradition, which is not beautiful. Traditional ways for women are punishing and bad for society. Maybe society even needs violence if tradition is oppressive."

The raising of the issue of the oppressive nature of traditional women's roles in society influenced a few people in Anne's direction. "In cleared ground, there can be new growth," offered Helena, thoughtfully, in her excellent English. "Making room for a better future might be a worthwhile sacrifice. But who chooses who will be sacrificed?"

"Old things, even wrong old things, should not be destroyed. They should be seen, understood and contribute to greater learning." Tyler's constant faith that learning would make everything better was always lovely to hear.

Allen began to whistle the French Revolutionary anthem, the *Marseillaise*. It's a very catchy tune, if a little bloody in the lyrics.

In China, in keeping with the merging of many contradictory stories into one story of pride in China's long history, there seemed to be a kind of practical resolution of the quarrel between tradition and reason being worked out. I heard it first when we visited the city of *Xī'ān*, where the terra cotta warriors are. We had hired a tour guide to take us through the city. He showed us wonderful things, including the Great Wild Goose Pagoda to which the monk *Xuánzàng* in *The Journey to the West* had brought the Buddhist scriptures after his long travels. We were standing in front of the statue of the monk *Xuánzàng* (I got a selfie with him), when talk turned to American politics. Barack Obama had just been re-elected to the presidency, and our tour guide said he was glad that had happened. "The last two emperors were re-elected," he observed, "It was right that Obama should be, too."

So, Obama was for him an emperor. The American cry of "no kings!" that we had taken from ancient Rome was not important beside the fact that Obama was a head of state, making him an Emperor. The same thing was working with *Máo*, too. The Great Helmsman may have condemned the exploitation of the workers that took place in the imperial era and not have worn the imperial yellow-colored robes, but, practically speaking, he had led China as an emperor. The balcony on which he had stood on October 1, 1949 to proclaim the People's Republic of China was the same on which the emperors before him had also stood to speak to the people. Acts of defying tradition, if looked at from a certain angle, joined the tradition or even paid tribute to it.

Through this principle, pieces of the Chinese past that had warred and shouted murderously at each other in years past had somehow today merged into one tradition. At a tourist place in Beijing, we saw an array of plasticine figurines for sale that showed Chinese people engaged in a variety of daily or historical activities and wearing many kinds of costumes from the past and present. There were emperors and empresses, warriors and beauties, courtiers, fishermen, farmers, cooks, sailors, merchants, and characters from operas, shows and books. Figurines danced, or seemed to be singing, or did calligraphy, or played games. Grant bought a little grouping of two ancient Chinese men playing 围棋 (*Wéi qí*, usually known in America by its Japanese name, *Go*). Near them was a Chinese man sitting on a stool with a dunce cap on his head, representing an accused counterrevolutionary accepting criticism— which was often deadly—during the Cultural Revolution. Now he had become another figurine being sold as a souvenir of China's long history. There was the crowd again, full of separate people living their own lives. Somehow these individual lives pushed along the movements of change and added up to China. The Empire divided, must unite.

Grant and I were invited to dinner at the home of one of our best students. There we learned how to make dumplings, which is a valuable life skill. Our student's mother spoke some English, but her French was excellent and she kindly gave Grant and me a chance to practice ours. She had studied French in high school, where her imagination had been caught by the French Revolution. "When I was young," she told us, "we were in revolutionary, communist times in China. The spirit of the French Revolution seemed … *sympathique* (sympathetic)." The teacher told them that French was "*la plus belle langue du monde* (the most beautiful language in the world)" and ended the class with the cry, "*Vive la France!*" Now times were more mixed, she said. The great inspirations that had fired her youth had disappeared somehow. Everyone just worked from day to day, uncertain that there was anything else worth doing. In that state of uncertainty, the main thing that people could be sure they wanted was money—a small and ugly goal, but one of the few left standing after more principled ones had ebbed. Also, in these mixed times it was harder for children to find a way forward. Helping her daughter, not politics, was what she cared about most, now.

I felt for her, mother to mother. There was a touch in the air of an unexpectedly strong human connection between two people who might have seemed far apart, like Achilles and Priam weeping together in the midst of the Greek army. She and I had grown up being shaped by vastly different political regimes—two cities. We had been stirred by contrasting societal dreams and radically opposing visions of what was the best life. We were one, though, in our worries for our children in a changing, incalculable world. The longing to make better lives for the people we loved made political differences about justice or tradition or revolution fade away. We filled up dumplings in companionable silence.

Dickens ends *A Tale of Two Cities* with that same longing for a better life. When the ne'er-do-well Sydney Carton takes the place of his doppelgänger, the virtuous Charles Darnay, and rides the

tumbril to the guillotine in Darnay's place, he is not making any
great political statement but is following the seemingly small aim
of doing good for particular people he loves. After all the cata-
strophic political upheaval in the book, Dickens gives the final
word in the book to Sydney Carton. Well, it is not exactly a final
word from Sydney Carton—it is stranger than that. At this cul-
minating end to the book, Dickens does not tell us what Sydney
Carton actually thought on the scaffold. Instead, slipping into the
conditional tense that points to hypothetical worlds outside of history, Dickens tells us what Sydney Carton *would have thought* **if**
his thoughts had been spoken and **if** those thoughts had been pro-
phetic. Entirely in that conditional tense, Sydney Carton envisions
a future in which a beautiful city and a brilliant people have risen
from the abyss of the days of the guillotine. Then he prophesies
about the lives of the people he loves, the Darnays, and calls up
a picture of them in the future remembering the events he now
undergoes. Generations from that day, a child, holding the hand
of his father, would be told the story. Only after he has imagined
this happy future from the perspective of his tragic present does
he speak the line for which he and the book are remembered best:
"It is a far, far better thing that I do, than I have ever done; it is a far,
far better rest that I go to than I have ever known."[24] Dickens has
put fiction, time, and reality in creative conversation.

I cannot convince myself that many of my students took in
much of this. The end of the year was near. Spring was unfolding.
The basketball court was full of shouting students and it was hard
to concentrate. What's more, the senior year students were being
accepted into American colleges and could not take high school
seriously anymore. Every day at least one rejoicing student would
bring in news of being admitted to a faraway place that had, until
then, been only an aspiration. For each of them it was a moment of

24   Charles Dickens, *A Tale of Two Cities* (Oxford: Oxford University Press 1949)
book 3, ch.15, 358.

pay-off, of arrival, after years and years of anxious fears and hard, hard work. With this going on in their individual lives, they could not keep their minds on the vast historical and philosophical tides of the world.

Grant and I, meanwhile, in between packing and planning for our trip home, talked over our two years in China. Grant, when asked pointblank to distill down to one thing what he had learned by coming to China, responded that he had learned never to use the word "exotic." He had come to China, he said, partly to try to understand better the students who came to St. John's College from there, and he had learned that either place could be home, that no places were exotic and that the world really could grow together.

As for me, I had begun our second year, the seminar on change, with a grand dream that reading classic texts with Chinese students would encourage a conversation between the classic traditions of the East and the West. I even dreamed in my moments of exalted fantasy that through that conversation there would be ushered in a new Axial Age of global exchange and creativity. I still have this dream, but it has more personality and color now; blankness has been filled in and I am humbler about what it might look like for the dream to be fulfilled. If there will be such a revolution at all, it is likely to be a quiet one, with conversation growing like the ring roads of Beijing until the world is embraced. "Hope," I told myself, firmly. "It always helps."

The two voyages that Grant and I undertook in China had stirred up eddies in me. I learned to read differently, with more attention to the stories and assumptions I bring to books. Currents must have gone the other way, too, into the reading experience of my students. There is no way to know how or whether these waves will join with others to make great changes, or whether they will ripple across individual lives with a smaller, subtler scope. Conversation cannot be controlled. There is nothing to do now but keep moving.

In the last few classes I held with my change students we read some poetry. The students' hearts and minds were rarely in the room and I had no heart or mind to try to pull them back. It was time to accept that the groundwork had been laid for whatever the class meant or would come to mean. There would be no wrapping up into a neat bundle of certainty—that's not what the liberal arts are about. Instead, I hoped that, in some future I could not imagine, these students would carry a memory of our time together and hear, always, all their lives, that it matters what they feel, think and believe.

Acknowledgments

There are many wonderful people to whom I am indebted for the production of this book. My husband Grant Franks, for example, is a traveling companion of many journeys, including this one. The chief heroes, however, are students and readers who are willing to embark on the adventure of ideas, both the particular students I had the privilege of teaching in China and all readers who care about finding something true. Thank you.

About the Author

Martha C. Franks teaches part time at St. John's College, an institution which centers on the study of great books, East and West, through conversation. In 2012-14 she taught at a high school in Beijing, China, offering classes on the great books of the Western world to Chinese students. Ms. Franks is also an environmental attorney specializing in water law. Her work concentrates on issues of drought and scarcity, water rights adjudication and administration, the Endangered Species Act, and interstate compacts. During her time in China, Ms. Franks offered a course in American law.

Ms. Franks has a JD from the University of New Mexico, a Masters in Theological Studies from the Virginia Theological Seminary, and a Masters in Eastern Classics from St. John's College. She has published articles on pedagogical, legal and theological subjects.